Beowulf

Revised edition

EDITED WITH AN INTRODUCTION,
NOTES AND NEW PROSE TRANSLATION

by Michael Swanton

Manchester University Press

Manchester and New York

distributed exclusively in the USA by Palgrave

First published by Manchester University Press 1978,
reprinted 1982, 1986, 1990, 1994

This edition published 1997
by Manchester University Press
Oxford Road, Manchester M13 9NR, UK
and Room 400, 175 Fifth Avenue, New York, NY 10010, USA
www.manchesteruniversitypress.co.uk

Distributed in the United States exclusively by
Palgrave Macmillan, 175 Fifth Avenue, New York,
NY 10010, USA

Distributed in Canada exclusively by
UBC Press, University of British Columbia, 2029 West Mall,
Vancouver, BC, Canada V6T 1Z2

British Library Cataloguing-in-Publication Data
A catalogue record for this book is available from the British Library

Library of Congress Cataloging-in-Publication Data applied for

ISBN 978 0 7190 5146 3

First published 1997

15 14 13 12 11 10 09 08   10 9 8 7 6 5

Printed in Great Britain
by Biddles Ltd, King's Lynn

Contents

Acknowledgment Since its 'rediscovery' and the appearance of the first printed editions in the middle of the last century, *Beowulf* has attracted considerable scholarly attention, generating something approaching three thousand learned papers, more, that is, than any other single work of literature, superseding *The Canterbury Tales* and threatening to outstrip even the whole of Shakespeare's tragedies. It is clear that any recent worker in this field will owe an enormous debt to his predecessors—whose views he will have adopted either consciously or unconsciously, and whose influence will be visible on every page.

Note to the Revised Edition The first edition appeared in a number of impressions. Now, although the high cost of resetting unfortunately precludes the accommodation of all the valuable points made to me in person and in the continually growing body of critical literature, the publication of this new edition permits the incorporation of corrections to the text and additions to the bibliography.

To my parents

This is the sense but not the actual order of the words the poet sang: for poems, however finely composed, cannot be translated literally without losing their grace and dignity. (*Bede*)

Introduction

Beowulf is to English what the *Odyssey* and *Iliad* are to Greek language and literature. The oldest piece of vernacular literature of any substance not only in England but the whole of Europe, it breathes the true spirit of the northern Heroic Age. We cannot tell how it might have compared with similar epics composed at this time, since no others have survived. The various vicissitudes through which the medieval libraries passed meant that the preservation of the *Beowulf*-manuscript itself was a matter of mere chance. Because of changes in language, spelling and hand-writing conventions, it would probably have ceased to be intelligible, or even legible, a mere two hundred years after it was written. But the poem was already several centuries old when this sole surviving copy was made, and close examination of the text suggests that it had a complex history of transmission, being copied several times in different parts of the country. *Beowulf* may have been very popular; certainly it was familiar enough for the name 'Grendel's pit' or 'pool' to have been used, presumably in fun, to describe boggy places in several parts of the country. And that the poem was highly regarded in literary circles is suggested by the fact that it seems to have been imitated in parts by certain writers of both poetry and prose.

The sole surviving text of *Beowulf* is found in a late tenth-century manuscript: British Library MS Cotton Vitellius Axv. Some time during the early seventeenth century, probably when in the possession of Sir Robert Cotton, the manuscript was bound up with an originally quite distinct twelfth-century copy of miscellaneous Old English prose. However, the *Beowulf*-manuscript proper (now ff. 94–209) is itself a composite volume. It begins with three short prose works: a legendary account of the dog-headed saint Christopher (the first two-thirds missing), an illustrated *Wonders of the East* and a translation of the Latin *Letter of Alexander to Aristotle* describing his adventures in the East. Each of these deal in various ways with monsters, and perhaps they were brought together with *Beowulf* on that account. The poem *Beowulf* begins at the top of f.132, written continuously like prose, at about twenty lines to the page. It ends at the very bottom of f. 201 ᵛ; this was the last leaf of a quire, and the crowded writing suggests that the scribe tried to get everything in on the one page. In the way it is now bound up, *Beowulf* is followed by a fragment of the Old English poem *Judith*. This was written by the same scribe as finished *Beowulf*. But a pattern of worm-holes found on the last leaves of *Beowulf* and not in the *Judith* fragment, together with the rubbed appearance of f. 201ᵛ, suggests that *Beowulf* ended the volume, and indicates that at one time at least, the *Beowulf* codex stood on the shelf unbound, as known to have been the case with some other Old English manuscripts.

Before coming into the Cotton library, the manuscript had passed through the hands of the sixteenth-century pioneer Saxonist Laurence Nowell, but nothing is known of its earlier history. Neither the styles of handwriting, nor the illustrations to the *Wonders* give any evidence as to its original provenance, although it should probably be ascribed to a southern English scriptorium like Winchester or Canterbury. Close examination of the text provides some evidence for the history of its transmission, however. Two scribes were involved in its production, writing distinct but contemporary hands of *c*. 1000 A.D. The first scribe was responsible for the pieces of prose which begin the manuscript, and then for the text of *Beowulf* up to line 1939—and then he broke off in mid sentence. Perhaps he fell ill, or was alloted some other task in the scriptorium. A second scribe, who was also responsible for the text of *Judith*, finished the poem off. Now the first scribe was a very careful writer, with a light, graceful hand, and was clearly interested in the work of producing a well turned-out book, even though it was a modest format by Anglo-Saxon standards—originally a mere 23 × 15 cm. He made a point of carefully regularising the spelling of his exemplar, using the classical koinė of literary late West Saxon and trying to avoid any dialectal or archaic features. The second scribe, who was given the job of carrying on the text, does not seem to have taken half as much interest in the work—and the difference is important. He wrote rapidly and vigorously, using more abbreviations. But at the same time he was the more conservative copyist of the two. He did not bother to modify the spelling of the text as he wrote it out, simply copying down what he saw in front of him. Both scribes to some extent, but the second especially, preserve archaic and dialectal features which are important in enabling us to ascribe the poem a cultural context. That these features are the result of faithful copying, rather than linguistic peculiarities of the scribe himself, is indicated by the fact that the text of *Judith*, for which he was also responsible, is written in a perfectly regular form of literary late West Saxon.

Most commonly such diagnostic features take the form of Anglian, i.e. Northumbrian or Mercian, spellings. It is true that the literary koinė of the age of Ælfric and Wulfstan contains a considerable admixture of other dialects, notably Anglian. But the pattern of their distribution in the *Beowulf* manuscript is significant. For example, the first scribe normally uses the late West Saxon form of the feminine personal pronoun, *heo*, whereas the second scribe regularly preserves the Anglian variant *hio*. The preservation of the Anglian diphthong *io* for West Saxon *eo* is characteristic of the second scribe, and the use of the diphthong *eo* where normal West Saxon would have had *ea* is found even in the hand of the first scribe, e.g. *eoletes*, 224, *deog*, 850. Cumulatively such indicators are strong evidence for an Anglian origin, but give no indication of the date, since they occur in the latest as well as the earliest known texts. However, one or two archaic forms, surviving the process of transmission like linguistic fossils embedded in the text, suggest that the original, at several stages removed from our manuscript, may have been written at least two centuries earlier than the surviving copy. For example, the instrumental suffix *-ini* preserved in *wundini*, 1382, was already old-fashioned when the Epinal–Erfurt glossaries were being written in the early to middle eighth-century, and is unlikely to have been freshly used after, say, some time in the second half of that century. Other textual details suggest that at least one copy was made at the time of King Alfred, and that at some stage after the middle of the ninth century a Kentish scribe probably had a hand in its transmission.

A date of composition some time during the eighth century might be supported on other than linguistic grounds. The common use of phrases such as *wuldur cyning, sigora waldend* 'King of glory, ruler of victories' to describe the Almighty shows that the author was familiar with poetry of the Cædmonian school, which is presumed to have flourished during the last decades of the seventh century and the opening of the eighth. And it might be supposed that the lay of creation which Hrothgar's minstrel is described singing during the inaugural ceremonies at Heorot, was a direct imitation of Cædmon's own creation hymn, which the historian Bede reliably states to have been the first vernacular Christian poem. From the time of the Conversion a sufficient period must certainly have elapsed for Latin loan-words such as *gigant* or *draca* (113, 892 etc.), and the originally purely ecclesiastical *non* (1600), all to be clearly intelligible to the lay audience. Biblical references to Cain and to the story of the destruction of the giants in the flood (106f, 1261f, 1688f) apparently occur naturally to the poet. And this might argue a *terminus post quem* of at least 700 A.D. But how far these may have been explicitly recognised by the poet's typical audience is far from clear; they would not be the only obscure references in what is a patchwork of esoteric allusions. Some critics have supposed a high degree of Christian understanding behind some of the allusions in the poem, arguing a relatively late date of composition. But even if this can be substantiated, a sophisticated poet does not necessarily predicate an equally sophisticated audience. With leisure and a reference library at our elbow, it is all too easy to recognise hints and subtleties in the printed text which the conditions of oral delivery would scarcely allow. Then as now, the poem 'means' what we choose to make it mean. The relatively homogeneous society of early Anglo-Saxon England meant that public poetry of this order had to be accessible at every level of understanding. No certain allusion in the poem actually requires theological subtlety on the part of the reader or the listener. And for every *soi-disant* Bede in the audience there must have been enough tough *comitatenses* to have ensured the minstrel an unhealthy reception should he fail to please.

It is difficult to argue for matter of date from a degree of assumed theological sophistication on the part of the *audience* rather than the *poet*: how many Anglo-Saxon clerics, let alone laymen, were familiar with all Old Testament details, still less the patristic commentaries on them, is far from clear. As late as the tenth century even the careful first scribe of the *Beowulf*-manuscript was apparently unfamiliar with so straightforward a name as that of Cain; in line 107 he had written first *cames*, crossing that out and then writing *caines*—and then in line 1261 wrote just *camp*—and left it at that, although the context demands the name Cain.

Whether or not the poem as a whole responds to 'Christian' interpretation may be disregarded in this respect. It is a viable if idiosyncratic view, but one dependent on the zones of reference of the reader rather than on the text. The question would almost certainly have been considered irrelevant by the typical Anglo-Saxon audience. 'What has Ingeld to do with Christ?' demanded Alcuin of the lax monks at Lindisfarne; faced with certain of the more *parti pris* modern interpretations of *Beowulf*, those same monks might be forgiven for replying 'What has Christ to do with Ingeld?' Of course an eighth-century Anglo-Saxon poet was nominally Christian: so was Dickens. But it makes no more sense to speak of *Beowulf* as 'Christian literature' than it does of *Bleak House*. The classification is simply unnecessary. Cain is annexed to Grendel together with all other evil progeny, as generously as the Anglo-Saxon kings included Noah in genealogies which they traced back to Woden.

Just as his language is inevitably coloured by Cædmonian epithets, the poet cannot avoid reference to the futility of worship at pagan shrines (175–8). He was, of course, a child of his time. But as a man with an undoubted feeling for antiquity, he could no more attribute specifically Christian piety to any of his characters than he could refer to the Trinity or the Atonement. To do so would seem both gratuitous and grotesque. Beowulf will naturally go to reap the reward of the righteous, despite his request for 'heathen' burial (the only type he could possibly have known), while those guilty of evil deeds will also receive their due reward—what else? Redwald, the great-hearted, defiantly half-pagan *bretwalda* of whom we read in Bede and who was buried at Sutton Hoo in a manner so reminiscent of Scyld's funeral as it is described in the opening to *Beowulf*, and who ensured that his silver baptismal spoons were buried with him, would have understood well enough.

In assessing the probable date of composition, we must seriously question what sort of an effect much of the material included in the poem would have had on an eighth-century audience—without benefit of index, or notes in the back, no reference-library or museum. The words and concepts had to be directly accessible to the audience, as they fell from the lips of the minstrel in the hall. The poem *Widsith* suggests that the major figures and peoples mentioned would have been known from countless stories and therefore well enough understood however allusive the reference. But certain Baltic tribes were soon lost to history; some, like Beowulf's own Geats, seem not to have survived the end of the sixth century; during the great Migration Age whole nations sometimes disappeared altogether, destroyed in war or merely subsumed in another culture. Perhaps, like some of the fine-sounding names in Marlowe's mighty line, the occasional reference was intended merely for effect. But wherever we can check them from external sources, all such references as the poet gives are quite correct. The work of historical scholars like Olrik has shown that the poem's historical details must be considered accurate. And recent archaeological research proves that the detailed material background to the narrative is pictured quite realistically. The poet speaks with obvious knowledge of helmets, swords, jewels, etc., all of which, like the burial customs he describes, belong firmly to the sixth-century scene. Yet details such as these are used in a way which suggests that they were old-fashioned, rather than totally archaic. Archaeological evidence indicates that the account of Beowulf's funeral at the end of the poem is accurate in the last detail—and yet, so far as we know, cremation was not practised in Anglo-Saxon England after the opening years of the seventh century.

A *terminus ante quem* is provided by the poetry of Cynewulf and his group, who are normally considered to have flourished during the earlier part of the ninth century, and who seem to have been familiar with *Beowulf*. Cynewulf's *Elene* shows strong influence from *Beowulf* both in its diction and in its treatment of story-material, while the author of *Andreas* was sufficiently impressed by the *Beowulf*-poet frequently to have imitated his phraseology (cf. note to *ealuscerwen*, 769).

Given a date some time in the eighth century, almost any part of Anglo-Saxon England would have provided a cultural context appropriate to the composition of such a poem. But in view of what seems to have been the original Anglian complexion of the dialect, it would be preferable to look to the midland or northern kingdoms. The Northumbria of Bede and Alcuin, of the Lindisfarne Gospels and Ruthwell Cross, with sophisticated aristocratic patrons of the arts like King Aldfrith, would certainly have supplied a fitting milieu for the poem. The discovery at Sutton Hoo in Suffolk of the magnificent memorial to the great *bretwalda*, Redwald, whose funeral in 625 A.D. bore such a remarkable similarity to that described in the preface to *Beowulf*, presents a strong case for composition in East Anglia. Redwald's forbears included people mentioned in the poem, and he may even have recognised kinship with Beowulf himself. It would be perfectly appropriate that the poem should first have been recited in the hall at Rendlesham in the presence of one or other of Redwald's successors. On the other hand the political, economic and cultural dominance of Mercia from the middle of the eighth century makes the west midlands an almost equally attractive candidate. Some scholars have supposed the allusion to Offa of Angeln (1944f) to be a flattering reference to his descendent Offa II of Mercia. As the *Vitae Offarum Duorum* shows, it later became conventional to draw literary parallels between the careers of these two kings, although in this case the further reference to his queen Thryth—whose name is so like that of Offa II's queen—would sound a little incongruous by modern standards of propriety (cf. note to 1931–62).

The social picture represented, like its material background, must have seemed decidely antique from the point of view of the eighth century. But this antique perspective had undoubted literary value. The narrative was provided with a setting appropriate to heroic action: the great Migration Age, to which the vernacular literatures of Europe long looked for their story-material. And if the incidents described were sufficiently far removed to seem simple and not a little larger than life, they were set not in some never-never land, but one well known to the poet's audience.

It might seem strange that the first great piece of English literature deals not with England, or Englishmen at all. The hero is a Geat, living somewhere in central Sweden, who is involved in adventures first in Denmark and later in his own country. But the lengthy catalogues of poetic allusions offered in *Deor* and *Widsith* show that the early English minstrel derived his topics from almost any part of Germanic Europe.

His heroes may have been Burgundians, Goths, Franks, or men from a host of lesser known tribes—for literary purposes even the eastern Huns were reckoned 'Germanic' in this sense. Most of the historical characters referred to in *Beowulf* are well-known figures from Migration times when the Germanic tribes of northern Europe began their great journeys south and west, land-taking, forming new kingdoms out of what had been the Roman Empire, and laying the foundations for medieval and modern Europe. The Anglo-Saxons recognized themselves part of this movement, and long preserved detailed traditions respecting their origins—much as European immigrants to modern America often preserve quite precise oral information as to their antecedents. Anglo-Saxon kings like Alfred who traced their genealogies back to the Gods, did so via various continental heroes, including some mentioned in *Beowulf*: Scyld, Scef and Heremod.

The Germanic peoples who settled in the Roman province of Britain were of very mixed origins. Many of them came from some part of the Baltic littoral: the Angles from what is now Schleswig-Holstein, and the Saxons from Mecklenburg; but already on the eve of the fourth- and fifth-century immigration, there is archaeological evidence for considerable mongrelisation of these peoples. Many different cultural groups seem to have taken part in the land-takings at this time, either on their own behalf or joining another's war-band. Merely ethnic loyalties belong to a far later age; the heroic *comitatus* consisted simply of those free warriors who chose to follow a leader for mutual benefit; the war-band of Hengest, which carved out the fifth-century kingdom of Kent, will have been composed of a wide variety of people including Franks, Frisians and Jutes. The leader of the 'Saxons' who are described fighting their way inland from Southampton Water was almost certainly a Celt. (Interestingly the first English Christian poet, Cædmon, also bore a Celtic name, although this might mean no more than that he had a British grandmother.)

Some of the *Beowulf*-poet's references are clearly intended to be historical, even in the context of the poem, like that to the famous Ostrogothic king Eormanric, who must have died somewhere about 375 A.D. when his kingdom was over-run by the Huns. More nearly contemporary was the Swedish king Ongentheow, who was killed in battle by the Geats early in the sixth century. But the latest externally corroborated historical reference in the poem is to the death of Hygelac, Beowulf's own lord and uncle. We know from reliable historical sources that Hygelac was killed during a piratical raid on Frisian territory under Frankish suzerainty about the year 521 A.D. (cf. note to lines 1202–14). It is possible to erect a chronology based on the known date of this raid on the Rhine. Hrothgar must have reigned in Heorot during the last decades of the fifth century. Then after Hygelac's death some time elapsed before Beowulf could be persuaded to take the Geatish throne—possibly as a puppet of the great Swedish king Onela; and then we are told that he had a long and successful reign before finally meeting his end confronting a dragon. If Beowulf can be said to have lived at all, then he must be reckoned to have died shortly after the middle of the sixth century, say between 550 and 570 A.D.

Of all the major characters mentioned in the poem, the hero is the only one for whom we do not have some external corroboration. Even if Beowulf actually had any real existence as king of the Geats, the last historic act ascribed to him by the poet is his raising of Eadgils to the Swedish throne in about 530—an event which all other sources attribute to a Danish force sent by Hrothulf. (Significantly, this is said in some accounts to have included the *berserkr* Bothvar Bjarki, who is sometimes identified with Beowulf as a literary type, see below, p. 12.) However, the remainder of Beowulf's long and reputedly glorious reign rests quite without historical substance. Of course the fact that he is described fighting fabulous monsters does not of itself discredit his historicity. The heroes of two analogues to *Beowulf*, Grettir and Orm, were both historical persons. And by the same yardstick, the feats popularly attributed to Richard Cœur de Lion would result in him being dismissed as a mere myth. It is possible that (with the sole exception of Unferth), all the major figures mentioned by the poet had some basis in actuality. But the question of Beowulf's historicity, like Arthur's, is unimportant. The effect of the poet's antiquarian distancing is very much like that Dickens achieved with *Pickwick Papers*. The author chose to set his theme in a time sufficiently close for its concerns to be clearly recognisable by the audience as relevant to their own age, and yet sufficiently far in the past for it to have entered that twilight period when heroes of gigantic stature could be believed to have lived in the earth—not occupying a never-never land, but stalking a real world with which we can still to some degree feel ourselves familiar.

Given the foregoing chronology, we may presume that the bulk of the story-material—the semi-historical or mythical lays out of which the author composed his poem—came to England from across the North Sea some time during the second half of the sixth century, that is, by the end of the Migration Age proper. The archaeological evidence suggests that by the end of the sixth century no very strong cultural links were maintained with Scandinavia. From the seventh century onwards Anglo-Saxon England looked to the Frankish Rhine rather than northern Europe. So probably the *Beowulf*-poet's story-materials were introduced just as the last strong ties with the Baltic were being abandoned.

The title by which the poem is known is merely a name of convenience. As usual with Old English literature, there is no title page, no introductory material, and the only preface takes the form of an exordium dealing with the death and burial of Scyld Scefing, which at first sight seems to have little to do with the main text. In the absence of any explanatory material, critical consideration of the poem is bedevilled from the very beginning. After all, how is it that we establish initial critical criteria with which to approach any work of literature? We would not think of applying the standards of the lyric to the novel, or the sonnet to the drama. This poem corresponds with none of the genres or kinds into which we are accustomed to divide modern or classical literature, and any attempt to judge it by classical criteria merely frustrates. Equally, we lack any comparative material. Of contemporary poems which might have been written on the same epic scale, we have left only the two leaves of *Waldere* and the slight fragment of the *Fight at Finnsburh*. And *Beowulf* antedates by several centuries any substantial piece of secular literature in other European vernaculars, like the *Chanson de Roland*, the *Nibelungenlied* or the Icelandic sagas.

Some light is thrown on the poem, however, by its relationship to an indigenous European folktale, known to folklorists as 'The story of Jean l'Ours', or 'The Bear's Son tale'. In this, the hero is a young man of exceptional physical strength, which is usually accounted for by his having been brought up as a child in a den of bears in the forest. Later in life he shares some of the ursine characteristics of his foster-parents—their enormous strength, and an ugly habit of hugging his enemies to death in battle. He may be something of a shape-shifter, that is, one able to change his outward appearance from that of a man—in this case to that of a bear. He may in fact be a *berserkr*; today this term survives only in the phrase 'to go berserk', but its original sense is simply 'bear-shirt'. That Beowulf's contemporary, the Swedish king Ohthere, wore a bearskin at his burial has been proved by excavation of his grave-mound at Vendel. The word *berserkr* was applied initially to those who wore the dress of a bearskin, and subsequently to warriors who shared the fighting characteristics of the animal. Perhaps such men supposed themselves actually capable of shape-shifting in battle; there is every reason to believe that they were terrible opponents, reputedly invulnerable to weapons, and characteristically crushing their enemies to death with their bare hands, presumably unable to moderate their excesses. They were apparently what we would regard as pathological killers—who exist in every age, of course, but have a natural outlet in time of war, and then gain praise for exploits which in peacetime would be unacceptable. It is easy enough to see just how the *berserkr* would have fitted into the heroic life of sixth- or seventh-century Europe. Later viking kings certainly considered themselves fortunate to number such warriors among their bodyguards, or the corps d'elite of their armies. If the hero of *Beowulf* were in fact such a man as this, we can readily understand his reputation in his homeland and why he should be so eagerly received at beleaguered Heorot. Whether or not the name Beowulf can be analysed as 'bee-wolf', i.e. 'honey-eater' or 'bear', as some scholars have maintained, the hero certainly exhibits some of the *berserk*'s characteristics. He is said to possess the strength of thirty men; he relates how he hugged the Frankish champion Dæghrefn to death; and when confronting the monster Grendel he explicitly scorns the use of weapons.

In the Bear's Son folktale, this young hero sets out on a series of adventures accompanied by several companions. He successfully combats a supernatural creature haunting a house, whom several others have failed to withstand, usually because they had fallen asleep. In the course of the struggle he commonly wrenches a limb off the monster. Later he is guided by bloodstained tracks to its lair, underground and sometimes under water also. The hero descends by means of a rope. He finds there his former enemy either wounded or dead, and also a female of the species, whom he overcomes with the aid of a magic sword which is found in the lair. Finally, his comrades on the surface, who were to have hauled him up by the rope, abandon the hero, either treacherously or because they think him dead. Nevertheless he manages to return, bringing with him a piece of the dead monster and occasionally the sword with which it was overcome, and is acclaimed victorious.

Scandinavian versions in particular, although found in their recorded form only from the fourteenth century, seem to preserve certain features of this folk tale in a relatively pristine form. It is clear from several versions that the marauding monsters are in fact trolls—that is, the living dead, who, because of some unhappiness in their lives or in the manner of their deaths, walk abroad in the dark at night creating havoc wherever they go. Being creatures of darkness, they are upset by any kind of light—which if shone in their eyes, causes them to lose their hideous strength, and so enables a hero to deal with them permanently. This is usually effected by cutting off their heads, although the feat is properly achieved only with the aid of a magic sword, since trolls are normally invulnerable to ordinary human weapons.

In addition to providing a general paradigm, comparison with certain of these Old Norse versions occasionally helps show how the *Beowulf*-poet has handled his received materials. For example, in *Grettis Saga* we can recognise a protagonist whose chief actions and functions are in principle identical with those of Beowulf. At different times in the course of a very eclectic tale, the hero Grettir is shown confronting three quite discrete monsters. First Grettir defeats and slays a male troll haunting a lonely farmstead by night. He feigns sleep until the monster's approach, and then there follows a battle in which much of the hall is destroyed in a manner very reminiscent of Beowulf's confrontation with Grendel at Heorot. The hero succeeds because he is able to take advantage of a moment of weakness on the part of the troll when the moon comes out from behind the clouds and shines in its eyes. Later, after much intervening matter, the hero plans to confront another troll, this time a female, haunting a different farmstead. On this occasion the fight goes harder, the she-troll dragging him towards her lair behind a waterfall; but the hero manages to draw a knife and hack off one of the monster's arms, whereupon she disappears dead down the ravine. Rather arbitrarily, Grettir is then made to seek out the underwater lair as the result of disbelief in his exploits. He descends by means of a rope, leaving a friend at the surface. He finds not the monster, but a third ogre, and it is the destruction of this third monster which bloodies the water so that his waiting friend thinks the worst and thereupon leaves.

In *Grettis Saga* the several incidents are quite unrelated, resulting in a loose picaresque effect, whereas the *Beowulf*-poet contrives to link his materials, making for a very much tighter overall structure. He simplifies the locale, associates the monsters and reduces their number to two. The loss of an arm is transferred to the male troll, who is allowed to make his escape, thus motivating the introduction of the second—now its mother—who comes in revenge; it is in consequence of this attack that the hero goes in search of her watery lair, and it is there that he is handled so severely. There is still a trail of blood to guide him; but there is no need of a rope—since Beowulf has already been established as a powerful swimmer—and thus no mechanism by which he may be betrayed; and the one significant friend is happily replaced by Beowulf's entire *comitatus* together with the Danes he has come to assist. *Beowulf* is clearly the more literary version, modifying the tale so as to provide unity, continuity and adequate motivation.

The *Beowulf*-poet adapts his source-material in detail as well as in overall structure to suit the literary taste of his audience. One example will suffice. When Beowulf *in extremis* is sat upon by the she-troll, God intervenes by allowing the hero to catch sight of a magic sword on the wall, with which he then manages to slay the troll—after which it is said, symbolically and perfectly appropriately, that light, the symbol of goodness, shone within the cave as brightly as the sun in heaven (1570–72). We are not told by what means Beowulf is able to free himself from the troll's grip. But, as with Grettir's first troll-fight, and several other Old Norse versions, we should probably assume that in the folktale original, the light shone *before* rather than *after* the event, simultaneously depriving the troll of its strength and enabling the hero to discover the instrument necessary for its despatch. The *Beowulf*-poet has recast the event, displaying less understanding of trolls but a superior sense of poetic function.

There is obviously much in these Scandinavian versions of the Bear's Son story that is paralleled in the first part of *Beowulf*. But the paradigm apparently says nothing of dragon-killing; dragons seem to belong to an altogether different kind of folktale, represented in its most extended and pertinent form by the saga of Sigurðr Vǫlsungr (see note to lines 874–97). Perhaps we would be right in supposing *Beowulf* to have been made by joining together two quite separate stories, one dealing with water-monsters and the other with a dragon, which were linked merely by virtue of having been slain by a hero with the same or similar name. But occasional Old Norse narratives are found which contain elements from both halves of the Beowulf story, suggesting that there may have been an original link of some kind. In *Harðar Saga*, for instance, the hero, a Geat named Hǫrðr, in company with twelve other men, seeks out a troll for the sake of the gold it possesses rather than because of its offensive character; the troll inhabits a grave-mound, rather than an underwater lair; when defeated, the troll lays a curse on the treasure, declaring that one ring in particular will be the death of Hǫrðr and anyone else who should own it. In *Gull-þóris Saga* also, the hero together with his companions attack a group of supernatural creatures for the sake of their treasure, which incidentally includes a remarkable sword-hilt. These creatures take the form of dragons, but are said to have been vikings in their lifetime; their lair is situated behind a water-fall and when light falls upon them they fall asleep. The dragon Fafnir whom Sigurðr Vǫlsungr killed for the sake of his gold had also once been human, and thus also shares troll-like characteristics in origin. In another, *Hrólfs Saga Kraka*, the hero, a man called Boðvarr Bjarki (which means 'bear', and who actually is a shape-shifter) is shown fighting a monster which is said to be a troll and yet flies like a dragon. Although the hero engages in only one fight, there is a subsidiary plot in which he props up the dead monster in order that a young warrior (a Wiglaf figure to whom he offers protection) may apparently kill it in the sight of the whole court, and thus win renown. Interestingly, this incident has exactly the same context as the first part of the Beowulf story; the hero is a Geat who comes to join Hrothulf's court at Lejre (i.e. Heorot), and there, like Beowulf at the hands of Unferth, is given a hostile reception until he displays his prowess.

Unless all these stories are themselves based ultimately on *Beowulf*, which is *a priori* unlikely, it seems probable that the composite story in one form or another was known commonly in northern Europe. Genetically, therefore, the two parts of *Beowulf* are probably to be regarded as a natural unity which came into the hands of the poet already made up. But we have no need to apologise for the *Beowulf*-poet's lack of originality in this respect. It is no longer necessary for us to believe that any masterpiece of literature represents the inspired utterance of undefiled genius. Behind *The Canterbury Tales*, *King Lear*, or the *Four Quartets*, we can recognise material sources and influences which it was the purpose of the poet, however adroitly, to adapt and develop. But *Beowulf* is very far from being simply an unqualified English version of the Scandinavian Bear's Son tale. Even at the level of simple narrative, the *Beowulf*-poet has contrived to produce something more highly wrought, more impelling and significant, than the rather provincial, hand-me-down analogues. The tone of the Icelandic sagas is very different: matter-of-fact and casual even when the most striking crises are at hand. And their setting is different; no great hall of Heorot, centre of the nation state, upon the survival of which so much depends—but small yeoman farmers being attacked in their lonely fields by night, their lives depending on themselves alone, with no dramatic or tragic consequences. They are ruled by heroic ideals, just as Beowulf is, but the net effect is personal rather than communal, individual rather than universal. Our interest in the picaresque adventures of a Grettir or Hǫrðr lies in the straightforward narrative relation of, for instance, the hand-to-hand combats in which the heroes engage as they move from one predicament to another. The *Beowulf*-poet on the other hand gives the earthy folktale an altogether wider, more significant context, and has composed from his inherited materials a remarkably original and possibly unique work of literature. It probably came into the poet's hands as an unembroidered folktale, a casual account of monsters and dragons with no deeper significance than that required for simple fireside entertainment. But the poet has left us with a highly-wrought dramatic structure, the thematic content of which has formed the subject of lengthy and continuing scholastic dispute.

No one could pretend that we read *Beowulf* for a racy story-line. The poet's style is by no means turgid in itself, but continual comment, allusion and digression detract from what 'plot' there is. In any case, if the poet's primary concern had been heroic narrative, there are curious omissions to account for. There is hardly any reference to normal battle events, and such as there is, is minimised. Beowulf has the reputation of heroic activity carefully built up around him, but the only direct descriptions of his prowess we are given are when he encounters three supernatural beings—only the first two of which does he survive. What was in origin a threefold repetition—three encounters with monsters that are essentially the same, each of which is successfully dealt with by the hero—has been turned into something not only more artistically contrived but more momentous in its significance. The *Beowulf*-poet separates out the trolls who maraud Heorot from the quite distinct dragon who guards the hoard—and presents the two parts as diagnostic stages in the hero's career: his rise to prominence, and his eventual fall. However, *Beowulf* is not obviously a narrative poem in anything like the usual sense of that term. Neither is it a continuous setting forth of the life and manners of its hero. The poem now goes by the name of its protagonist, and not without some reason; but it is not necessarily 'about' Beowulf in the way that we normally consider *Hamlet* to be about Hamlet. Nevertheless, the author's object is apparently to be achieved by our contemplation of Beowulf's glorious youth, and later of the same hero's inevitable doom and death in old age.

It is the means of setting out these two contrasted stages in Beowulf's life that makes for the major bipartite division of the poem—and which has caused problems for those twentieth-century critics who reckon it falls apart in the middle. But, as the late J. R. R. Tolkien observed, the two halves are as integral to the whole as are the two parts of the Old English verse line. The structure of the poem, being thematic rather than narrative, is just as rhythmic and just as complete in itself as the rise and fall of the individual verse line. And like its unstressed but cumulatively significant metrical elements, there occur a wide variety of narrative digressions. These are often disturbing to the classically-educated reader, but of course the structure of *Beowulf* cannot be judged by classical criteria any more than we can analyse the Old English line in terms of classical syllabic metrics. Just as Old English verse allows for functional hypermetric elements, each allusion can be shown to be tightly tied in to the whole, and properly subordinate to the central theme, serving to illustrate, explain or emphasise. While the classically-trained reader may criticise the *Beowulf*-poet for a supposed looseness in construction, for his delight in a plethora of digressions which seem only to impede the progress of his narrative, the frustrated historian, who seeks to use the poem merely as an antiquarian mine, may accuse the poet of placing trivial myths at the centre of his composition while relegating important matters to a vague and allusive periphery. But although it is now sometimes difficult to reconstruct all of the various stories to which the poet alludes, it is clear that the so-called 'digressions' of *Beowulf* are not irrelevant and peripheral, but legitimate and highly appropriate parts of a deliberately constructed artistic whole.

The reader encounters one such episode at the very beginning of the poem—that dealing with the death and burial of Scyld Scefing. Standing outside the numbered sectional divisions of the poem, these lines have no obvious connection with the main narrative, and in the past were sometimes considered to be either the beginning of another poem, or perhaps a complete separate poem, which somehow got tacked on to the beginning of *Beowulf* because both seemed to deal with the kings of Denmark. But pursuing the metrical analogy, this sequence can be shown to be viable as a kind of structural anacrusis, functionally comparable with the extrametrical introductory *Hwæt* at the beginning of the first line. In fact the Scyld Scefing episode provides the *leitmotif* to the whole poem, evoking the noble, heroic, glorious and tragic atmosphere of the courts of Migration Age Europe. It reminds an informed audience with aristocratic and antiquarian interests of the noble origins of those whose exploits the poet is about to relate. Scyld Scefing had come to the Danish people in their hour of need, and had established the glory of their kingdom: 'That', says the poet, 'was a great king'. It is important for the poet to establish the heroic might of the Danish kingdom in order to heighten the contrast of Grendel's onslaught, bringing chaos to the land of Scyld, threatening to destroy all that he had built, and bring to an end the reign of his grandson and heir, Hrothgar. Had we plunged straight into the account of Grendel's attacks, the Danes would have given the impression of mere weakness, and Beowulf's subsequent achievements would have seemed the less heroic. It is not only the terrible nature of the monsters, but the imperium of their victims that enhance the hero. The audience of course knew from the genealogies that Scyld had been preceded by the savage and avaricious king Heremod whose exile and destruction reduced the Danish people to a state of misery. The poet has no need to mention the fact; he can rely on this knowledge and at the same time contrive to make it appear that Scyld's arrival marks the very foundation of the Danish state and the springtime of its fortunes. However, just as Scyld Scefing came to the Danes alone over the waves at their hour of need, so now another young hero comes to them from over the waves, another stranger who will also cleanse their land and re-establish the glory of their kingdom—but again only for a time, for in this life all is corruptible, every glory transient. This young man will also one day prove a great king, and the remembrance of Scyld offers a sad anticipation of the eventual fate of Beowulf himself, in the sure knowledge that, however laden with treasures and renown, death (and perhaps before death, failure) comes to all men. No man, counsellor or hero, was so wise as to know Scyld's ultimate destination. 'Sad was their mind', says the poet, 'mourning their mood'—and ours also, because this is the burden of the poem: the overriding fact of mutability in the world.

This symbolic arrival and departure in the prelude to the poem is a literary mechanism commonly employed to distance an event and set it in a more universal perspective. The mysterious arrival and departure of a national folk hero by boat is by no means without parallel in heroic literature. Tennyson's Arthur comes and goes thus, and so also many later heroes, although latterly the ship is often replaced by a horse, and the sea by a western sunset. This episode of the poem dealing with the beginnings and the end of the greatest of the kings of Denmark thus foreshadows the substance of the larger poem, which deals with the rise and fall of the greatest of Geatish kings—the establishment of his reputation with the troll-fights at Heorot and finally his death, facing the dragon at Eagles' Crag. The events of Beowulf's long and prosperous reign, half a century full of incident no doubt, are all passed over without comment. It is perhaps surprising that we should be given no account of the type of successful kingship. Instead we are brought rapidly to his final battle with the dragon, his death and the subsequent destruction of his kingdom. This structural telescoping of the narrative so as to bring the hero's downfall into deliberate juxtaposition with the struggle involved in his rise to prominence suggests that the two parts are intended to be compared in some way. The contrast is significant. *Beowulf* is a poem of beginnings and ends. It begins with the rise of the Danes under the leadership of Scyld Scefing; it ends with the very certain destruction of the Geats after the death of their leader Beowulf. And to this the opening fifty lines of the poem provide a totally apposite exordium, evoking the atmosphere of mystery, transitoriness and inscrutable destiny, both of individuals and of entire nations. Just as no man knew what became of Scyld Scefing, neither did they know—nor do we know—what became of Beowulf's Geats; they both just drift out of history.

Broadly speaking, the allusions intercalated with the first part of the poem are legendary, while those of the second part deal with more definitely historical events. In the first part we have allusions to, or summaries of legends about such figures as Sigemund the dragonslayer, Hama who stole the necklace of the Brosings, the avaricious Heremod and others. The second half refers more precisely to what was known of the history of the Danes under the Scylding dynasty, and the causes of their downfall, and of the history of the Geatish wars until the final destruction of the Geats following the joint invasion of Franks and Swedes. This division is quite appropriate. The first part deals with the legendary rise of the hero, remote in time, appropriately linking him with other great heroes of the past; the second part concerns his actual effect upon the people, the historical references being immediate and concrete, to events occurring within the hero's own lifetime, and touching himself or his people closely. Legendary matter builds up the heroic perspective; the stories of Hama and Ingeld encrust a rich surface like jewels; they do not motivate the action of the plot, but add immeasurable resonances to an already dense structure. Beowulf's exploits are compared with those of the great Sigemund, and contrasted with those of the wicked and tight-fisted Heremod. There is no need for the poet to describe at length the great value of the necklace which Queen Wealhtheow gives to the hero; it is simply compared (perhaps identified) with the rich necklace of the Brosing dwarves which Hama stole from the tyrant Eormanric—thus gaining lasting fame. The reference incidentally allows the poet to refer to the recurrent theme of Hygelac's downfall and death. On Beowulf's return he had given Wealhtheow's present to Queen Hygd, who in turn apparently gave it to her husband. Certainly it was this same necklace that Hygelac wore on his last fateful raid against the Frisians, which event ultimately led to Beowulf's taking on the burden of kingship, but which only temporarily postpones its ultimate consequence of bringing about the destruction of the Geatish kingdom by its enemies.

The historical allusions of the later part are rather different in their functions. The first part had seen Beowulf's preparation and initiation into leadership; the second provides the setting and background for his actual adoption of kingship. Their function here is dramatic and vital, motivating the progress of Beowulf's life and tricking out his inevitable doom. The digressions of the first part had defined the movement of the poem in blocks of colour—a dignified circumspect dance; those of the second part in no way impede the progress of swifter narrative, but are actually involved in hastening its end. The historical traditions deal with the decline and fall of the Danish and Geatish kingdoms, both of which it had been Beowulf's life-work to maintain. The whole elaborately investigated matter of the Geat–Swedish wars is structurally significant as part of a moving framework within which the tragedy of the hero can be enacted, provoking a universal quality.

The resonant nature of the slightest digression is usefully illustrated by an allusion to the ultimate fate of Heorot in the very midst of its present glories (82–5). The destruction of Heorot as a result of the Danish–Heathobard feud, like Hrothulf's ousting of Hrothgar's sons, touch upon events that were well known to the contemporary audience —both gaining their dramatic effect from being uttered at the very moment of secure and prosperous triumph. They are used to provoke a tragic atmosphere of foreboding. The lofty gold-adorned palace of Heorot, the glory of the kingdom of Denmark, is newly completed—it awaits only the furious surges of hateful flame, which are destined to reduce it to ashes. Just so, the ruling kinsmen, the noble Hrothgar and the heroic Hrothulf, sit together at the banquet, in high spirits and in friendship—for the time being. Queen Wealhtheow is confident that Hrothulf will act nobly towards her sons—if he remembers all the advantages he was given in his own youth. But the audience already knew that Hrothulf would need to slay the young princes before taking the throne. Such examples of ironic anticipation are used throughout the poem to reinforce the note of impending doom struck at the very beginning.

Similar in its effect is the reference to Sigemund Wælsing (874f). This is introduced easily enough with the author's usual fluidity in transition between one narrative element and another. Beowulf has defeated Grendel—his renown is proclaimed, and the nobles of Hrothgar's court amuse themselves by letting their horses run on the sands, and telling each other stories of great monster-killings of the past. A minstrel is said first to compose a lay about the achievement of Beowulf himself, and then to devise an apt parallel. The parallel he chooses is that of Sigemund the dragon-slayer. This Sigemund, as the audience knew, slew a dragon and seized its treasure; but the treasure had a curse laid upon it which ultimately brought about the death of the hero. Only the slaying of the dragon and the taking of the treasure are mentioned in *Beowulf*, but it is certain that the audience would be familiar with the entire story. The point of the Sigemund digression is to suggest parallels between Sigemund's career and that of Beowulf, both in the past, as a monster-slayer, and also in anticipation of the future, as a prospective dragon-killer too. The minstrel pays a proper compliment to Beowulf in choosing to compare him with the greatest of monster-slayers known to the Germanic world. It is left to the audience of the poem to recall the tragic consequence of Sigemund's action, and to think of what will happen to Beowulf in later life when he is fated to face the same situation, and the same doom. Such digressions have their virtue not in the stories themselves, which were already well known and needed only to be partially related, but in the way they are employed to achieve a cumulative end. Unlike its Old Norse analogues, *Beowulf* presents not a straightforward narrative, but a series of vivid pictorial splashes against an unstable moving background, the allusions adding both colour and depth to the structure while never breaking its overall organic unity. The poem's structure, like its verbal style, progresses by a series of deliberative parallels and variations towards a unified whole. The net effect is monumental. A narrative poem does not necessarily lose anything by our being already familiar with the plot. It gains enormously in that kind of ironic anticipation peculiar to earlier Germanic literature. The poet is not concerned with suspense; he is, after all, writing not a detective story but a stately exposition of a particular theme.

The poet's theme is the nature of the heroic life—more specifically, the function and character of leadership in heroic society. The didactic content of the poem is high. Even where the poet is not directly moralising, it is easy enough to see the poem advancing through a series of *sententiae* culminating in Hrothgar's so-called 'sermon' or 'homily' (1687f). In the beginning we are presented with an image of strong Germanic kingship in the person of Scyld Scefing, the founder of his nation's prosperity; in the face of hostile armies, he struck terror into his neighbours, forcing them to pay tribute in submission. This is greeted in terms of unqualified praise: 'that was a great king!' It is the worst possible fate, insists the poet, for a nation to be without a strong king. Subsequently we are shown a son born to Scyld, who by goodness and generosity won the support and loyalty of his people. Among all nations, says the poet, it is only through those actions which merit praise that a man may prosper. This is the key to the heroic ethic: action which leads to glory and praise, *lof* and *dom*, to the attainment of which all men should direct themselves. Life is fleeting: we shall all die; let us therefore so act as to merit the praise and remembrance of men. Scyld's great grandson, Hrothgar, had been a fine example of the heroic king in his youth. Such success in arms and so great a fame attended him, we are told, that kinsmen were eager to serve him, and his *comitatus* increased in size to a formidable army. Princes from distant lands flocked to a court which seems to have been a northern equivalent of that of Arthur in the sub-Roman west.

It is against this background that we see the introduction of the hall Heorot, the major symbol of the first half of the poem—the integrity of which it is Beowulf's object to preserve. The power of the hall as a poetic image is attested throughout Old English literature; it was the practical and emotional centre of heroic society, all that a man could wish; and its destruction therefore represented the negation of all that society stood for. The symbol of Heorot is introduced with great care by the poet. The home of Hrothgar's people, their source of joy and national harmony, it is shown to be less the palace of a king than the symbol of Denmark as a nation state. It is given a princely name: Heorot; it would be known to occupy a site of extreme sacred antiquity in the Germanic north. At its inauguration there is feasting and music, the universal symbols of order and harmony; the minstrel sings a hymn of creation. And yet at the very moment of its erection we are fore-warned of its eventual destruction. The audience in any case knew very well what the end would be—and Beowulf has not yet entered into his business of saving it from the monsters. The implication is not that his actions are so much futile, as transient. All the glories of mankind are temporary; it is necessary to recognise the reality of this before we can begin to understand the nature of the heroic life.

In his youth, then, Hrothgar had been the type of the ideal Germanic leader, possessed of both wisdom and courage, the mental and physical strength that such a position demands. But while old and full of years, and still the archetypal wise king, Hrothgar now no longer possesses the physical strength he once had. Thus it is that he has need of Beowulf's services. He is not a feeble king: he has had a great career behind him; and it would not be a worthily heroic picture if he were seen to be in any way weak or cowardly, a lame dog to be helped over a stile. He allows himself to accept Beowulf's offer of assistance, since it merely represents just repayment of help the young Hrothgar had once been able to afford the hero's father in an hour of need. At a time when Hrothgar's physical strength is failing with age, his court apparently falls prey to an external force of disruption. This takes the form of depredation by the monster Grendel, a wretched and unnatural outcast, creature of chaos and outer darkness.

Early medieval society felt itself closely surrounded by the whole paraphernalia of common pagan fear: hobgoblins, trolls, elves, things that go bump in the night, which dwelt in the wastelands, swamps and deep forests, approaching human awareness only at night, in darkness—and against which the warmth of the hall and its society offered the only security. This belief is not quite so naive as it might at first seem to the average twentieth-century man—who also believes in a whole range of things he has not personally seen, from bacteria to men on the moon, and in literary terms a host of science-fiction wonders. This was not necessarily a belief in the supernatural as such; the poet's trolls and dragons are firmly embedded in a matrix of realism and normality. It is interesting that where the *Letter of Alexander to Aristotle* speaks of water-monsters it uses the word *nicor*, as in *Beowulf*, whereas the original Latin was *hippopotamus*. That hippopotami were not found in sixth-century Europe is irrelevant; the fact is, water-monsters exist for a hero like Alexander or Beowulf to confront. Early medieval Europe had no alternative but to externalise its personal and institutional neuroses, and the monster provided a convenient mechanism for fear, then as now. Whatever their origins, physical or mental, it is clear that such monsters represent an evil that could, and should, be encountered and opposed. Not that monsters like Grendel can be defeated once for all; for as the perpetuation of the feud by Grendel's mother demonstrates, the price of freedom is eternal vigilance.

The main outline of Grendel's function within the poem is plain: a creature of darkness and night, outcast by God from the society of men, together with hobgoblins and all other monstrous progenies hostile to human happiness. Associated by the poet with Cain, primordial kinslayer and therefore symbol of elemental social disunity, he stalks abroad, ravaging only by night when the sun, *Godes candel*, is far from the sky. He has made his home with all that is antithetical to Heorot, inhabiting an unvisited land, solitary paths, perilous swamps and the misty wastelands. His lair is a place very like Hell, a dreadful region shunned by all that is good in nature like the noble hart, *heorot*, a major Germanic symbol of both regality and purity. Banished from the society of men, obliged to take the paths of an outcast, he treads the wilderness as an exile, a solitary figure. Such loneliness has none of the romantic aura that a later age might ascribe to it. For heroic society, the solitary figure is invariably suspect and probably vicious, an object of fear and distrust. Although this monster has been proscribed by God, Danish society seems still to be subject to his depredation. He is not effectively banished for ever. Haunting the borders of human society, he is always present, neither in nor fully out of it, the corporeal substance of fear, always ready to intrude given opportunity enough. Well known to both the people and the councillors of the king, Grendel and his dam tread the wastelands in the likeness of men, but misshapen, a mockery of the form of human society, and a public enemy. In this shape, then, some sort of evildoer is found amongst the Danes, a hidden enemy inflicting unheard of injury, havoc and disgrace. It is not the physical splendour of Heorot which so angers Grendel, but the order and peace he discerns there. Above all, it is the sweet sound of the harp, archetypal symbol of harmony, that the creature of chaos is unable to bear. Thus it was that the outcast Satan beheld the newly-created Eden, according to the Cædmonian *Genesis*. Grendel has centred his destructive spite on the heroic society that inhabited the hall Heorot, and apparently without encountering any effective opposition.

The ancient order seems to have proved ultimately inadequate to oppose such an enemy. Heorot's king, although once a renowned war-leader and still both valiant and wise, is now incapable in his own person of bearing the brunt of the attacks. Those to whom he might have looked for support in such a situation, the councillors of his people or his own *comitatus*, both fail him. As with the ancient Swedes or the East Saxons in times of national adversity, war or famine, all the Danish witan can suggest to alleviate public misery is to promise sacrifices at heathen shrines. But this will obviously be of no avail. The poet at least seems well aware of the futility of this course of action. Hrothgar's *comitatus* is no more successful than his witan. Although composed of a great number of noble young warriors like Wulfgar, they are none of them able to put an end to Grendel's encroachments. Asleep in Heorot, grown fat with feasting, they prove all too easy a prey; and the monster has become accustomed to wreak havoc among them, taking up thirty thanes at a time. Despite boasting in their cups, the hollowness of heroic Scylding society based on a free *beot* is soon apparent, and the *comitatus* dwindles, partly through sheer inactivity and partly through simple lack of courage. The onslaught is so forceful and persistent that the old pattern of free loyalties as represented by the company in Heorot breaks up, and the hall is abandoned.

It is plain that external vulnerability is merely symptomatic of internal debility, however; and as Beowulf himself is later to point out, Grendel could not have wrought such havoc unless the seeds of spiritless discord were not already present in the state of Denmark. This disease is epitomised for us in the person of Unferth, the court orator who seats himself at Hrothgar's feet and in whom the king is said to place implicit trust. The name, literally 'Discordia', or perhaps simply 'Lacking spirit', sounds fictional, and possibly the figure was an invention of the author. The conventional 'wicked councillor' is a common literary device employed to account for errors made by otherwise good rulers without compromising their greatness. It was at the instance of such personae that an otherwise good king might be prompted to embark on some disastrous course of action, to court defeat in war or to slay his own offspring.

The old pattern of loyalties proving unable to contain these new conditions, a new 'kind' of hero is required; and indeed, his reputation has preceded him. Beowulf is already the subject of travellers' tales, a greater man than any other. The introduction of this hero into the decayed Danish kingdom is like the advent of a saviour—a breath of new and vigorous life. He is a stranger to the land, but is immediately recognisable for his plain virtues. Through the eyes of Hrothgar's coast-warden, the hero is seen from the beginning as an essentially active agent, clothed in the fine, bright armour of his business. He is in every way remarkable, singled out from other men as a strong-willed leader. He is a man with a personal sense of mission. His fine war-gear is not merely the affection of pride, but the outward promise of strong action, equipment deserving respect. Arms and armour form a persistent and powerful symbol of heroic activity throughout the poem. And in contrast to the current Danish malaise, this is a man of decisive, strong and vital action who can distinguish between words and deeds. To such a one, the coast-warden recognises, it will be given successfully to survive the hostile encounter. Nevertheless, as Beowulf himself admits, wyrd will go as it must. Returning victorious from his second fight against the underwater monsters, the hero concedes that this time his sole strength would have been insufficient without the intervention of Providence, the ruler of victories. He brings with him as proof of his exploit not only Grendel's head, but the hilt of the sword with which the deed was accomplished—and which significantly bears a pictorial allusion to the giants who had warred against God and were thus destroyed in the flood. Hrothgar closely examines the hilt, so eloquent of the ever-present possibility of sudden change in fortune; and it is this he uses as the starting point for his so-called sermon, which forms both the structural and thematic hinge of the poem. He contrasts Beowulf's virtues with the miserable savagery of the treacherous King Heremod, prophesying the hero's likely accession to power. Beowulf has both strength and wisdom, but must be warned of the cardinal heroic sin of arrogance. Worldly success will often lull the conscience to sleep, and then a hero proves particularly vulnerable to the attacks of evil—and then suddenly, in a variety of ways, death may come upon him —either violently through sword or arrow, or simply through the inevitable decay of old age. Beowulf is therefore urged to take the better part, which is eternal gain—avoiding pride. Only a little while will he be at the height of his powers before old age, disease or the edge of the sword will plunder his strength: its transience is inevitable.

The second half of the poem might be expected to assess how far the hero lives up to Hrothgar's prophecy of him in face of the inevitable facts of reality. But in fact we are shown very little of his subsequent career, although various allusions hint at such matters as his presence at the death of Hygelac and his role in the Swedish wars. If, as some have supposed, *Beowulf* was intended as a 'mirror for princes', in which young men might encounter in imagination a variety of ennobling situations and thus learn the attitudes appropriate to their place in heroic society, we might have expected the poet to have given full rein to a taste for battle scenes, showing the hero engaged in noble exploits. But there are only oblique allusions to actual physical battles, and the poet seems deliberately to have minimised any battle scene in which the hero might possibly have taken part. Although he has a whole aura of courageous action built round him, the only enemies we see our hero confront are not even human, but incredible monsters and supernatural beings. This then is a curious kind of heroism in some ways. We are soon aware that Beowulf's struggles have broader implications than their outward appearance, involving not merely physical but moral courage. And if there is any moral content, then the conflict with monsters provides a more suitable vehicle than any human battle, however well described, could ever be, simply because the forces of evil are better seen in monstrous shapes. The age had not yet arrived when any human enemy could be considered entirely vicious—the Antichrist. The open society of Migration Age Europe recognised no such concept as lèse-majesté, so that Hrothulf's displacement of Hrothgar's sons would be regarded as natural, and his subsequent reign was long remembered as a golden age in Scandinavian tradition. The greatness of an Ohthere or Ongentheow can be readily acknowledged because, though avowed enemies of Beowulf's people, they conform to the heroic ethic. Mere hostility is understandable, and inevitable, whereas greed and the swearing of false oaths are abhorrent because they corrode the fabric of heroic society. It is significant that in the event Beowulf is not destroyed by any human foe but by a dragon.

The monsters of the first part and the dragon of the second are similar in some respects. Both are elemental, primeval enemies; and both are public scourges, intent upon the humiliation of men, destroying their dwellings and ultimately the courts of their kings. Both are creatures of the night, unwilling to engage in their depredations by the light of day. However, whereas Grendel's enmity was self-motivated and aroused instinctively not by the material wealth and prosperity of Heorot but by its harmonious and joyful order, the dragon remains happily inactive until its anger is provoked by the theft of a jewelled goblet which the dragon believes to belong to itself alone. The man who rifles the dragon's hoard is not described by the poet as any kind of hero, but as an outlaw and a sin-perplexed soul. That dragons, like trolls, have some ulterior significance is obvious; as the tenth-century scientific writer Byrhtferth of Ramsey would say: 'What are dragons, but people who are evil and contentious and enemies of God, and the ruin of their own souls.' Those well read in the Bible could find confirmation for the Satanic associations of dragons. But dragons had a long-established mythological history in the north, and any contemporary audience would readily have identified the beast of popular tradition. Their origins could be traced to those 'gold-guarding griffins' which Herodotus thought occupied the extreme north of Europe. This function is well-defined by the Old English verse maxim: 'The dragon dwells in a barrow, ancient and proud in treasures.' Their maiden-devouring propensities were a later romantic innovation. Conventionally in early Germanic literature dragons act as the miserly hoarders of material wealth, concerned not to use it, but simply to allow it to moulder while they sleep, coiled round both it and the barrows, the graves of dead men, that traditionally contain it. This image of elemental parsimony, the sin of Heremod which Beowulf had been adjured to shun, closely overlaps with the potent symbols of arms rusting through inaction, and the derelict hall. The so-called 'lay of the lone survivor' lists those features of the orderly and active life which are now lacking. Those who formerly delighted in the dragon's treasure, as in all the joys of hall, are now all passed away; there is none to wield the sword, nor to polish the cup. The arms and armour moulder and decay, like the warriors who had worn them.

There is neither music of the harp, nor any stamping of swift steeds in the courtyard; no hawk swoops through this empty and desolate hall. All active agents are now dead, and the treasure is buried with the dead, useless. This is where the dragon finds it and covets it. It is simple, profitless greed that the dragon here represents, a slumbering in possession, which, as Hrothgar's sermon had insisted, is fatal to men.

The end comes about suddenly, almost accidentally. As Hrothgar had warned, one can never tell what change of fortune may occur. It is significant that when this trouble comes to Beowulf—the destruction of his own, like Hrothgar's court—he is in much the same position the Danish king had been in when, as a young man, the hero had lent the old king his strong aid. Beowulf has ruled his kingdom well and strongly for fifty years—just the length of time that Hrothgar had reigned—but now he too is old and subject to the weakness of age. But although old, Beowulf is still personally courageous. His weakness is of a different order from Hrothgar's inactivity. But the foe that now oppresses his kingdom is of a different order also. Contrary to his usual spirit, Beowulf falls prey to dismal thoughts. Although no coward, the hero is no longer resolute and self-confident, now despairing of God's strength to support his arm. Uneasy and restless, he gloomily anticipates his doom. Only one reminiscence comes to mind—again linked with the image of a ruined and desolate hall. He recalls how it was that Hygelac himself had first come to the throne through an act of kin-killing—his elder brother slaying the eldest, a futile and profitless death which necessarily went unavenged. It was, of course, this death which ultimately led to Beowulf's assuming the throne. Former warriors now lying in the grave, their hall lies waste, the only sound heard being not that of the harp but of the rushing wind. The armour in which Beowulf trusts will prove no greater protection than the walls of the barrow in which the dragon puts its faith.

If the great king finally fails, however, there is another who does not. There comes to him *in extremis*, just as he himself once came to the aid of the elderly Hrothgar, a strong prince and heir to his spirit, Wiglaf. His action in joining battle is both an appeal to the heroic code and a recognition of the old king's personal stature. He is certain that, for as long as Beowulf had ruled the kingdom, he had been the most honoured hero in the world. And when at last Wiglaf ignores the express wishes of his leader in coming to his aid, it was because the old hero did not now deserve to die alone—if only for the sake of all his past deeds.

But Beowulf's death is merely the climax of the poem. The tragic denouement is to follow. Now, of course, as Wiglaf knows, the giving of swords and all the joys of native land must end, with the dispersal of Beowulf's people into enforced and despised exile (2884–90). Whether the entire Geatish nation was actually annihilated at this point, as some historians suppose, is immaterial; for the purpose of the narrative the issue is clear. The messenger who announces the death of the king to his people serves to confirm both Beowulf's great *dom* and the dangerous vulnerability of the nation consequent upon the passing of so strong a ruler. Just as in his pride Hygelac had aroused the hostility of the Franks to the south, Hæthcyn had been slain for the similarly arrogant attack on the Swedes to the north. And now the destruction of the kingdom is inevitable, the messenger gloomily prophesying a simultaneous invasion from both north and south. His theme is taken up by the Geatish woman—perhaps Beowulf's queen—to whom falls the office of singing the dead king's dirge. Nevertheless, whatever may result, no one can deny that Beowulf had been a great king. As he had wished, his people erect for him a great barrow high up on Whale's Cape to be recognised from afar as both a memorial and a landmark for all those who in future will urge their ships from afar over the darkness of the seas. The gold, which the hero had died to win, they again commit to the earth 'as useless to men as it was before'. But the final words of the poem belong to Beowulf's *comitatus*. They declare him to have been the greatest of heroes, of all kings in the world the gentlest and most gracious, kindest to his people and most desirous of renown—one who had truly achieved that *lof* and *dom* for which, as we learned in the beginning, all men should strive.

Death in some fashion or another must come at last to even the greatest of heroes. Given the ultimate fact of mutability, the Germanic hero is invariably a tragic hero; his virtues are characteristically seen in defence—and often in defeat. But his tragedy has far greater consequences than the merely personal tragedy we associate with the classical or Shakespearian tragic hero. Hamlet, for example, moves in a neurotic world of inner conflict and self-doubt; between his values and those of society at large there exists a wide gulf. Beowulf, on the other hand, does not feel Hamlet's need constantly to question his motives; he and his people share a community of interests. Although his personal stature is so great, and although in the end he goes out alone to face his fate, he nevertheless has the strongest ties with his people. He is the one hope of their culture—the culmination of a tradition, identifying and embodying the fundamental values and aspirations of his nation. Hamlet's disaster is individual to himself. At his fall Denmark is not destroyed; if anything, the kingdom is cleansed by Hamlet's death. Beowulf's death has epic implications: it marks the end of a way of life, the destruction of a civilisation. The death of Hector resulted in the fall of Troy. Arthur's death meant the end of the Round Table. Beowulf's death will bring with it the demise of the kingdom of the Geats.

Hamlet's death ends the play—there's nothing more to say. But Beowulf's death, as the poet knew, meant the Geats would disappear without trace in the culture of sixth-century Sweden. The poet puts into the mouth of the messenger a full awareness of the fate Beowulf had gone so willingly to meet, and which as a result his people will have to meet. In classical tragedy the hero struggles against the fate which some personal tragic flaw has brought about. In this kind of epic literature, however, evil is usually confined to agents external to the hero: Arthur's Mordred or Beowulf's monsters. The epic hero knows his opponent as well as the source of his own strength, though in the end this knowledge is of no use to him. The epic hero goes willingly to his fate, even though the awful consequences of his choice must be as clear to himself as anyone else. Beowulf dismisses his *comitatus*, but continues to act in the light of the ethical requirements of that group. He believes for an instant—the instant of *beot*—that he *may* overcome the dragon, that he *may* preserve the way of life they all know. The hero defies his fate, but in a spirit of resignation: fate will go always as it must; a man can achieve so much, and no more; he cannot, after all, live for ever. His decision may seem to be brought about by pride but, unlike the classical hubris, it is external and clear, not what he but society expects. And whether victorious or defeated, therefore, the end will be that glory, *lof* and *dom*, for which Beowulf, of all men, was the most eager.

A note on the text and translation

Two facsimile editions of the *Beowulf*-manuscript are available: *The Nowell Codex: British Museum Cotton Vitellius A.XV, Second MS.*, ed. Kemp Malone, Early English Manuscripts in Facsimile, XII, Copenhagen 1963; *Beowulf: Reproduced in Facsimile from the unique manuscript British Museum MS. Cotton Vitellius A.XV*, ed. Julius Zupitza, revised N. Davis, Early English Text Society, CCXLV, London, 1959.

The manuscript was badly scorched during a fire which damaged the Cotton Library in 1731; the margins of the vellum have crumbled and many words at the outer edges are now missing or only partly legible. However, two transcripts made in 1786–7 before the condition of the manuscript had deteriorated too far, supply valuable evidence for restoring some readings. One transcript was made by a professional copyist on behalf of the Icelandic philologist G. J. Thorkelin (Thorkelin A), and then a second copy was made by Thorkelin himself (Thorkelin B): *The Thorkelin Transcripts of 'Beowulf' in Facsimile*, ed. Kemp Malone, Early English Manuscripts in Facsimile, I, Copenhagen, 1951.

Some parts of the manuscript, and two folios in particular, 182^r and 201^v, were already badly rubbed, and here the Thorkelin transcripts afford little or no additional information. But close examination of the manuscript using ultraviolet light enables us to postulate certain additional restorations. See generally: A. H. Smith, *London Mediaeval Studies*, I (1938), 179–207; J. C. Pope, *The Rhythm of Beowulf*, New Haven, 1966, pp. xxivf, 232f.

I have presented as conservative a text as possible, retaining manuscript readings wherever they are tenable. Corrections in the hands of the Anglo-Saxon scribes are silently admitted. Difficult readings have been checked with the original, using ultraviolet light where appropriate. Where Thorkelin readings have become part of the 'textus receptus', they have been adopted without comment. Space forbids full textual commentary and only the most notorious *loci desperati* can be described in the notes. For a full account of the various scholarly interpretations of the text, see: *Beowulf and Judith*, ed. E.v.K. Dobbie, The Anglo-Saxon Poetic Records, IV, New York, 1953; *Beowulf and The Fight at Finnsburg*, ed. F. Klaeber, 3rd edn., Boston, 1950.

The translator, especially one attempting to translate from poetry into prose, is confronted by innumerable problems too well known to require rehearsal here; whole books have been written about them. Of its nature, translation is unsatisfactory. The number of possible interpretations, not simply of substance but of tone and texture, is often large. And the decisions which must be taken are more often than not purely subjective. Ultimately translation cannot reproduce, or even adequately reflect, the style of the original without departing from its substance to an unacceptable degree. Particularly frustrating are places where density of meaning or ambiguity is simply unavailable in Modern English. Repeatedly the translator is obliged to plump for one simplistic sense, when he knows that several are present in the original. Much of the force of the original depends on the economic vigour of poetic compounds, which prosaic periphrasis merely dissipates, and I have tried not to 'clarify' by over-expansion. The range of vocabulary presents special problems since the choice of words available in Modern English is often too limited to accommodate the various terms a warlike society needed for such concepts as weapons or soldiers, which were not necessarily technical variants but which presumably offered differing emotive connotations. The *Beowulf*-poet uses no less than ten separate synonyms for 'man', although how far their various etymologies were still meaningful by the time the poet was writing we cannot know. I have avoided the antique verbal register employed by Scott or Morris, eschewing so far as possible words like 'knight' or 'lord', since these evoke the romantic world of feudal chivalry—as far removed from the heroic society of Beowulf as from our own. Recourse to the terms 'warrior' and 'chief' seems inescapable however, and I can only hope that recurrent use will reduce any Red Indian or Zulu connotations they may have, and accustom the reader to their use in a heroic context. Since the overall texture of the poem depends to some extent on a regular pattern of synonyms, I have thought it important to render word for word consistently throughout, departing from this only where the poet's cumulative listing would have resulted in a repetition not present in the original.

Less easy to resolve satisfactorily are problems of syntax. The poet's general style is reflected in the appearance of the manuscript, where the verse is written out continuously like prose but punctuation and capitals are used only very sparingly. Anacoluthon is common. The favoured mode of construction is paratactic. As in his overall structure, so in his verbal constructions, the poet has an associative habit of mind. Rather than dividing his ideas logically in the manner of modern prose writers, he presents his thoughts in a complex interlaced flow. Incremental and annexive, clauses and phrases are added one after another resulting in an epithetical cumulative subject hung about with multiple predications. And loose correlatives allow the poet to develop elaborate paragraphs where a modern writer might consider it proper to use only two or three logically connected clauses. The development of such a style was presumably necessitated by the conditions of oral delivery. 'Elegant variation' would ensure that nothing essential to the plot was lost to individual members of the audience momentarily distracted by other delights and necessities of hall, while those following the poet's line with greater concentration might appreciate its ingenuity and verbal dexterity. The net effect was to achieve a medium able to sustain the epic flow of a long narrative poem, quite unlike the more staccato movement appropriate to slighter literary forms.

To render all this satisfactorily into a modern prose style of which Fowler might approve, and at the same time without doing any real disservice to the poem, is wellnigh impossible. I have tried to cut through a Gordian tangle by presenting as close a translation as the language will allow without being awkwardly over-literal. But the task is one which causes the experienced reader to despair as readily as the first-year undergraduate. It is comforting to recall that even so practised an exponent as Bede himself, in translating the first English Christian hymn into Latin prose, acknowledged the impossibility of such a feat. But it was, and is, none the less worth attempting for all that.

The presence of an asterisk in the translation indicates the existence of an explanatory note (see p. 188ff). These notes are used largely to expand the poet's more esoteric allusions and to offer background

SWEDES

VANDALS

GEATS

DANES

rot

Wulfings

ONS

Gifthas

VANDALS

NORTHERN EUROPE IN
THE SIXTH CENTURY

information on contemporary manners and customs without which the text might prove obscure.

Select bibliography

R. E. Bjork and J. D. Niles, ed., *A Beowulf Handbook*, Exeter, 1997.

H. Bloom, ed., *Modern Critical Interpretations: Beowulf*, New York, 1987.

A. Bonjour, *The Digressions in Beowulf*, Oxford, 1950.

A. G. Brodeur, *The Art of Beowulf*, Berkeley, 1959.

R. W. Chambers, *Beowulf: an Introduction*, 3rd ed. revised by C. L. Wrenn, Cambridge, 1959.

G. Clark, *Beowulf*, Boston, 1990.

B. S. Cox, *Cruces of Beowulf*, The Hague, 1970.

J. W. Earl, *Thinking about Beowulf*, Stanford, 1994.

D. K. Fry, *The Beowulf Poet*, Englewood Cliffs, 1968.

G. N. Garmonsway et al., *Beowulf and its Analogues*, London, 1968.

M. E. Goldsmith, *The Mode and Meaning of Beowulf*, London, 1970.

E. B. Irving, *A Reading of Beowulf*, New Haven, 1968.

— *Rereading Beowulf*, Philadelphia, 1989.

L. E. Nicholson, ed., *An Anthology of Beowulf Criticism*, Notre Dame, Indiana, 1963.

K. Sisam, *The Structure of Beowulf*, Oxford, 1965.

D. Whitelock, *The Audience of Beowulf*, Oxford, 1951.

Beowulf

Hwæt, we Gar-Dena   in geardagum
þeodcyninga   þrym gefrunon,
hu ða æþelingas   ellen fremedon.
    Oft Scyld Scefing   sceaþena þreatum,
monegum mægþum   meodosetla ofteah;   5
egsode Eorle.   Syððan ærest wearð
feasceaft funden,   (he þæs frofre gebad)
weox under wolcnum,   weorðmyndum þah,
oðþæt him æghwylc   þara ymbsittendra
ofer hronrade   hyran scolde,   10
gomban gyldan: þæt wæs god cyning!
    Ðæm eafera wæs   æfter cenned
geong in geardum,   þone God sende
folce to frofre.   Fyrenðearfe ongeat,
þæt hie ær drugon   aldorlease   15
lange hwile.   Him þæs Liffrea,
wuldres Wealdend,   woroldare forgeaf;
Beowulf wæs breme   —blæd wide sprang—
Scyldes eafera,   Scedelandum in.
Swa sceal geong guma   gode gewyrcean,   20
fromum feohgiftum   on fæder bearme,
þæt hine on ylde   eft gewunigen
wilgesiþas,   þonne wig cume,
leode gelæsten.   Lofdædum sceal
in mægþa gehwære   man geþeon.   25
    Him ða Scyld gewat   to gescæphwile,
felahror, feran   on Frean wære.
Hi hyne þa ætbæron   to brimes faroðe,
swæse gesiþas,   swa he selfa bæd,
þenden wordum weold   wine Scyldinga.   30
Leof landfruma   lange ahte.
    Þær æt hyðe stod   hringedstefna,
isig ond utfus,   æþelinges fær.
Aledon þa   leofne þeoden,

Indeed, we have heard of the glory of the Spear-Danes, kings of the nation in days gone by—how those princes performed deeds of courage.

Often Scyld Scefing dragged away the mead benches from bands of foes, from many tribes—struck terror into the Heruli.* From the time when first he was found destitute (he received consolation for that) he flourished beneath the skies, prospered in honours until every one of those who dwelt around about him across the whale's road had to obey him, pay him tribute. That was a great king!

Later a son was born to him, a young man in the court, whom God sent to be a comfort to the people. He had perceived the cruel distress they once suffered when for a long time they lacked a king. Therefore the Lord of Life, the Ruler of Glory, granted him honour in the world; Beowulf* was renowned, the fame of Scyld's son spread widely throughout the Danish lands. So it is that a young man while still in his father's protection ought to do good deeds, making liberal rich gifts, so that when he comes of age good companions will stand by him, lend aid to the people when war comes. Among all nations it is by praiseworthy deeds that a man shall prosper.

Then at his destined hour Scyld, still very active, passed away to go into the keeping of the Lord. Those who were his dear companions carried him down to the surge of the sea as he himself had instructed when, friend of the Scyldings, he governed with words. The beloved leader of the land had been long in possession.

There at the landing-place stood the curved prow, ice-covered, ready to put out, a prince's vessel.* Then they laid down the

---

4 sceaþena: MS sceaþen.; Humphrey Wanley (1705) sceaþena   6 Eorle: MS eorl   15 aldorlease: MS aldor . . ase   20 geong guma: MS . . . . uma   21 bearme: MS . . . rme

beaga bryttan   on bearm scipes,   35
mærne be mæste. Þær wæs madma fela
of feorwegum,   frætwa, gelæded.
Ne hyrde ic cymlicor   ceol gegyrwan
hildewæpnum   ond heaðowædum,
billum ond byrnum. Him on bearme læg   40
madma mænigo, þa him mid scoldon
on flodes æht   feor gewitan.
Nalæs hi hine læssan   lacum teodan,
þeodgestreonum, þon þa dydon,
þe hine æt frumsceafte   forð onsendon   45
ænne ofer yðe   umborwesende.
Þa gyt hie him asetton   segen gyldenne
heah ofer heafod; leton holm beran,
geafon on garsecg. Him wæs geomor sefa,
murnende mod. Men ne cunnon   50
secgan to soðe,   selerædende,
hæleð under heofenum,   hwa þæm hlæste onfeng.

I   Ða wæs on burgum   Beowulf Scyldinga,
leof leodcyning,   longe þrage
folcum gefræge,   (fæder ellor hwearf,   55
aldor of earde),   oþþæt him eft onwoc
heah Healfdene. Heold, þenden lifde,
gamol ond guðreouw,   glæde Scyldingas.
Ðæm feower bearn   forðgerimed
in worold wocun,   weoroda ræswan: 60
Heorogar ond Hroðgar   ond Halga til;
hyrde ic þæt Yrse wæs   Onelan cwen,
Heaðo-Scilfingas   healsgebedda.
Þa wæs Hroðgare   heresped gyfen,
wiges weorðmynd,   þæt him his winemagas   65
georne hyrdon,   oððþæt seo geogoð geweox
magodriht micel. Him on mod bearn
þæt healreced   hatan wolde,
medoærn micel   men gewyrcean,
þonne yldo bearn   æfre gefrunon,   70
ond þær on innan   eall gedælan
geongum ond ealdum,   swylc him God sealde—
buton folcscare   ond feorum gumena.
Ða ic wide gefrægn   weorc gebannan
manigre mægþe   geond þisne middangeard,   75
folcstede frætwan. Him on fyrste gelomp,

beloved ruler, the distributor of rings, in the bosom of the ship, the famous man by the mast. Many treasures, jewels from distant lands, were brought there. I have not heard of a craft more splendidly furnished with weapons of war and battle garments, with swords and coats of mail. On his breast lay many treasures which were to go with him far out into the power of the flood. In no way did they provide him with lesser gifts, treasures of the nation, than did those who at the beginning when he was still a child sent him off alone over the waves. Furthermore they set up a golden banner high over his head; they let the sea carry him, gave him up to the ocean. Their spirits were sad, their hearts sorrowful. Men cannot say for certain, neither councillors in the hall nor warriors beneath the skies, who received that cargo.

1   Then in that stronghold the beloved king of the people, Beowulf of the Scyldings, was for a long time famous among the nations (his father had passed elsewhere, the chief from his land) until to him in turn was born lofty Healfdene. He ruled the noble Scyldings for as long as he lived, old and savage in war. To him, the leader of armies, there were born into the world in succession four children: Heorogar and Hrothgar and Halga the Good; I have heard that Yrse was Onela's queen,* the beloved bed-fellow of the War-Scylfing.

Then success in war, glory in battle, was granted to Hrothgar, so that his friends and kinsmen gladly obeyed him until the youthful band of companions grew into a mighty troop of young warriors. It came into his mind that he would instruct men to build a greater mead-hall than the children of men had ever heard of, and therein he would distribute to young and old everything which God had given him—except for public land and the lives of men. I have heard how then orders for the work were given to many peoples throughout this world to adorn the nation's palace. So in time—

47 gyldenne: MS g . . denne   51 selerædende: MS selerædenne   60 ræswan:
MS ræswa   62 Yrse wæs On- supplied   70 þonne: MS þone

ædre mid yldum,   þæt hit wearð ealgearo,
healærna mæst.   Scop him Heort naman,
se þe his wordes geweald   wide hæfde.
He beot ne aleh,   beagas dælde,   *80*
sinc æt symle.   Sele hlifade
heah ond horngeap: heaðowylma bad,
laðan liges.   Ne wæs hit lenge þa gen,
þæt se ecghete   aþumswerian
æfter wælniðe   wæcnan scolde.   *85*
    Ða se ellengæst   earfoðlice
þrage geþolode,   se þe in þystrum bad,
þæt he dogora gehwam   dream gehyrde
hludne in healle.   Þær wæs hearpan sweg,
swutol sang scopes.   Sægde, se þe cuþe   *90*
frumsceaft fira   feorran reccan;
cwæð þæt se Ælmihtiga   eorðan worhte,
wlitebeorhtne wang,   swa wæter bebugeð,
gesette sigehreþig   sunnan ond monan
leoman to leohte   landbuendum,   *95*
ond gefrætwade   foldan sceatas
leomum ond leafum,   lif eac gesceop
cynna gehwylcum,   þara ðe cwice hwyrfaþ.
Swa ða drihtguman   dreamum lifdon,
eadiglice,   oððæt an ongan   *100*
fyrene fremman   feond on helle.
Wæs se grimma gæst   Grendel haten,
mære mearcstapa,   se þe moras heold,
fen ond fæsten.   Fifelcynnes eard
wonsæli wer   weardode hwile,   *105*
siþðan him Scyppend   forscrifen hæfde
in Caines cynne.   Þone cwealm gewræc
ece Drihten,   þæs þe he Abel slog.
Ne gefeah he þære fæhðe,   ac he hine feor forwræc,
Metod for þy mane,   mancynne fram.   *110*
Þanon untydras   ealle onwocon,
eotenas ond ylfe   ond orcneas,
swylce gigantas,   þa wið Gode wunnon
lange þrage;   he him ðæs lean forgeald.

II   Gewat ða neosian,   syþðan niht becom,   *115*
hean huses,   hu hit Hring-Dene
æfter beorþege   gebun hæfdon.
Fand þa ðær inne   æþelinga gedriht

rapidly as men reckon it—it came about that it was fully completed, the greatest of hall buildings. He who ruled widely with his words gave it the name Heorot.* He did not neglect his vow; he distributed rings, treasure at the banquet. The hall rose up high, lofty and wide-gabled: awaited the furious surge of hostile flames.* The day was not yet near when violent hatred between son-in-law and father-in-law should be born of deadly malice.

Then the powerful demon, he who abode in darkness, found it hard to endure this time of torment, when every day he heard loud rejoicing in the hall. There was the sound of the harp, the clear song of the minstrel. He who could recount the creation of men in far off times, spoke; he told how the Almighty made the earth, a bright-faced plain which the waters encircle, set up in triumph the radiance of sun and moon as light for those dwelling on land, and adorned the corners of the earth with branches and leaves, how also he created life for every kind of thing that moves about alive. Thus these noble men lived blessedly in joy, until a certain fiend from hell began to wreak evil. That grim demon was called Grendel, a notorious prowler of the borderlands, who held the wastelands, swamp and fastness. Unhappy creature, he lived for a time in the home of the monster race after God had condemned them as kin of Cain. The Eternal Lord avenged the murder whereby he killed Abel;* he got no joy from that feud, but Providence drove him far away from mankind for that crime. Thence were born all evil broods: ogres and elves and goblins—likewise the giants who for a long time strove against God; he paid them their reward for that.

2   Then, after night had come, Grendel went to seek out the lofty house to see how, after their beer-drinking, the Ring-Danes had settled into it. Inside he found a band of noblemen, asleep after

swefan æfter symble;   sorge ne cuðon,
wonsceaft wera.   Wiht unhælo,   *120*
grim ond grædig,   gearo sona wæs,
reoc ond reþe,   ond on ræste genam
þritig þegna.   Þanon eft gewat
huðe hremig   to ham faran,
mid þære wælfylle   wica neosan.   *125*
   Ða wæs on uhtan   mid ærdæge
Grendles guðcræft   gumum undyrne;
þa wæs æfter wiste   wop up ahafen,
micel morgensweg.   Mære þeoden,
æþeling ærgod,   unbliðe sæt;   *130*
þolode ðryðswyð,   þegnsorge dreah,
syðþan hie þæs laðan   last sceawedon
wergan gastes.   Wæs þæt gewin to strang,
lað ond longsum.   Næs hit lengra fyrst,
ac ymb ane niht   eft gefremede   *135*
morðbeala mare   ond no mearn fore,
fæhðe ond fyrene;   wæs to fæst on þam.
Þa wæs eaðfynde   þe him elles hwær
gerumlicor   ræste sohte,
bed æfter burum,   ða him gebeacnod wæs,   *140*
gesægd soðlice   sweotolan tacne
healðegnes hete.   Heold hyne syðþan
fyr ond fæstor   se þæm feonde ætwand.
Swa rixode   ond wið rihte wan
ana wið eallum,   oðþæt idel stod   *145*
husa selest.
               Wæs seo hwil micel:
twelf wintra tid   torn geþolode
wine Scyldinga,   weana gehwelcne,
sidra sorga.   Forðam secgum wearð,
ylda bearnum,   undyrne cuð,   *150*
gyddum geomore,   þætte Grendel wan
hwile wið Hroþgar,   heteniðas wæg,
fyrene ond fæhðe   fela missera,
singale sæce.   Sibbe ne wolde
wið manna hwone   mægenes Deniga,   *155*
feorhbealo feorran,   fea þingian;
ne þær nænig witena   wenan þorfte
beorhtre bote   to banan folmum.
Ac se æglæca   ehtende wæs,
deorc deaþscua   duguþe ond geogoþe,   *160*

the banquet; they had no thought of sorrow, of the misery destined for men. Straightaway the creature of damnation was ready, grim and greedy, savage and cruel, and seized thirty thanes from their rest. From there he turned, exulting in plunder, to go back home, to seek out his dwelling with that glut of slaughter.

Then in the half-light before dawn Grendel's war-strength was revealed to men; then after the feast arose weeping, a great cry in the morning. The famous prince, a leader of proven merit, sat joyless; when they examined the tracks of that loathsome, accursed demon, the mighty one suffered, grieved for his thanes. That struggle was too fierce, loathsome and long-lasting. Nor was there longer interval, but the next night he again wrought more murderous havoc, vengeful acts and wickedness, and felt no remorse; he was too intent on it. Then it was easy to find the man who was seeking a couch for himself elsewhere, a bed among the outbuildings farther away,* once this 'hall-thane's' hatred was made clear by manifest proof. Whoever escaped the fiend held himself afterwards farther off and more securely. Thus one held sway over all and strove against right until the best of houses stood deserted.

This went on for a long time: for a period of twelve years the Scyldings' friend suffered affliction, every kind of woe and deep sorrows. Wherefore sadly in songs it became generally known among the children of men that Grendel had long waged war on Hrothgar, maintained fierce malice, feud and enmity, constant conflict over many seasons. He wanted no friendship with any man of the Danish force, would not withdraw his deadly hostility, or pay compensation; nor need any of the councillors there expect a handsome reparation at the killer's hands. But the monster, dark shadow of death, went on persecuting both tried warriors and

139 sohte *supplied*   148 Scyldinga: MS scyldenda   149 secgum *supplied*
158 banan: MS banū   159 Ac se *restored*

seomade ond syrede;   sinnihte heold
mistige moras.   Men ne cunnon
hwyder helrunan   hwyrftum scriþað.
   Swa fela fyrena   feond mancynnes,
atol angengea,   oft gefremede,   165
heardra hynða.   Heorot eardode,
sincfage sel   sweartum nihtum.
No he þone gifstol   gretan moste,
maþðum for Metode,   ne his myne wisse.
   Þæt wæs wræc micel   wine Scyldinga,   170
modes brecða.   Monig oft gesæt
rice to rune,   ræd eahtedon,
hwæt swiðferhðum   selest wære
wið færgryrum   to gefremmanne.
Hwilum hie geheton   æt hærgtrafum   175
wigweorþunga,   wordum bædon,
þæt him gastbona   geoce gefremede
wið þeodþreaum.   Swylc wæs þeaw hyra,
hæþenra hyht;   helle gemundon
in modsefan;   Metod hie ne cuþon,   180
dæda Demend,   ne wiston hie Drihten God
ne hie huru heofena Helm   herian ne cuþon,
wuldres Waldend.   Wa bið þæm ðe sceal
þurh sliðne nið   sawle bescufan
in fyres fæþm,   frofre ne wenan,   185
wihte gewendan!   Wel bið þæm þe mot
æfter deaðdæge   Drihten secean
ond to Fæder fæþmum   freoðo wilnian!

III   Swa ða mælceare   maga Healfdenes
singala seað,   ne mihte snotor hæleð   190
wean onwendan;   wæs þæt gewin to swyð,
laþ ond longsum,   þe on ða leode becom,
nydwracu niþgrim,   nihtbealwa mæst.
   Þæt fram ham gefrægn   Higelaces þegn
god mid Geatum,   Grendles dæda.   195
Se wæs moncynnes   mægenes strengest
on þæm dæge   þysses lifes,
æþele ond eacen.   Het him yðlidan
godne gegyrwan;   cwæð, he guðcyning
ofer swanrade   secean wolde,   200
mærne þeoden,   þa him wæs manna þearf.
Ðone siðfæt him   snotere ceorlas

youths, lay in wait and ensnared them; in perpetual darkness he ruled the misty wastelands. Men do not know where those who share hell's secrets will direct their paths.

Thus the enemy of mankind, this dreadful solitary, would often commit many crimes, bitter humiliations. On dark nights he dwelt in the treasure-decked hall, Heorot. Because of Providence he could not approach the precious throne, the source of gifts; nor did he feel his love.*

That was a great misery and heartbreak for the Scyldings' friend. Many a powerful man often sat in council, sought a plan, what action would be best for a stout-hearted man to take against the terror of sudden onslaughts. At times they took vows of idol-worship at heathen shrines,* prayed aloud that the slayer of souls would render aid against the nation's calamities. Such was their custom, the hope of heathens; they turned their minds towards hell; they were ignorant of Providence, the Judge of deeds, they knew not the Lord God, nor indeed did they know how to worship the Protector of Heaven, the Ruler of Glory. It will go ill for him who as a result of terrible malice must thrust his soul into the fire's embrace—to expect no comfort, nothing to change. Well will it be for him who after the day of his death may seek out the Lord and ask for peace in the embrace of the Father.

3   Thus the son of Healfdene constantly brooded on the sorrow of his time, nor could the wise hero set aside his grief; that strife which had befallen the people, cruel and malicious distress, worst of night-horrors, was too harsh, loathsome and long-lasting.

At home, a great man among the Geats, a thane of Hygelac, heard of Grendel's deeds. In strength he was the mightiest among mankind in that day and age, noble and powerful. He ordered a good seagoing vessel to be made ready for him; he said that he wished to seek out over the swan's road the war-king, the famous prince, since he had need of men. Wise men in no way reproached

lythwon logon,   þeah he him leof wære;
hwetton higerofne,   hæl sceawedon.
Hæfde se goda   Geata leoda   205
cempan gecorone,   þara þe he cenoste
findan mihte;   fiftyna sum
sundwudu sohte.   Secg wisade,
lagucræftig mon,   landgemyrcu.
    Fyrst forð gewat;   flota wæs on yðum,   210
bat under beorge.   Beornas gearwe
on stefn stigon;   streamas wundon,
sund wið sande;   secgas bæron
on bearm nacan   beorhte frætwe,
guðsearo geatolic;   guman ut scufon,   215
weras on wilsið,   wudu bundenne.
    Gewat þa ofer wægholm,   winde gefysed,
flota famiheals,   fugle gelicost,
oðþæt ymb antid,   oþres dogores
wundenstefna   gewaden hæfde,   220
þæt ða liðende   land gesawon,
brimclifu blican,   beorgas steape,
side sænæssas.   Þa wæs sund liden,
eoletes æt ende.   Þanon up hraðe
Wedera leode   on wang stigon,   225
sæwudu sældon   —syrcan hrysedon,
guðgewædo.   Gode þancedon,
þæs þe him yþlade   eaðe wurdon.
    Þa of wealle geseah   weard Scildinga,
se þe holmclifu   healdan scolde,   230
beran ofer bolcan   beorhte randas,
fyrdsearu fuslicu.   Hine fyrwyt bræc
modgehygdum,   hwæt þa men wæron.
Gewat him þa to waroðe   wicge ridan
þegn Hroðgares;   þrymmum cwehte   235
mægenwudu mundum,   meþelwordum frægn:
    'Hwæt syndon ge   searohæbbendra,
byrnum werede,   þe þus brontne ceol
ofer lagustræte   lædan cwomon,
hider ofer holmas?   Ic hwile wæs   240
endesæta,   ægwearde heold,
þe on land Dena   laðra nænig
mid sciþherge   sceðþan ne meahte.
No her cuðlicor   cuman ongunnon
lindhæbbende;   ne ge leafnesword   245

him for that venture, though he was dear to them; they encouraged
the man renowned for his spirit, examined the omens.* From the
people of the Geats the great man had picked champions, the
bravest he could find; he went down to the water-borne timbers as
one of fifteen. A skilled seaman pointed out the line of the coast.

The time came; the boat lay on the waves, afloat beneath the
cliff. Eager heroes stepped aboard at the prow; the tide turned,
sea against the sand; soldiers carried bright trappings, splendid
battle-gear, into the bosom of the vessel; men shoved out the
well-braced timbers, warriors on a willing journey.

Then driven by the wind, the ship travelled over the sea-waves,
floating foamy-necked, just like a bird, until in due course on the
following day* its curved prow had come to where the voyagers
could sight land, shining sea-cliffs, steep promontories and broad
headlands. The sea then was crossed, the voyage at an end. The
men of the Weders quickly set foot on level ground, moored the
sea-borne timbers; their mail-shirts, the garments of war, rang out.
They thanked God that the sea voyage had been easy for them.

Then from the rampart the Scyldings' watchman, whose duty
it was to guard the sea-cliffs, saw bright shields carried over the
bulkhead, war-equipment ready for use. Curiosity pricked his mind
as to who these men were. So Hrothgar's thane went down to the
shore, riding on horseback; he forcefully brandished the mighty
shaft in his hands, questioned them in formal words:

'What manner of armed men are you who have come thus
protected by mail, bringing a tall ship over the seaways, over the
water to this place? For a long time I have been guardian of this
frontier, kept watch on the sea, so that no enemies might harry the
land of the Danes with a shipborne force. Never have shield-
bearers made so open an approach; and yet you had no ready

---

204 higerofne: MS hige . . . . .; Thorkelin A hige þofne
240 Ic hwi- supplied

guðfremmendra   gearwe ne wisson,
maga gemedu.   Næfre ic maran geseah
eorla ofer eorþan,   ðonne is eower sum,
secg on searwum.   Nis þæt seldguma,
wæpnum geweorðad,   næfne him his wlite leoge,   *250*
ænlic ansyn.   Nu ic eower sceal
frumcyn witan,   ær ge fyr heonan
leassceaweras   on land Dena
furþur feran.   Nu ge feorbuend,
mereliðende,   mine gehyrað   *255*
anfealdne geþoht: ofost is selest
to gecyðanne   hwanan eowre cyme syndon.'

IV   Him se yldesta   andswarode,
werodes wisa,   wordhord onleac:
'We synt gumcynnes   Geata leode   *260*
ond Higelaces   heorðgeneatas.
Wæs min fæder   folcum gecyþed,
æþele ordfruma   Ecgþeow haten.
Gebad wintra worn,   ær he on weg hwurfe,
gamol of geardum;   hine gearwe geman   *265*
witena welhwylc   wide geond eorþan.
We þurh holdne hige   hlaford þinne,
sunu Healfdenes,   secean cwomon,
leodgebyrgean;   wes þu us larena god!
Habbað we to þæm mæran   micel ærende,   *270*
Deniga frean;   ne sceal þær dyrne sum
wesan, þæs ic wene.
                        Þu wast—gif hit is
swa we soþlice   secgan hyrdon—
þæt mid Scyldingum   sceaðona ic nat hwylc,
deogol dædhata,   deorcum nihtum   *275*
eaweð þurh egsan   uncuðne nið,
hynðu ond hrafyl.   Ic þæs Hroðgar mæg
þurh rumne sefan   ræd gelæran,
hu he frod ond god   feond oferswyðeþ—
gyf him edwendan   æfre scolde   *280*
bealuwa bisigu,   bot eft cuman—
ond þa cearwylmas   colran wurðaþ.
Oððe a syþðan   earfoðþrage,
þreanyd þolað,   þenden þær wunað
on heahstede   husa selest.'   *285*
      Weard maþelode,   ðær on wicge sæt,

knowledge of the soldiers' password approved by kinsmen. I have never seen a mightier warrior on earth than is a certain one among you, a hero in armour. That is no mere serving-man decked out with weapons, unless his appearance and unique form belie him. Now I must know your origin before you go any further from here as spies, deeper into the land of the Danes. Now you foreigners, sea-voyagers, pay attention to my frank opinion: you would do best to announce quickly where you are coming from.'

4   The chief of them, the leader of the company, answered him, unlocked his store of words: 'We are men of the Geatish people and the companions of Hygelac's hearth. My father was well known among the nations, a noble war-leader called Ecgtheow. He lived on for many years before in old age he passed away from his court; every councillor throughout all parts of the earth remembers him well. We have come in good faith to seek out your leader, Healfdene's son, defender of his people; advise us well. We have important business with the famous lord of the Danes; there should be no secret from what I understand of it.

You will know, if what we have heard tell is in fact so, that among the Scyldings some kind of ravager, mysterious persecutor, displays in the terror he creates on dark nights, unheard of malice, humiliation and carnage. I can give Hrothgar advice about this from a generous heart, how he, wise and good, might overcome the enemy, and his surging anxieties grow cooler—if change is ever to come to him, relief from the affliction of miseries. Otherwise he will ever after suffer great hardship, times of distress, for as long as the best of houses remains there in its lofty position.'

The watchman, fearless officer, spoke from where he sat on his

250 næfne: MS næfre

ombeht unforht: 'Æghwæþres sceal
scearp scyldwiga   gescad witan,
worda ond worca,   se þe wel þenceð.
Ic þæt gehyre,   þæt þis is hold weorod   290
frean Scyldinga.   Gewitaþ forð beran
wæpen ond gewædu;   ic eow wisige.
Swylce ic maguþegnas   mine hate
wið feonda gehwone   flotan eowerne,
niwtyrwydne   nacan on sande   295
arum healdan,   opðæt eft byreð
ofer lagustreamas   leofne mannan
wudu wundenhals   to Wedermearce.
Godfremmendra   swylcum gifeþe bið,
þæt þone hilderæs   hal gedigeð.'   300
    Gewiton him þa feran.   Flota stille bad,
seomode on sale   sidfæþmed scip,
on ancre fæst.   Eoforlic scionon
ofer hleorbergan,   gehroden golde;
fah ond fyrheard,   ferhwearde heold.   305
Guþmod grummon;   guman onetton,
sigon ætsomne,   oþþæt hy sæl timbred,
geatolic ond goldfah   ongyton mihton;
þæt wæs foremærost   foldbuendum
receda under roderum,   on þæm se rica bad;   310
lixte se leoma   ofer landa fela.
Him þa hildedeor   hof modigra
torht getæhte,   þæt hie him to mihton
gegnum gangan;   guðbeorna sum
wicg gewende,   word æfter cwæð: 315
'Mæl is me to feran.   Fæder alwalda
mid arstafum   eowic gehealde
siða gesunde!   Ic to sæ wille,
wið wrað werod   wearde healdan.'

v   Stræt wæs stanfah,   stig wisode   320
gumum ætgædere.   Guðbyrne scan,
heard, hondlocen,   hringiren scir
song in searwum.   þa hie to sele furðum
in hyra gryregeatwum   gangan cwomon,
setton sæmeþe   side scyldas,   325
rondas regnhearde,   wið þæs recedes weal;
bugon þa to bence   —byrnan hringdon,
guðsearo gumena.   Garas stodon,

horse: 'A sharp shield-fighter who thinks clearly must know the difference between the two things: words and deeds. I gather, then, that here is a troop loyal towards the lord of the Scyldings. Proceed, bearing weapons and armour; I will guide you. Moreover, I will instruct my young thanes to guard your ship honourably against all enemies, the newly-tarred vessel on the sand, until the timbers with curved prow carry back the beloved man over the sea's currents to the Weders' coastline. May it be granted to one of such noble deeds that he survive the onslaught of battle unharmed.'

Then they proceeded to journey onwards. The boat lay quietly, rode on its moorings, a broad-bosomed ship fast at anchor. Above their cheek-guards, adorned with gold, shone the boar image; bright and fire-hardened, it stood guard over men's lives.* Warlike hearts were excited; the men hastened, moved onwards together until they could see the timbered hall, splendid and decked with gold. Of all buildings beneath the skies, this in which the great ruler dwelt was the most famous to those who inhabit the earth; its radiance shone over many lands. The battle-brave man then pointed out to them the splendid bright dwelling of proud men, so that they might proceed directly to it. The notable warrior turned his horse and thereupon spoke these words: 'It is time for me to leave. May the Almighty Father keep you in grace, safe in your exploit! I will return to the sea to keep watch against hostile bands.'

5   The road was paved with stone,* a path guiding the group of men. The war-mail shone, hard with hand-forged links; the bright iron rings sang on their armour. When they first arrived, striding up to the hall in their grim gear, the sea-weary men laid broad shields, wonderfully strong discs, against the wall of the building; then they sank to the bench—coats of mail, the battle-dress of men, rang out. The javelins that were the seamen's arms, stood all together, a

302 sale: MS sole   304 hleorbergan: MS hleor beran   307 sæl timbred: MS æltimbred   312 hof: MS of

sæmanna searo,   samod ætgædere,
æscholt ufan græg;   wæs se irenþreat   *330*
wæpnum gewurþad.

                Þa ðær wlonc hæleð
oretmecgas   æfter æþelum frægn:
'Hwanon ferigeað ge   fætte scyldas,
græge syrcan   ond grimhelmas,
heresceafta heap?   Ic eom Hroðgares   *335*
ar ond ombiht.   Ne seah ic elþeodige
þus manige men   modiglicran.
Wen ic þæt ge for wlenco,   nalles for wræcsiðum,
ac for higeþrymmum   Hroðgar sohton.'
Him þa ellenrof   andswarode,   *340*
wlanc Wedera leod,   word æfter spræc,
heard under helme: 'We synt Higelaces
beodgeneatas;   Beowulf is min nama.
Wille ic asecgan   sunu Healfdenes,
mærum þeodne   min ærende,   *345*
aldre þinum,   gif he us geunnan wile,
þæt we hine swa godne   gretan moton.'
Wulfgar maþelode: —þæt wæs Wendla leod,
wæs his modsefa   manegum gecyðed,
wig ond wisdom: 'Ic þæs wine Deniga   *350*
frean Scildinga   frinan wille,
beaga bryttan,   swa þu bena eart,
þeoden mærne,   ymbe þinne sið,
ond þe þa andsware   ædre gecyðan,
ðe me se goda   agifan þenceð.'   *355*
     Hwearf þa hrædlice   þær Hroðgar sæt,
eald ond unhar,   mid his eorla gedriht;
eode ellenrof   þæt he for eaxlum gestod
Deniga frean: cuþe he duguðe þeaw.
Wulfgar maðelode   to his winedrihtne: *360*
'Her syndon geferede,   feorran cumene
ofer geofenes begang   Geata leode.
Þone yldestan   oretmecgas
Beowulf nemnað.   Hy benan synt
þæt hie, þeoden min,   wið þe moton   *365*
wordum wrixlan.   No ðu him wearne geteoh
ðinra gegncwida,   glædman Hroðgar:
hy on wiggetawum   wyrðe þinceað
eorla geæhtlan;   huru se aldor deah
se þæm heaðorincum   hider wisade.'   *370*

forest of ash-wood shafts, steel-grey above. The iron-clad troop was well-equipped with weapons.

Then a proud hero there questioned the champions about their lineage: 'From whence do you bring these gold-plated shields, grey mail-shirts and visored helmets, this pile of battle-shafts? I am Hrothgar's messenger and officer. I have never seen foreigners— so many men—more brave in bearing. I imagine that it was through daring and greatness of heart that you sought out Hrothgar, and in no way as a result of banishment! The proud prince of the Weders, renowned for courage, answered him; stern beneath his helmet, he spoke these words in reply: 'We are the companions of Hygelac's table; Beowulf is my name. I wish to tell my errand to Healfdene's son, the famous commander your chief, if, good as he is, he will grant that we might approach him.' Wulfgar spoke—he was a prince of the Vandals,* his bold spirit, valour and wisdom known to many: 'Respecting this, I will ask the friend of the Danes, the Scyldings' lord, distributor of rings, famous prince, about your venture, as you have requested, and rapidly make known to you the answer the noble man thinks fit to give me.'

Then he turned away swiftly to where Hrothgar, old and quite grey, sat with his band of warriors; the man renowned for courage went forward till he stood squarely in front of the lord of the Danes —he knew the custom of the company. Wulfgar spoke to his friend and leader: 'Men of the Geats have journeyed here, come from afar over the ocean's expanse. These champions call their chief Beowulf. They have asked that they might exchange words with you, my prince. Do not refuse them your response, gracious Hrothgar: from their fighting-gear they seem worthy of the respect of warriors; at any rate the chief who has led these warlike men is valiant.'

---

332 æþelum: MS hæle þum

VI   Hroðgar maþelode,   helm Scyldinga:
          'Ic hine cuðe   cnihtwesende.
          Wæs his ealdfæder   Ecgþeo haten;
          ðæm to ham forgeaf   Hreþel Geata
          angan dohtor;   is his eafora nu   375
          heard her cumen,   sohte holdne wine.
          Ðonne sægdon þæt   sæliþende,
          þa ðe gifsceattas   Geata fyredon
          þyder to þance,   þæt he þritiges
          manna mægencræft   on his mundgripe,   380
          heaþorof, hæbbe.   Hine halig God
          for arstafum   us onsende
          to West-Denum,   þæs ic wen hæbbe,
          wið Grendles gryre.   Ic þæm godan sceal
          for his modþræce   madmas beodan.   385
          Beo ðu on ofeste,   hat in gan,
          seon sibbegedriht   samod ætgædere.
          Gesaga him eac wordum   þæt hie sint wilcuman
          Deniga leodum!'
                          Þa to dura healle
          Wulfgar eode,   word inne abead: 390
          'Eow het secgan   sigedrihten min,
          aldor East-Dena,   þæt he eower æþelu can,
          ond ge him syndon   ofer sæwylmas,
          heardhicgende,   hider wilcuman.
          Nu ge moton gangan   in eowrum guðgetawum,   395
          under heregriman,   Hroðgar geseon;
          lætað hildebord   her onbidan,
          wudu, wælsceaftas,   worda geþinges.'
          Aras þa se rica,   ymb hine rinc manig,
          þryðlic þegna heap;   sume þær bidon,   400
          heaðoreaf heoldon,   swa him se hearda bebead.
          Snyredon ætsomne,   þa secg wisode,
          under Heorotes hrof.   Eode hildedeor,
          heard under helme,   þæt he on heorðe gestod.
          Beowulf maðelode   —on him byrne scan,   405
          searonet seowed   smiþes orþancum:
          'Wæs þu, Hroðgar, hal!   Ic eom Higelaces
          mæg ond magoþegn.   Hæbbe ic mærða fela
          ongunnen on geogoþe.   Me wearð Grendles þing
          on minre eþeltyrf   undyrne cuð;   410
          secgað sæliðend   þæt þæs sele stande,
          reced selesta,   rinca gehwylcum
          idel ond unnyt,   siððan æfenleoht

6   Hrothgar spoke, protector of the Scyldings: 'I knew him when he was a boy. His late father was called Ecgtheow; it was to him that Hrethel of the Geats gave in marriage his only daughter; now his son has come here, a strong man, to visit a faithful friend. Moreover, seafarers who have carried rich gifts there to the Geats as a token of our regard, have said that he has in the grip of his hand the strength of thirty men, one renowned in battle. Holy God in his mercy has sent him to us, the West Danes, to meet the terror of Grendel, or so I hope. I shall offer the great man treasures for his impetuous courage. Make haste, bid them enter to see the noble company of kinsmen assembled together. Say also to them in your speech that they are welcome to the Danish people!'

Then Wulfgar went to the door of the hall and from inside announced these words: 'My victorious leader, the chief of the East Danes, has bidden me tell you that he knows of your lineage, and you are welcome to him here, brave-hearted men from across the surging sea. You may now go to see Hrothgar in your war-dress and beneath battle-visors; leave here your war-shields and spears, deadly shafts, to await the outcome of your talk.'

The mighty one then arose with many a warrior about him, a splendid band of thanes; some waited there to guard their war-trappings as the bold man instructed them. Together they hastened as the warrior directed under Heorot's roof. The battle-brave man, bold beneath his helmet, advanced till he stood by the hearth.* Beowulf spoke—the mail-coat on him shone, an armour net woven with a smith's ingenuity:

'Hail to you, Hrothgar! I am kinsman and young thane of Hygelac. In my youth I have undertaken many glorious deeds. The affair of Grendel became well known to me on my native soil; seafarers say that this hall, the best of buildings, stands empty and useless to all warriors once the evening light is hidden beneath

---

³⁷⁵ eafora: MS eaforan   ^{389b–390a} *supplied*   ³⁹⁵ guðgetawum: MS guð geata wum   ³⁹⁷ onbidan: MS onbidman   ^{403b} *supplied*   ⁴⁰⁴ heorðe: MS heoðe

under heofenes hador   beholen weorþeð.
Þa me þæt gelærdon   leode mine,   *415*
þa selestan,   snotere ceorlas,
þeoden Hroðgar,   þæt ic þe sohte,
forþan hie mægenes cræft   mine cuþon.
Selfe ofersawon,   ða ic of searwum cwom,
fah from feondum,   þær ic fife geband,   *420*
yðde eotena cyn,   ond on yðum slog
niceras nihtes;   nearoþearfe dreah,
wræc Wedera nið   —wean ahsodon—
forgrand gramum.   Ond nu wið Grendel sceal,
wið þam aglæcan   ana gehegan   *425*
ðing wið þyrse.
                Ic þe nu ða,
brego Beorht-Dena,   biddan wille,
eodor Scyldinga,   anre bene:
þæt ðu me ne forwyrne,   wigendra hleo,
freowine folca,   nu ic þus feorran com,   *430*
þæt ic mote ana   ond minra eorla gedryht,
þes hearda heap,   Heorot fælsian.
Hæbbe ic eac geahsod   þæt se æglæca
for his wonhydum   wæpna ne recceð.
Ic þæt þonne forhicge,   swa me Higelac sie,   *435*
min mondrihten,   modes bliðe,
þæt ic sweord bere   oþðe sidne scyld,
geolorand to guþe;   ac ic mid grape sceal
fon wið feonde   ond ymb feorh sacan,
lað wið laþum.   Ðær gelyfan sceal   *440*
Dryhtnes dome   se þe hine deað nimeð.
    Wen ic þæt he wille,   gif he wealdan mot,
in þæm guðsele   Geotena leode
etan unforhte,   swa he oft dyde,
mægen hreðmanna.   Na þu minne þearft   *445*
hafalan hydan,   ac he me habban wile
dreore fahne,   gif mec deað nimeð;
byreð blodig wæl,   byrgean þenceð.
Eteð angenga   unmurnlice,
mearcað morhopu;   no ðu ymb mines ne þearft   *450*
lices feorme   leng sorgian.
Onsend Higelace,   gif mec hild nime,
beaduscruda betst,   þæt mine breost wereð,
hrægla selest;   þæt is Hrædlan laf,
Welandes geweorc.   Gæð a wyrd swa hio scel!'   *455*

heaven's firmament. Thereupon my people, the noblest, wise men, advised me that I should seek you out, prince Hrothgar, because they knew the power of my strength. They themselves had looked on when, stained with the blood of foes, I came back from the struggle in which I destroyed a race of ogres, bound five of them, and killed water-monsters in the waves by night; I suffered dire straits, avenged the Weders' wrong, utterly crushed those fierce creatures—they asked for trouble. And now I alone shall settle matters with that monster, with the demon Grendel.

Now therefore, chief of the Bright-Danes, bulwark of the Scyldings, I wish to make one request of you: that you do not refuse me, defence of fighting men, noble friend of nations, now that I have come so far, that I alone may cleanse Heorot with my company of warriors, this band of brave men. Also, I have heard that in his recklessness the monster disdains weapons. Therefore, so that my leader Hygelac may be glad at heart on my account, I scorn to carry sword or broad shield, yellow disc, into battle; but I shall grapple with the enemy with my bare hands and fight to the death, foe against foe. He whom death then takes must trust to the judgement of the Lord.

I imagine that, if he is able to prevail, he will fearlessly devour the people of the Geats in the war-hall, as he has often done to a force of triumphant men. You will have no need to cover my head* if death takes me, for he will have me dripping with gore; he will carry away the bloody corpse, intent on eating it. The lone prowler will devour it remorselessly, staining his wasteland retreat; you will no longer need to trouble yourself about caring for my body.* If war should take me, send to Hygelac this best of battle-clothing, most excellent of garments, that protects my breast; it is a legacy from Hrethel, the work of Weland.* Fate will always go as it must!'

431-2 ond *transposed from before* þes   447 dreore: MS deore

VII Hroðgar maþelode, helm Scyldinga:
'For werefyhtum þu, wine min Beowulf,
ond for arstafum usic sohtest.
Gesloh þin fæder fæhðe mæste,
wearþ he Heaþolafe to handbonan   *460*
mid Wilfingum. Ða hine Wedera cyn
for herebrogan habban ne mihte.
Þanon he gesohte Suð-Dena folc
ofer yða gewealc, Ar-Scyldinga.
Ða ic furþum weold folce Deniga   *465*
ond on geogoðe heold gimmerice,
hordburh hæleþa. Ða wæs Heregar dead,
min yldra mæg unlifigende,
bearn Healfdenes: se wæs betera ðonne ic!
Siððan þa fæhðe feo þingode;   *470*
sende ic Wylfingum ofer wæteres hrycg
ealde madmas; he me aþas swor.
  Sorh is me to secganne on sefan minum
gumena ængum, hwæt me Grendel hafað
hynðo on Heorote mid his heteþancum,   *475*
færniða gefremed. Is min fletwerod,
wigheap gewanod; hie wyrd forsweop
on Grendles gryre. God eaþe mæg
þone dolsceaðan dæda getwæfan!
  Ful oft gebeotedon beore druncne   *480*
ofer ealowæge oretmecgas,
þæt hie in beorsele bidan woldon
Grendles guþe mid gryrum ecga.
Ðonne wæs þeos medoheal on morgentid,
drihtsele dreorfah, þonne dæg lixte,   *485*
eal bencþelu blode bestymed,
heall heorudreore. Ahte ic holdra þy læs
deorre duguðe, þe þa deað fornam.
Site nu to symle, ond on sælum eow
sige hreðsecgum, swa þin sefa hwette!'   *490*
  Þa wæs Geatmæcgum geador ætsomne
on beorsele benc gerymed;
þær swiðferhþe sittan eodon,
þryðum dealle. Þegn nytte beheold,
se þe on handa bær hroden ealowæge,   *495*
scencte scir wered. Scop hwilum sang
hador on Heorote. Þær wæs hæleða dream,
duguð unlytel Dena ond Wedera.

7 Hrothgar spoke, protector of the Scyldings: 'Beowulf my friend, you have sought us out to fight in our defence and out of good will. A blow by your father brought about the greatest of feuds, when with his own hand he killed Heatholaf among the Wylfings. After that the kindred of the Weders could not keep him for fear of war. Thence he sought out the people of the South Danes, the Honoured-Scyldings, over the rolling waves. At that time I was first ruling the nation of the Danes, and in my youth held a broad kingdom, a rich stronghold of heroes. By then my elder brother Heorogar, Healfdene's son, was dead and lifeless—he was better than I! Thereupon I settled the feud by payment; I sent ancient treasures over the crest of the waves to the Wylfings—he swore oaths to me.

It grieves my heart to tell any man what humiliation, sudden violence, Grendel has inflicted on me in Heorot with his notions of hatred. My hall-troop, fighting-band, has shrunk; fate has swept them away in Grendel's terror. God could easily sever the mad ravager from his deeds!

So often champions, drunk with beer, have vowed over the ale-cups that they would await Grendel's attack in the beer-hall with terrible blades. Then in the morning when day dawned, this mead-hall, noble court, was stained with gore, all the bench-boards drenched with blood, the hall full of gore fallen from swords. I had all the fewer faithful men, dear companions, for death had taken them off. Now, sit down to the banquet and in happiness reveal victorious deeds to the triumphant men, as your mood may prompt you.'*

Then a bench in the beer-hall was cleared for the men of the Geats all together; the stout-hearted men went to sit there, proud in their strength. The thane who carried in his hands a decorated ale-cup did his duty, poured out the sweet drink. From time to time a minstrel sang, a clear voice in Heorot. There was rejoicing among heroes, no small company of Danes and Weders.

457 For werefyhtum: MS fere fyhtum   461 Wedera: MS gara   465 Deniga: MS deninga   489b-490a see note

VIII   Unferð maþelode, Ecglafes bearn,
þe æt fotum sæt frean Scyldinga,   500
onband beadurune; wæs him Beowulfes sið,
modges merefaran, micel æfþunca,
forþon þe he ne uþe þæt ænig oðer man
æfre mærða þon ma middangeardes
gehedde under heofenum þonne he sylfa: 505
'Eart þu se Beowulf se þe wið Brecan wunne,
on sidne sæ ymb sund flite,
ðær git for wlence wada cunnedon
ond for dolgilpe on deop wæter
aldrum neþdon? Ne inc ænig mon,   510
ne leof ne lað, belean mihte
sorhfullne sið, þa git on sund reon.
Þær git eagorstream earmum þehton,
mæton merestræta, mundum brugdon,
glidon ofer garsecg; geofon yþum weol,   515
wintrys wylmum. Git on wæteres æht
seofon niht swuncon. He þe æt sunde oferflat,
hæfde mære mægen. Þa hine on morgentid
on Heaþo-Ræmes holm up ætbær.
Ðonon he gesohte swæsne eðel,   520
leof his leodum, lond Brondinga,
freoðoburh fægere, þær he folc ahte,
burh ond beagas. Beot eal wið þe
sunu Beanstanes soðe gelæste.
Ðonne wene ic to þe wyrsan geþingea,   525
ðeah þu heaðoræsa gehwær dohte,
grimre guðe, gif þu Grendles dearst
nihtlongne fyrst nean bidan.'
    Beowulf maþelode, bearn Ecgþeowes:
'Hwæt, þu worn fela, wine min Unferð,   530
beore druncen, ymb Brecan spræce,
sægdest from his siðe. Soð ic talige
þæt ic merestrengo maran ahte,
earfeþo on yþum, ðonne ænig oþer man.
Wit þæt gecwædon cnihtwesende   535
ond gebeotedon —wæron begen þa git
on geogoðfeore— þæt wit on garsecg ut
aldrum neðdon; ond þæt geæfndon swa.
Hæfdon swurd nacod, þa wit on sund reon,
heard on handa; wit unc wið hronfixas   540
werian þohton. No he wiht fram me

8   Unferth* spoke, Ecglaf's son who sat at the feet of the Scyldings'
lord, let loose hostile thoughts; the bold seafarer Beowulf's venture
caused him great vexation, for he did not wish that any other man
in the world should ever achieve more glorious deeds beneath the
heavens than himself: 'Are you the Beowulf who contended
against Breca, competed in swimming on the open sea, where in
your pride you two explored the flood, and risked your lives in deep
water for the sake of a foolish boast? Nor could any man, neither
friend nor foe, dissuade the both of you from that disastrous venture
when you swam out to sea. There you both embraced the tides
with your arms, measured the seaways, struck out with your hands,
glided across the ocean; the sea surged with waves, with winter's
swell. For seven days you two toiled in the power of the water.* He
beat you at swimming, had the greater strength; then in the morning the water carried him to the coast of the Heatho-Ræmas.
From there, beloved of his people, he sought out his dear country,
the land of the Brondings, the fair peaceful stronghold where he
ruled over a nation, fortress and treasures. The son of Beanstan in
fact accomplished all he had boasted against you. So although you
have been successful everywhere in the onslaught of battle, in
grim warfare, I imagine the outcome will be the worse for you if you
dare wait all night long near at hand for Grendel.'

Beowulf spoke, the son of Ecgtheow: 'Well, Unferth my friend,
drunk with beer you have talked a great deal about Breca, told of
his adventure. I claim for a fact that I had greater strength in the
sea, hardship on the waves, than any other man. As boys we two
came to an agreement and boasted—we were both then still in our
youth—that we would risk our lives out on the ocean; and we did
just that. As we swam in the sea we each took a naked sword,
strong in our hands; we meant to defend ourselves against whales.
He was quite unable to float far away from me across the waves of

flodyþum feor   fleotan meahte,
hraþor on holme;   no ic fram him wolde.
Ða wit ætsomne   on sæ wæron
fif nihta fyrst,   oþþæt unc flod todraf,   *545*
wado weallende;   wedera cealdost,
nipende niht,   ond norþan wind
heaðogrim ondhwearf.
                              Hreo wæron yþa;
wæs merefixa   mod onhrered.
þær me wið laðum   licsyrce min,   *550*
heard, hondlocen,   helpe gefremede;
beadohrægl broden   on breostum læg
golde gegyrwed.   Me to grunde teah
fah feondscaða,   fæste hæfde
grim on grape.   Hwæþre me gyfeþe wearð,   *555*
þæt ic aglæcan   orde geræhte,
hildebille;   heaþoræs fornam
mihtig meredeor   þurh mine hand.

VIIII   Swa mec gelome   laðgeteonan
þreatedon þearle;   ic him þenode   *560*
deoran sweorde,   swa hit gedefe wæs.
Næs hie ðære fylle   gefean hæfdon,
manfordædlan,   þæt hie me þegon,
symbel ymbsæton   sægrunde neah.
Ac on mergenne   mecum wunde   *565*
be yðlafe   uppe lægon,
sweordum aswefede,   þæt syðþan na
ymb brontne ford   brimliðende
lade ne letton.
                      Leoht eastan com,
beorht beacen Godes;   brimu swaþredon   *570*
þæt ic sænæssas   geseon mihte,
windige weallas.   Wyrd oft nereð
unfægne eorl,   þonne his ellen deah.
Hwæþere me gesælde,   þæt ic mid sweorde ofsloh
niceras nigene.   No ic on niht gefrægn   *575*
under heofones hwealf   heardran feohtan,
ne on egstreamum   earmran mannon;
hwæþere ic fara feng   feore gedigde,
siþes werig.   Ða mec sæ oþbær,
flod æfter faroðe   on Finna land,   *580*
wadu weallendu.

the flood, to move more quickly in the water; nor would I leave him. So we stayed together on the sea for the space of five days until the flood, the surging sea, drove us apart; the coldest of weather, darkening night and the battle-fierce north wind turned against us.

The waves were savage; the anger of the sea-fish was aroused. My body-armour, hard with hand-forged links, afforded help against the enemies there; the woven war-garment, decked with gold, lay on my breast. A fierce, hostile ravager dragged me to the bottom, held fast in the grasp of the grim creature. Nevertheless it was given to me that I should reach the monster with the point of my war-sword; the onslaught of battle carried off the mighty sea-beast by my hand.

9   Frequently these loathsome assailants pressed hard upon me thus; I served them with my dear sword, as was fitting. The wicked evildoers had no joy whatever in that glut, feeding off me sitting round a banquet at the bottom of the sea. But in the morning, wounded by blades, they lay along the sand of the shore, put to sleep by swords, so that never again would they hinder the passage of ocean voyagers across the high seas.

Light came from the east, the bright beacon of God; the ocean grew calm so that I could see promontories, windswept ramparts of the sea. Fate will often spare a man not yet destined for death, when his courage is good. In any case it befell me that I struck down nine sea-monsters with the sword. I have not heard tell of a harder fight by night beneath the vault of heaven, nor of a man under greater stress in the tides; yet I escaped from the grasp of foes alive, exhausted from the exploit. Then the sea, the flood with its currents, the surging waters, carried me away to the land of the Lapps.

567 sweordum: MS swe . . . .; Thorkelin A speodū   578 hwæþere: MS hwaþere
581 wadu: MS wudu

No ic wiht fram þe
swylcra searoniða   secgan hyrde,
billa brogan.   Breca næfre git
æt heaðolace,   ne gehwæþer incer,
swa deorlice   dæd gefremede   585
fagum sweordum   —no ic þæs fela gylpe—
þeah ðu þinum broðrum   to banan wurde,
heafodmægum;   þæs þu in helle scealt
werhðo dreogan,   þeah þin wit duge!
    Secge ic þe to soðe,   sunu Ecglafes,   590
þæt næfre Grendel swa fela   gryra gefremede,
atol æglæca   ealdre þinum,
hynðo on Heorote,   gif þin hige wære,
sefa swa searogrim,   swa þu self talast.
Ac he hafað onfunden   þæt he þa fæhðe ne þearf,   595
atole ecgþræce   eower leode
swiðe onsittan,   Sige-Scyldinga.
Nymeð nydbade,   nænegum arað
leode Deniga;   ac he lust wigeð,
swefeð ond sendeþ,   secce ne weneþ   600
to Gar-Denum.   Ac ic him Geata sceal
eafoð ond ellen   ungeara nu,
guþe gebeodan.   Gæþ eft se þe mot
to medo modig,   siþþan morgenleoht
ofer ylda bearn   oþres dogores,   605
sunne sweglwered   suþan scineð!'
    Þa wæs on salum   sinces brytta,
gamolfeax ond guðrof;   geoce gelyfde
brego Beorht-Dena,   gehyrde on Beowulfe
folces hyrde   fæstrædne geþoht.   610
    Ðær wæs hæleþa hleahtor;   hlyn swynsode,
word wæron wynsume.   Eode Wealhþeow forð,
cwen Hroðgares,   cynna gemyndig;
grette goldhroden   guman on healle,
ond þa freolic wif   ful gesealde   615
ærest East-Dena   eþelwearde;
bæd hine bliðne   æt þære beorþege,
leodum leofne;   he on lust geþeah
symbel ond seleful,   sigerof kyning.
Ymbeode þa   ides Helminga   620
duguþe ond geogoþe   dæl æghwylcne,
sincfato sealde,   oþþæt sæl alamp,
þæt hio Beowulfe,   beaghroden cwen

I have never heard ought of such skilful conflicts, such terror of swords, told about you. I do not boast too much in saying that in the game of war never yet has Breca—nor either of you—performed so valuable a deed with shining swords—although *you* became the slayer of your brothers, your closest kin; for that you shall suffer damnation in hell, clever as you are!

I tell you for a fact, son of Ecglaf, that the dreadful monster Grendel would never have committed so many terrible deeds against your chief, humiliation in Heorot, if your heart and mind were as warlike as you yourself claim. But he has found out that he need not fear a feud, a dreadful storm of blades, from your people, not be so frightened of the Victorious-Scyldings. He takes his toll, shows mercy to none of the people of the Danes; but he takes his pleasure, puts to sleep and despatches, expecting no opposition from the Spear-Danes. But very soon now I shall show him the Geats' strength and courage in battle. Then when the morning light of another day, the sun clothed in radiance, shines from the south over the children of men, he who will may again go brave to the mead-drinking!'

Then, grey-haired and renowned in battle, the distributor of treasure was joyful; the prince of the Bright-Danes, the shepherd of his nation, counted on help, having heard in Beowulf a steadfast resolve.

There was laughter among the heroes; a jubilant sound rose up, talk was cheerful. Wealhtheow, Hrothgar's queen, stepped forth, mindful of etiquette;* decked with gold, she greeted the men in the hall, and then the noble woman gave the goblet first to the guardian of the East Danes' homeland; bade him who was loved by the people be happy at the beer-drinking. He, the king renowned for victories, gladly partook of the banquet and hall-goblet. Then the lady of the Helmings went about everywhere among both tried warriors and youths, passed round the precious cup, until the moment arrived when she, a noble-hearted queen, circlet-adorned,

---

mode geþungen,   medoful ætbær.
Grette Geata leod,   Gode þancode   625
wisfæst wordum,   þæs ðe hire se willa gelamp,
þæt heo on ænigne   eorl gelyfde
fyrena frofre.   He þæt ful geþeah,
wælreow wiga,   æt Wealhþeon,
ond þa gyddode   guþe gefysed;   630
Beowulf maþelode,   bearn Ecgþeowes:
'Ic þæt hogode,   þa ic on holm gestah,
sæbat gesæt   mid minra secga gedriht,
þæt ic anunga   eowra leoda
willan geworhte,   oþðe on wæl crunge,   635
feondgrapum fæst.   Ic gefremman sceal
eorlic ellen,   oþðe endedæg
on þisse meoduhealle   minne gebidan.'
Ðam wife þa word   wel licodon,
gilpcwide Geates;   eode goldhroden   640
freolicu folccwen   to hire frean sittan.
    Þa wæs eft swa ær   inne on healle
þryðword sprecen,   ðeod on sælum,
sigefolca sweg,   oþþæt semninga
sunu Healfdenes   secean wolde   645
æfenræste.   Wiste þæm ahlæcan
to þæm heahsele   hilde geþinged,
siððan hie sunnan leoht   geseon ne meahton,
oþðe nipende   niht ofer ealle,
scaduhelma gesceapu   scriðan cwoman,   650
wan under wolcnum.   Werod eall aras.
Gegrette þa   guma oþerne,
Hroðgar Beowulf,   ond him hæl abead,
winærnes geweald,   ond þæt word acwæð:
'Næfre ic ænegum men   ær alyfde,   655
siþðan ic hond ond rond   hebban mihte,
ðryþærn Dena   buton þe nu ða.
Hafa nu ond geheald   husa selest;
gemyne mærþo,   mægenellen cyð,
waca wið wraþum!   Ne bið þe wilna gad   660
gif þu þæt ellenweorc   aldre gedigest.'

x   Ða him Hroþgar gewat   mid his hæleþa gedryht,
        eodur Scyldinga   ut of healle;
        wolde wigfruma   Wealhþeo secan,

carried the mead-goblet to Beowulf. She greeted the prince of the Geats and, perfect in speech, thanked God that her wish was fulfilled, that she might count on some warrior for help against wickedness.

A fighter, savage in slaughter, he took the goblet from Wealhtheow and then, eager for battle, made a speech; Beowulf spoke, son of Ecgtheow: 'When I put to sea, occupied an ocean-going boat with my band of men, I resolved that I should once for all carry out the wish of your people, or else fall in slaughter, fast in the grip of the enemy. I shall achieve this deed of heroic courage, or else meet my final hour in this mead-hall.' These words, the Geat's vaunting speech, pleased the woman well; decked with gold, the noble queen of the nation went to sit by her lord.

Then again as of old, brave words were spoken within the hall, the nation joyful, the sound of a victorious people, until presently the son of Healfdene determined to seek his evening's rest. He knew that the monster had planned an attack on the lofty hall from the time they should be unable to see the light of the sun and, night growing dark over everything, the shadowy shapes of dusk should stride forth, black under the clouds. The whole company rose. Then one man saluted the other, Hrothgar Beowulf, and wished him good luck, mastery of the wine-hall, and spoke these words: 'Never before, since I could lift hand and shield, have I entrusted the Danes' glorious hall to any man, except now to you. Now take and guard the best of houses; think of fame, show great courage, keep watch against the enemy! You shall lack nothing you desire if you escape this courageous deed alive.'

10 Then Hrothgar, the Scyldings' refuge, with his band of heroes went out of the hall; the war-leader wished to seek out Wealhtheow the

648 ne *supplied*   652 Gegrette: MS grette

cwen to gebeddan.   Hæfde Kyningwuldor   665
Grendle togeanes,   swa guman gefrungon,
seleweard aseted;   sundornytte beheold
ymb aldor Dena: eotonweard abead.
Huru Geata leod   georne truwode
modgan mægnes,   Metodes hyldo,   670
ða he him of dyde   isernbyrnan,
helm of hafelan,   sealde his hyrsted sweord,
irena cyst   ombihtþegne,
ond gehealdan het   hildegeatwe.

   Gespræc þa se goda   gylpworda sum,   675
Beowulf Geata,   ær he on bed stige:
'No ic me an herewæsmun   hnagran talige
guþgeweorca   þonne Grendel hine;
forþan ic hine sweorde   swebban nelle,
aldre beneotan,   þeah ic eal mæge.   680
Nat he þara goda,   þæt he me ongean slea,
rand geheawe,   þeah ðe he rof sie
niþgeweorca.   Ac wit on niht sculon
secge ofersittan,   gif he gesecean dear
wig ofer wæpen.   Ond siþðan witig God   685
on swa hwæþere hond,   halig Dryhten,
mærðo deme,   swa him gemet þince.'
   Hylde hine þa heaþodeor,   hleorbolster onfeng
eorles andwlitan,   ond hine ymb monig
snellic særinc   selereste gebeah.   690
Nænig heora þohte   þæt he þanon scolde
eft eardlufan   æfre gesecean,
folc oþðe freoburh,   þær he afeded wæs,
ac hie hæfdon gefrunen,   þæt hie aer to fela micles
in þæm winsele   wældeað fornam,   695
Denigea leode.   Ac him Dryhten forgeaf
wigspeda gewiofu,   Wedera leodum,
frofor ond fultum,   þæt hie feond heora
ðurh anes cræft   ealle ofercomon,
selfes mihtum.   Soð is gecyþed,   700
þæt mihtig God   manna cynnes
weold wideferhð.
                     Com on wanre niht
scriðan sceadugenga.   Sceotend swæfon,
þa þæt hornreced   healdan scoldon,
ealle buton anum.   Þæt wæs yldum cuþ,   705
þæt hie ne moste,   þa Metod nolde,

queen for his bed-fellow. The King of Glory, so men heard tell, had appointed a hall-guard against Grendel; he discharged a special duty on behalf of the chief of the Danes: mounted guard against ogres. Indeed, the prince of the Geats readily trusted in his brave strength, the favour of Providence, as he put off his iron mail, the helmet from his head, gave his decorated sword, the choicest of iron, to an attendant, and bade him take charge of the war-gear.

Then before the great man got on to his bed, Beowulf of the Geats spoke vaunting words: 'I do not reckon myself inferior in warlike vigour, for deeds of battle, than Grendel does himself; therefore I will not put him to sleep, take away his life, with a sword, although I easily could. He knows nothing of such noble matters—that he might strike against me, hew at the shield— renowned though he may be for hostile deeds. But in the night we both shall dispense with the sword, if he dare seek a fight without weapons. And then may the wise God, the holy Lord, assign the glory to whichever side seems to him appropriate.'

The battle-brave man then laid himself down, a pillow received the hero's cheek, and around him many a bold seaman sank to his couch in the hall. Not one of them thought that he would ever return from there to seek out his beloved country, nation and noble stronghold where he was raised; for they had heard that deadly slaughter had already carried off all too many of the Danish people in that wine-hall. But to these, the people of the Weders, the Lord granted comfort and support, success in battle to be woven into their destiny, inasmuch as through the might of one man, his sole powers, they all overcame their foe. The truth was made known that Almighty God has ruled mankind down the ages.

The creature that prowls in shadows came stalking through the black night. The marksmen who had to guard that gabled building were asleep—all but one.* It was known to men that, if Providence did not wish it, the spectral ravager could not drag them

---

684 he: MS het   702 wide *restored from* Thorkelin A and B ride

se scynscaþa   under sceadu bregdan.
Ac he wæccende   wraþum on andan,
bad bolgenmod   beadwa geþinges.

Ða com of more   under misthleoþum   710
Grendel gongan;   Godes yrre bær.
Mynte se manscaða   manna cynnes
sumne besyrwan   in sele þam hean.
Wod under wolcnum   to þæs þe he winreced,
goldsele gumena,   gearwost wisse,   715
fættum fahne.   Ne wæs þæt forma sið
þæt he Hroþgares   ham gesohte.
Næfre he on aldordagum   ær ne siþðan
heardran hæle   healðegnas fand.
    Com þa to recede   rinc siðian   720
dreamum bedæled.   Duru sona onarn
fyrbendum fæst,   syþðan he hire folmum gehran;
onbræd þa bealohydig,   ða he gebolgen wæs,
recedes muþan.   Raþe æfter þon
on fagne flor   feond treddode,   725
eode yrremod.   Him of eagum stod
ligge gelicost   leoht unfæger.
Geseah he in recede   rinca manige,
swefan sibbegedriht   samod ætgædere,
magorinca heap.   Þa his mod ahlog;   730
mynte þæt he gedælde,   ær þon dæg cwome,
atol aglæca,   anra gehwylces
lif wið lice,   þa him alumpen wæs
wistfylle wen.
                Ne wæs þæt wyrd þa gen,
þæt he ma moste   manna cynnes   735
ðicgean ofer þa niht.   Þryðswyð beheold,
mæg Higelaces,   hu se manscaða
under færgripum   gefaran wolde.
Ne þæt se aglæca   yldan þohte,
ac he gefeng hraðe   forman siðe   740
slæpendne rinc,   slat unwearnum,
bat banlocan,   blod edrum dranc,
synsnædum swealh;   sona hæfde
unlyfigendes   eal gefeormod,
fet ond folma.   Forð near ætstop,   745
nam þa mid handa   higeþihtigne
rinc on ræste;   him ræhte ongean

away beneath the shadows. But he, lying awake in anger for the enemy, awaited the outcome of the conflict, his heart swollen with rage.

11 Then out of the wasteland came Grendel, advancing beneath the misty slopes; he carried the wrath of God. The wicked ravager intended to ensnare someone of the human race in that lofty hall. He strode beneath the clouds until he could most clearly make out the wine-hall, the treasure-house of men, gleaming with gold plate. That was not the first time he had sought out the home of Hrothgar. Never in all the days of his life, before nor since, did he have worse luck in meeting thanes in a hall.

The creature, bereft of joys, came on, making his way to the hall. The door, fastened with fire-forged bars, gave way immediately once he touched it with his hands; intent on evil, swollen with rage he thrust open the mouth of the building. After that the fiend advanced, angry at heart, swiftly stepped on to the patterned floor.* From his eyes, very like fire, there gleamed an ugly light. Within the hall he saw many warriors, a band of kinsmen sleeping, a troop of young warriors all together. Then his heart laughed; the dreadful monster intended that, before day came, he should have severed life from the body of each one of them, now the chance of a glut of feasting had come his way.

It was not his destiny that, when that night was over, he should taste more of mankind. Very powerful, Hygelac's kinsman watched for how the wicked ravager would set about his sudden onslaughts. The monster did not think to delay it, but for a start he quickly seized a sleeping warrior, tore him apart without resistance, bit into the bones' links, drank the blood from the veins, swallowed great chunks; he had soon devoured all of the lifeless man—feet and fists. He stepped forward closer, then clutched with his hand at the stout-hearted warrior on his couch; the fiend groped towards

707 scynscaþa: MS synscaþa   722 gehran: MS . . hran   723 he gebolgen: MS . . . . . bolgen   747 him *restored*

feond mid folme.   He onfeng hraþe
inwitþancum   ond wið earm gesæt.
Sona þæt onfunde   fyrena hyrde,   750
þæt he ne mette   middangeardes,
eorþan sceatta   on elran men
mundgripe maran.   He on mode wearð
forht on ferhðe;   no þy ær fram meahte.
Hyge wæs him hinfus,   wolde on heolster fleon,   755
secan deofla gedræg.   Ne wæs his drohtoð þær,
swylce he on ealderdagum   ær gemette.
    Gemunde þa se goda   mæg Higelaces
æfenspræce,   uplang astod
ond him fæste wiðfeng.   Fingras burston;   760
eoten wæs utweard;   eorl furþur stop.
Mynte se mæra,   þær he meahte swa,
widre gewindan   ond on weg þanon
fleon on fenhopu;   wiste his fingra geweald
on grames grapum.   Þæt wæs geocor sið   765
þæt se hearmscaþa   to Heorute ateah.
    Dryhtsele dynede;   Denum eallum wearð,
ceasterbuendum,   cenra gehwylcum,
eorlum ealuscerwen.   Yrre wæron begen,
reþe renweardas.   Reced hlynsode;   770
þa wæs wundor micel   þæt se winsele
wiðhæfde heaþodeorum,   þæt he on hrusan ne feol,
fæger foldbold;   ac he þæs fæste wæs
innan ond utan   irenbendum
searoþoncum besmiþod.   Þær fram sylle abeag   775
medubenc monig,   mine gefræge,
golde geregnad,   þær þa graman wunnon.
Þæs ne wendon ær   witan Scyldinga,
þæt hit a mid gemete   manna ænig,
betlic ond banfag   tobrecan meahte,   780
listum tolucan,   nymþe liges fæþm
swulge on swaþule.
                    Sweg up astag
niwe geneahhe.   Norð-Denum stod
atelic egesa,   anra gehwylcum
þara þe of wealle   wop gehyrdon,   785
gryreleoð galan   Godes andsacan,
sigeleasne sang,   sar wanigean
helle hæfton.   Heold hine fæste,
se þe manna wæs   mægene strengest

him with open palm. He promptly realised this malicious intention and sat right up so as to drive back the arm. The patron of crimes soon discovered that nowhere in the world, in no corner of the earth, had he encountered a mightier hand-grip in any other man. In his mind he grew fearful in spirit; for all that, he could not escape any sooner. His spirit longed to be gone, wanted to flee into the darkness, seek out the company of devils. His plight there was unlike anything he had ever encountered in all the days of his life.

Then Hygelac's great kinsman recalled his speech of that evening, stood erect and laid firm hold on him. Fingers cracked; the ogre was striving to escape; the warrior took a step forward. The notorious creature intended to slip into the open whenever he could, and thence flee away into the swamp retreat; he knew his fingers' power to be in the grip of a wrathful man. That was a sorry journey that the pernicious ravager had taken to Heorot.

The noble hall resounded—became for all the Danes, those who dwelt in the city, for each valiant man, for warriors, a bitter cup.* Both fierce occupants of the house were enraged. The building re-echoed; it was a miracle that the wine-hall withstood those bold in battle—that it did not fall to the ground, the fair earthly dwelling; but inside and out it was too firmly made fast with iron bands, skilfully forged. There, as I have heard, where the fierce ones struggled, many a mead-bench set with gold collapsed from its base. The councillors of the Scyldings had never imagined that any man could ever shatter it in any way, tear it apart by cunning, splendid and adorned with antlers—unless the embrace of fire should swallow it up in flame.

A strange sound rose up, repeatedly. Dire terror came upon the North Danes, upon every one of those who from the rampart heard that shriek, heard the enemy of God chant his terrible lay, a song of defeat, the thrall of hell howl with pain. He who was the

---

on þæm dæge   þysses lifes.   790

XII   Nolde eorla hleo   ænige þinga
þone cwealmcuman   cwicne forlætan:
ne his lifdagas   leoda ænigum
nytte tealde.
                þær genehost brægd
eorl Beowulfes   ealde lafe,   795
wolde freadrihtnes   feorh ealgian,
mæres þeodnes,   ðær hie meahton swa.
Hie þæt ne wiston,   þa hie gewin drugon,
heardhicgende   hildemecgas,
ond on healfa gehwone   heawan þohton,   800
sawle secan: þone synscaðan
ænig ofer eorþan   irenna cyst,
guðbilla nan   gretan nolde,
ac he sigewæpnum   forsworen hæfde,
ecga gehwylcre.   Scolde his aldorgedal   805
on ðæm dæge   þysses lifes
earmlic wurðan,   ond se ellorgast
on feonda geweald   feor siðian.
Ða þæt onfunde   se þe fela æror
modes myrðe   manna cynne,   810
fyrene gefremede   —he fag wið God—
þæt him se lichoma   læstan nolde,
ac hine se modega   mæg Hygelaces
hæfde be honda;   wæs gehwæþer oðrum
lifigende lað.   Licsar gebad   815
atol æglæca;   him on eaxle wearð
syndolh sweotol;   seonowe onsprungon,
burston banlocan.   Beowulfe wearð
guðhreð gyfeþe.   Scolde Grendel þonan
feorhseoc fleon   under fenhleoðu,   820
secean wynleas wic;   wiste þe geornor,
þæt his aldres wæs   ende gegongen,
dogera dægrim.
                Denum eallum wearð
æfter þam wælræse   willa gelumpen.
Hæfde þa gefælsod,   se þe ær feorran com,   825
snotor ond swyðferhð,   sele Hroðgares,
genered wið niðe.   Nihtweorce gefeh,
ellenmærþum.   Hæfde East-Denum
Geatmecga leod   gilp gelæsted,

strongest of men in might in that day and age held him fast.

12   The warriors' defence did not wish that murderous visitant to leave alive on any account: he did not reckon his life of use to any people.

Then many a warrior of Beowulf's drew out an ancient heirloom, wished to defend the life of the noble leader, famous prince, if they could. One thing they did not know, stern-minded men of battle, when they joined in the struggle and thought to hack at him on every side, to seek his life —no war-sword, not the choicest of iron in the world, would touch the evil ravager, for with a spell he had rendered victorious weapons, all blades, useless. His departure from life at that time was to be wretched, and the alien visitant would have to travel far away into the power of fiends. Then he who, wicked in heart, had committed crimes against mankind for so long—he was in feud with God—found that his flesh would not serve him, but Hygelac's bold kinsman had him by the hand. As long as he was alive, each was hateful to the other. The dreadful monster suffered bodily pain; a huge wound appeared plain on his shoulder; sinews sprang apart, the bones' links broke. Triumph in battle was allotted to Beowulf. Grendel, mortally wounded, had to flee from there beneath the swampy slopes, to seek out a joyless dwelling; he knew all too well that the end of his life had come, the full number of his days.

As a consequence of that deadly onslaught, the desire of all the Danes was achieved. He who had recently come from afar, wise and stout-hearted, had thus cleansed Hrothgar's hall, saved it from persecution. He rejoiced in that night's work, in deeds of famous courage. The prince of the Geatish men had fulfilled his boast to the East Danes, and so remedied all the distress, the evil sorrow

swylce oncyþðe   ealle gebette,   *830*
inwidsorge,   þe hie ær drugon
ond for þreanydum   þolian scoldon,
torn unlytel. Þæt wæs tacen sweotol,
syþðan hildedeor   hond alegde,
earm ond eaxle   —þær wæs eal geador   *835*
Grendles grape—   under geapne hrof.

XIII   Ða wæs on morgen,   mine gefræge,
ymb þa gifhealle   guðrinc monig;
ferdon folctogan   feorran ond nean
geond widwegas   wundor sceawian,   *840*
laþes lastas. No his lifgedal
sarlic þuhte   secga ænegum,
þara þe tirleases   trode sceawode:
hu he werigmod   on weg þanon,
niða ofercumen,   on nicera mere,   *845*
fæge ond geflymed   feorhlastas bær.
Ðær wæs on blode   brim weallende,
atol yða geswing   eal gemenged
haton heolfre,   heorodreore weol.
Deaðfæge deog,   siððan dreama leas   *850*
in fenfreoðo   feorh alegde,
hæþene sawle;   þær him hel onfeng.
Þanon eft gewiton   ealdgesiðas,
swylce geong manig   of gomenwaþe,
fram mere modge   mearum ridan,   *855*
beornas on blancum. Ðær wæs Beowulfes
mærðo mæned;   monig oft gecwæð,
þætte suð ne norð   be sæm tweonum
ofer eormengrund   oþer nænig
under swegles begong   selra nære   *860*
rondhæbbendra,   rices wyrðra.
Ne hie huru winedrihten   wiht ne logon,
glædne Hroðgar,   ac þæt wæs god cyning.
Hwilum heaþorofe   hleapan leton,
on geflit faran   fealwe mearas,   *865*
ðær him foldwegas   fægere þuhton,
cystum cuðe. Hwilum cyninges þegn,
guma gilphlæden,   gidda gemyndig,
se ðe ealfela   ealdgesegena
worn gemunde,   word oþer fand   *870*
soðe gebunden;   secg eft ongan

which they earlier endured and had to suffer through dire necessity —no little trouble. It was manifest proof when the battle-brave man set the hand, arm and shoulder, up under the curved roof— there was the whole of Grendel's grasp complete.

13   Then in the morning, as I have heard, there was many a warrior around that gift-hall; leaders of the nation travelled from far and near, through distant regions, to examine that marvel, the tracks of the foe. His separation from life was in no way thought sorrowful by any of the men who examined the footprints of the inglorious creature—how, weary at heart, overcome in violence, doomed and put to flight, he left traces of his life-blood from there all the way to the water-monsters' lake. There the water was welling with blood, the dreadful swirl of waves all mingled with hot gore, welled with sword-blood. Doomed to death he hid himself when, bereft of joys, he laid down his life, the heathen soul, in the swamp refuge; there hell received him.

From there old companions, and many a young man also, returned again from their joyful journey, riding from the lake, high-spirited on horseback, warriors on glossy steeds. Then Beowulf's fame was proclaimed; many repeatedly declared that nowhere in the wide world, south or north between the seas, was there any shield-bearer nobler than he under the expanse of heaven, nor more worthy of power. Yet in no way did they reproach their friend and leader, the gracious Hrothgar, for he was a great king.

At times, where the paths seemed fair, were known to be good, those renowned in battle allowed their steeds to gallop, to run races. At times one of the king's thanes, a man filled with high-sounding words, with a memory for stories, who remembered a multitude of all kinds of old legends, improvised a new poem linked in true metre; again the man began by his art to relate

836 hrof: MS h . . .; Thorkelin B hr . . .

siŏ Beowulfes   snyttrum styrian
ond on sped wrecan   spel gerade,
wordum wrixlan.

        Welhwylc gecwæŏ
þæt he fram Sigemunde   secgan hyrde,   *875*
ellendædum,   uncuþes fela,
Wælsinges gewin,   wide siŏas,
þara þe gumena bearn   gearwe ne wiston,
fæhŏe ond fyrena,   buton Fitela mid hine,
þonne he swulces hwæt   secgan wolde,   *880*
eam his nefan,   swa hie a wæron
æt niŏa gehwam   nydgesteallan;
hæfdon ealfela   eotena cynnes
sweordum gesæged.   Sigemunde gesprong
æfter deaŏdæge   dom unlytel,   *885*
syþŏan wiges heard   wyrm acwealde,
hordes hyrde.   He under harne stan,
æþelinges bearn,   ana geneŏde
frecne dæde;   ne wæs him Fitela mid;
hwæþre him gesælde   ŏæt þæt swurd þurhwod   *890*
wrætlicne wyrm,   þæt hit on wealle ætstod,
dryhtlic iren;   draca morŏre swealt.
Hæfde aglæca   elne gegongen,
þæt he beahhordes   brucan moste
selfes dome;   sæbat gehleod,   *895*
bær on bearm scipes   beorhte frætwa,
Wælses eafera;   wyrm hat gemealt.

    Se wæs wreccena   wide mærost
ofer werþeode,   wigendra hleo,
ellendædum   —he þæs ær onŏah—   *900*
siŏŏan Heremodes   hild sweŏrode,
eafoŏ ond ellen;   he mid Eotenum wearŏ
on feonda geweald   forŏ forlacen,
snude forsended.   Hine sorhwylmas
lemede to lange;   he his leodum wearŏ,   *905*
eallum æþellingum   to aldorceare.
Swylce oft bemearn   ærran mælum
swiŏferhþes siŏ   snotor ceorl monig,
se þe him bealwa to   bote gelyfde,
þæt þæt ŏeodnes bearn   geþeon scolde,   *910*
fæderæþelum onfon,   folc gehealdan,
hord ond hleoburh,   hæleþa rice,
eŏel Scyldinga.   He þær eallum wearŏ,

Beowulf's exploit and skilfully to tell an apt tale, varying his words.*

He spoke of all he had heard tell about Sigemund,* about courageous deeds—many strange things—of the struggle of the son of Wæls, his remote journeys, feuds and crimes, about which the children of men knew little except for Fitela, to whom he would speak of such matters, as uncle to nephew, since they were always friends in need in every conflict; they had laid low with their swords very many of the race of ogres. No little glory accrued to Sigemund after the day of his death, since, bold in battle, he had slain a serpent, guardian of a treasure-hoard. He, a prince's son, had ventured alone on that daring deed beneath the grey rock; Fitela was not with him; nevertheless it befell him that his sword pierced the wondrous serpent so that it stuck in the wall, noble iron; the dragon died a violent death. By his courage the terrifying man had brought it about that he might enjoy the hoard of rings at his own pleasure; the offspring of Wæls loaded a seagoing boat, carried bright treasure into the bosom of the ship; heat consumed the serpent.

Of all exiles, he, the defence of fighting men, was the most widely renowned among the nations for deeds of courage—so much had he prospered of old—after the battle-prowess, the strength and courage of Heremod ceased;* among the Jutes he was betrayed into the power of enemies, and quickly despatched. Surging misery had crippled him too long; he became a cause for deadly anxiety to his people, to all the nobles. For in earlier times many a prudent man often grieved over the stout-hearted one's career—the same who had counted on him for a remedy against disasters, counted on the fact that the prince's son should prosper, succeed to his father's rank, guard the people, treasure-hoard and stronghold, the realm of heroes, homeland of the Scyldings. The kinsman of

---

⁹⁰² eafoð: MS earfoð

mæg Higelaces,   manna cynne,
freondum gefægra: hine fyren onwod!   915
   Hwilum flitende fealwe stræte
mearum mæton. Ða wæs morgenleoht
scofen ond scynded. Eode scealc monig
swiðhicgende to sele þam hean,
searowundor seon. Swylce self cyning   920
of brydbure, beahhorda weard,
tryddode tirfæst getrume micle,
cystum gecyþed; ond his cwen mid him
medostigge mæt mægþa hose.

XIIII   Hroðgar maþelode —he to healle geong,   925
stod on stapole, geseah steapne hrof
golde fahne ond Grendles hond:
'Ðisse ansyne Alwealdan þanc
lungre gelimpe! Fela ic laþes gebad,
grynna æt Grendle: a mæg God wyrcan   930
wunder æfter wundre, wuldres Hyrde.
Ðæt wæs ungeara, þæt ic ænigra me
weana ne wende to widan feore
bote gebidan, þonne blode fah
husa selest heorodreorig stod,   935
wea widscofen witena gehwylcum
ðara þe ne wendon þæt hie wideferhð
leoda landgeweorc laþum beweredon
scuccum ond scinnum. Nu scealc hafað
þurh Drihtnes miht dæd gefremede,   940
ðe we ealle ær ne meahton
snyttrum besyrwan. Hwæt, þæt secgan mæg
efne swa hwylc mægþa, swa ðone magan cende
æfter gumcynnum, gyf heo gyt lyfað,
þæt hyre Ealdmetod este wære   945
bearngebyrdo.
                 Nu ic, Beowulf, þec,
secg betsta, me for sunu wylle
freogan on ferhþe; heald forð tela
niwe sibbe. Ne bið þe nænigre gad
worolde wilna, þe ic geweald hæbbe.   950
Ful oft ic for læssan lean teohhode,
hordweorþunge hnahran rince,
sæmran æt sæcce. Þu þe self hafast
dædum gefremed, þæt þin dom lyfað

Hygelac became the dearer to his friends, to all mankind: crime took possession of the other!

Racing at times, they measured the yellow road with their steeds. By then the morning light was advanced and hastening on. Many a strong-minded man went to the great hall to look at the strange wonder. The king himself, guardian of ring-hoards, famed for his virtues, also stepped forth majestically from his marriage-bower with a large troop; and his queen with him measured the path to the mead-hall with a company of maidens.

14 Hrothgar spoke—he went to the hall, stood on the steps,* gazed at the steep roof shining with gold, and at Grendel's hand: "For this sight thanks may at once be given to the Almighty! I have endured many afflictions, violence at the hands of Grendel: God, the Guardian of Glory, can always work marvel upon marvel. It was only recently that I despaired of ever living to see any remedy for my woes, since the best of houses stood bloodstained with sword-gore, a far-reaching woe to every one of the councillors who despaired of ever defending the peoples' fortress from its enemies, from demons and evil spirits. Now through the might of the Lord, a man has accomplished the deed that previously all of us with our skill could not contrive. Indeed, whichever maiden gave birth to such a son among mankind may well say—if she is still alive—that eternal Providence was kind to her in her child-bearing.

Now Beowulf, best of men, I will cherish you in my heart as a son; keep true henceforth to this new friendship. You shall lack nothing in the world you desire if it lies in my power. I have often enough conferred rewards for lesser deeds, honouring with riches a slighter warrior, weaker in combat. You yourself have ensured with deeds that your glory will live for ever. May the Almighty reward

---

⁹³⁶ gehwylcum: MS gehwylcne   ⁹⁴⁹ nænigre: MS ænigre   ⁹⁵⁴ dom *supplied.*

awa to aldre. Alwalda þec   955
gode forgylde, swa he nu gyt dyde!'
    Beowulf maþelode, bearn Ecgþeowes:
'We þæt ellenweorc estum miclum,
feohtan fremedon, frecne geneðdon
eafoð uncuþes. Uþe ic swiþor   960
þæt ðu hine selfne geseon moste,
feond on frætewum fylwerigne!
Ic hine hrædlice heardan clammum
on wælbedde wriþan þohte,
þæt he for mundgripe minum scolde   965
licgean lifbysig, butan his lic swice.
Ic hine ne mihte, þa Metod nolde,
ganges getwæman, no ic him þæs georne ætfealh,
feorhgeniðlan; wæs to foremihtig
feond on feþe. Hwæþere he his folme forlet   970
to lifwraþe last weardian,
earm ond eaxle; no þær ænige swa þeah
feasceaft guma frofre gebohte;
no þy leng leofað laðgeteona
synnum geswenced, ac hyne sar hafað   975
in nidgripe nearwe befongen,
balwon bendum. Ðær abidan sceal
maga mane fah miclan domes,
hu him scir Metod scrifan wille.'
    Ða wæs swigra secg, sunu Ecglafes,   980
on gylpspræce guðgeweorca,
siþðan æþelingas eorles cræfte
ofer heanne hrof hand sceawedon,
feondes fingras. Foran æghwylc wæs,
stedenægla gehwylc style gelicost,   985
hæþenes handsporu, hilderinces
egl unheoru. Æghwylc gecwæð
þæt him heardra nan hrinan wolde
iren ærgod, þæt ðæs ahlæcan
blodge beadufolme onberan wolde.   990

XV   Ða wæs haten hreþe Heort innanweard
folmum gefrætwod; fela þæra wæs,
wera ond wifa, þe þæt winreced,
gestsele gyredon. Goldfag scinon
web æfter wagum, wundorsiona fela   995
secga gehwylcum þara þe on swylc starað.

you with good things, as he has just done!'

Beowulf spoke, the son of Ecgtheow: 'We undertook the fight, that deed of courage, with great good will, daringly risked the strength of an unknown creature. I dearly wish that you could have seen him, the foe himself in his trappings, exhausted to the point of death! I thought to bind him quickly on his deathbed with a firm grasp so that, unless his body should slip away, he would have to lie struggling for life in the grip of my hand. I could not prevent him going, since Providence did not wish it, nor did I hold him, mortal enemy, closely enough for that; the fiend was too exceedingly strong in his movement. Nevertheless, to save his life he relinquished his fist—the arm and shoulder—to remain behind, although the wretched creature bought no comfort at all by that; weighed down with sins, the loathsome despoiler will not live any the longer, for pain has clutched him close in a forceful grip, in deadly fetters. There, stained with crime, the creature must await the great Judgement, whatever resplendent Providence should wish to impose on him.'

Ecglaf's son was then the more silent a man in boasting talk about deeds of war, when, thanks to the hero's might, princes examined the hand, the fingers of the fiend, up towards the high roof. From in front, each fixed nail was just like steel, every talon on the hand of the heathen warrior a hideous spike. Everyone agreed that there was no old and ancient iron of stern men would touch him, would sever the monster's bloody battle-fist.

15 Then it was quickly commanded that Heorot should be decorated within by hands; there were many, both men and women, who made ready that wine-hall, a building for guests. Along the walls tapestries shone adorned with gold, many a wonderful thing to look at for all men who gaze at such things. That bright house, all made

957 Ecgþeowes: MS ecþeowes   963 hine: MS him   965 mundgripe: MS handgripe   976 nidgripe: MS mid gripe   980 Ecglafes: MS eclafes   985 stedenægla: MS steda nægla

Wæs þæt beorhte bold   tobrocen swiðe,
eal inneweard   irenbendum fæst,
heorras tohlidene;   hrof ana genæs
ealles ansund,   þe se aglæca   1000
fyrendædum fag   on fleam gewand,
aldres orwena.   No þæt yðe byð
to befleonne   —fremme se þe wille—
ac gesecan sceal   sawlberendra
nyde genydde,   niþða bearna,   1005
grundbuendra   gearwe stowe,
þær his lichoma,   legerbedde fæst,
swefeþ æfter symle.
                    þa wæs sæl ond mæl
þæt to healle gang   Healfdenes sunu;
wolde self cyning   symbel þicgan.   1010
Ne gefrægen ic þa mægþe   maran weorode
ymb hyra sincgyfan   sel gebæran.
Bugon þa to bence   blædagande,
fylle gefægon;   fægere geþægon
medoful manig   magas þara,   1015
swiðhicgende   on sele þam hean,
Hroðgar ond Hroþulf.   Heorot innan wæs
freondum afylled;   nalles facenstafas
Þeod-Scyldingas   þenden fremedon.

    Forgeaf þa Beowulfe   brand Healfdenes   1020
segen gyldenne   sigores to leane,
hroden hildecumbor,   helm ond byrnan;
mære maðþumsweord   manige gesawon
beforan beorn beran.   Beowulf geþah
ful on flette;   no he þære feohgyfte   1025
for sceotendum   scamigan ðorfte.
Ne gefrægn ic freondlicor   feower madmas
golde gegyrede   gummanna fela
in ealobence   oðrum gesellan.
Ymb þæs helmes hrof   heafodbeorge   1030
wirum bewunden   walu utan heold,
þæt him fela laf   frecne ne meahton
scurheard sceþðan,   þonne scyldfreca
ongean gramum   gangan scolde.
Heht ða eorla hleo   eahta mearas   1035
fætedhleore   on flet teon,
in under eoderas.   Þara anum stod
sadol searwum fah,   since gewurþad:

firm within by iron bands, was much damaged, its hinges sprung apart; only the roof escaped entirely sound when the monster, guilty of criminal deeds, turned in flight, despairing of life. That is not easy to flee from—let him try it who will—but compelled by necessity one must seek out the place prepared for those who dwell on the earth, those who bear souls, the children of men, where, after the banquet, one's flesh shall sleep fast in its bed of death.

Then was occasion and time for the son of Healfdene to go into the hall; the king himself would share in the banquet. I have never heard that a nation behaved more nobly around their treasure-giver in so large a company. Then men of high renown sat at the benches, rejoiced in the feast; those kinsmen, stout-hearted Hrothgar and Hrothulf, courteously partook of many a goblet of mead in that lofty hall. Heorot was filled with friends; in no way, as yet, did the race of Scyldings practise treacherous arts.*

Then, as a reward for victory, Healfdene's brand* presented Beowulf with a golden banner, decorated war-standard, a helmet and coat of mail; many saw a famous costly sword carried before the hero. Beowulf partook of a goblet in the hall; he had no need to be ashamed in front of the marksmen for that rich gift. I have not heard of many men more heartily giving to others on the ale-bench four such treasures decked with gold. Across the crown of the helmet a crest bound with wires gave protection to the head from without, so that no storm-hardened* legacy of files might badly injure him when the bold shield-warrior had to advance against fierce foes. Then the defence of warriors commanded eight steeds with gold-plated bridles to be led into the hall through the precincts. On one of them lay a skilfully decorated saddle, enriched

1004 gesecan: MS gesacan   1022 hildecumbor: MS hiltecumbor   1026 sceotendum: MS scotenum   1031 walu: MS walan   1051 brimlade: MS brimleade

þæt wæs hildesetl   heahcyninges,
ðonne sweorda gelac   sunu Healfdenes   *1040*
efnan wolde;   næfre on ore læg
widcuþes wig,   ðonne walu feollon.
Ond ða Beowulfe   bega gehwæþres
eodor Ingwina   onweald geteah,
wicga ond wæpna;   het hine wel brucan.   *1045*
Swa manlice   mære þeoden,
hordweard hæleþa   heaþoræsas geald
mearum ond madmum,   swa hy næfre man lyhð,
se þe secgan wile   soð æfter rihte.

XVI   Ða gyt æghwylcum   eorla drihten   *1050*
þara þe mid Beowulfe   brimlade teah,
on þære medubence   maþðum gesealde,
yrfelafe;   ond þone ænne heht
golde forgyldan,   þone ðe Grendel ær
mane acwealde,   swa he hyra ma wolde,   *1055*
nefne him witig God   wyrd forstode
ond ðæs mannes mod.   Metod eallum weold
gumena cynnes,   swa he nu git deð;
forþan bið andgit   æghwær selest,
ferhðes foreþanc.   Fela sceal gebidan   *1060*
leofes ond laþes,   se þe longe her
on ðyssum windagum   worolde bruceð.
    Þær wæs sang ond sweg   samod ætgædere
fore Healfdenes   hildewisan,
gomenwudu greted,   gid oft wrecen,   *1065*
ðonne healgamen   Hroþgares scop
æfter medobence   mænan scolde:
    Finnes eaferum,   ða hie se fær begeat,
hæleð Healf-Dena,   Hnæf Scyldinga,
in Freswæle   feallan scolde.   *1070*
Ne huru Hildeburh   herian þorfte
Eotena treowe;   unsynnum wearð
beloren leofum   æt þam lindplegan
bearnum ond broðrum;   hie on gebyrd hruron
gare wunde;   þæt wæs geomuru ides!   *1075*
Nalles holinga   Hoces dohtor
meotodsceaft bemearn,   syþðan morgen com,
ða heo under swegle   geseon meahte
morþorbealo maga,   þær heo ær mæste heold
worolde wynne.
                Wig ealle fornam   *1080*

with jewels: that had been the high-king's war-seat when Healfdene's son wished to take part in the play of swords; the valour of
the far-famed man never failed at the front, when the slaughtered
were falling. And then the refuge of Ing's Friends conferred
possession of the both, horses and weapons, on Beowulf; he bade
him make good use of them. So manfully did the famous prince,
guardian of the treasure-hoard of heroes, reward the onslaught of
battle with steeds and jewels,* that no one who wishes to speak the
truth in fairness will ever disparage them.

16   In addition the leader of warriors bestowed a treasure, an heirloom,
on each of those on the mead-benches who had undertaken the
ocean voyage with Beowulf; and he caused gold to be paid in
recompense for the one whom earlier Grendel in his wickedness
had killed—as he would more of them if wise God and the man's
courage had not averted that fate. Providence governed all mankind,
just as it still does now; wherefore discernment, forethought of
mind, is best in everything. He who is going to enjoy the world for
long in these troublesome times must live through much of good
and of evil.

   There in the presence of Healfdene's war-leader, song and
music joined together, the joyful wood was plucked, a story often
rehearsed when, to entertain the hall, Hrothgar's minstrel would
recite down the mead-benches:

   Together with Finn's offspring, Hnæf of the Scyldings, hero of
the Half-Danes, had to fall in a Frisian slaughter, when the disaster
befell them.* Indeed, Hildeburh had no cause to praise the loyalty
of the Jutes; guiltless, she was deprived of her loved ones, a son and
a brother, in that shield-play; wounded by the javelin, they fell to
their fate; she was a sad woman! Not without cause did the daughter of Hoc lament the decree of Providence when, after morning
came, she could see beneath the heavens the violent slaughter of
kinsmen, where earlier she possessed the greatest of earthly
pleasure.

   The conflict carried off all Finn's thanes, save for only a few, so

1073 lindplegan: MS hildplegan   1079 heo: MS he

Finnes þegnas,   nemne feaum anum,
þæt he ne mehte   on þæm meðelstede
wig Hengeste   wiht gefeohtan,
ne þa wealafe   wige forþringan
þeodnes ðegne.   Ac hig him geþingo budon: *1085*
þæt hie him oðer flet   eal gerymdon,
healle ond heahsetl,   þæt hie healfre geweald
wið Eotena bearn   agan moston;
ond æt feohgyftum   Folcwaldan sunu
dogra gehwylce   Dene weorþode,   *1090*
Hengestes heap   hringum wenede
efne swa swiðe,   sincgestreonum
fættan goldes,   swa he Fresena cyn
on beorsele   byldan wolde.
Ða hie getruwedon   on twa healfa   *1095*
fæste frioðuwære.   Fin Hengeste
elne unflitme   aðum benemde
þæt he þa wealafe   weotena dome
arum heolde,   þæt ðær ænig mon
wordum ne worcum   wære ne bræce,   *1100*
ne þurh inwitsearo   æfre gemænden,
ðeah hie hira beaggyfan   banan folgedon
ðeodenlease,   þa him swa geþearfod wæs;
gyf þonne Frysna hwylc   frecnen spræce
ðæs morþorhetes   myndgiend wære,   *1105*
þonne hit sweordes ecg   syððan scolde.
    Ad wæs geæfned,   ond icge gold
ahæfen of horde: Here-Scyldinga
betst beadorinca   wæs on bæl gearu.
Æt þæm ade wæs   eþgesyne   *1110*
swatfah syrce,   swyn ealgylden,
eofer irenheard,   æþeling manig
wundum awyrded;   sume on wæle crungon.
Het ða Hildeburh   æt Hnæfes ade
hire selfre sunu   sweoloðe befæstan,   *1115*
banfatu bærnan   ond on bæl don
eame on eaxle.   Ides gnornode,
geomrode giddum.   Guðrinc astah;
wand to wolcnum   wælfyra mæst,
hlynode for hlawe;   hafelan multon,   *1120*
bengeato burston,   ðonne blod ætspranc,
laðbite lices.   Lig ealle forswealg,
gæsta gifrost,   þara ðe þær guð fornam

that he could in no way in that meeting-place fight to a finish the battle with Hengest the prince's thane, nor by warfare dislodge the survivors of the disaster. So they offered them terms: that they should entirely clear for them another building, a hall and throne, so that they might share equal power with the children of the Jutes; and the son of Folcwalda should every time honour the Danes with rich gifts, treat Hengest's troop well with rings, precious treasures of plated gold, to the same extent as he would have wished to encourage the Frisian kin in the beer-hall.

Then on both sides they put their trust in a firm peace-treaty. Finn declared to Hengest, with oaths of indisputable sincerity, that in accordance with the judgement of his councillors he would treat the survivors of the disaster with honour, provided that no man there should break the treaty by word or deeds, nor ever complain by means of a malicious contrivance, that, having lost their prince, they were following their ring-giver's slayer, since this was forced on them by necessity; if, however, any of the Frisians by rash speech should continually call the deadly hatred to mind, then it would have to be settled with the edge of the sword.

The funeral pyre was prepared, and fine gold brought from the hoard: the finest of the warriors of the War-Scyldings was ready on the fire. Upon the pyre was easily to be seen: blood-stained mail-shirt, the swine-image all golden, a boar as hard as iron, many a prince destroyed by wounds; notable men had fallen in the slaughter. Then Hildeburh commanded her own son to be committed to the flames on Hnæf's pyre, the body to be burned, and to be placed on the fire shoulder to shoulder with his uncle. The woman mourned, chanted a dirge. The warrior ascended; the greatest of funeral-fires curled up towards the clouds, roared in front of the burial-mound; heads melted away, gaping wounds, terrible bites in the body, burst open as the blood gushed out. Fire, the most ravenous of spirits, swallowed up all those of both nations

---

bega folces; wæs hire blæd scacen.

XVII   Gewiton him ða wigend   wica neosian   *1125*
freondum befeallen, Frysland geseon,
hamas ond heaburh. Hengest ða gyt
wælfagne winter wunode mid Finne
eal unhlitme. Eard gemunde,
þeah þe ne meahte on mere drifan   *1130*
hringedstefnan. Holm storme weol,
won wið winde; winter yþe beleac
isgebinde, oþðæt oþer com
gear in geardas, swa nu gyt deð
þa ðe syngales sele bewitiað,   *1135*
wuldortorhtan weder.
            Ða wæs winter scacen,
fæger foldan bearm. Fundode wrecca,
gist of geardum; he to gyrnwræce
swiðor þohte þonne to sælade,
gif he torngemot þurhteon mihte,   *1140*
þæt he Eotena bearn inne gemunde.
Swa he ne forwyrnde woroldrædenne,
þonne him Hunlafing Hildeleoman,
billa selest, on bearm dyde;
þæs wæron mid Eotenum ecge cuðe.   *1145*
  Swylce ferhðfrecan Fin eft begeat
sweordbealo sliðen æt his selfes ham,
siþðan grimne gripe Guðlaf ond Oslaf
æfter sæsiðe sorge mændon,
ætwiton weana dæl; ne meahte wæfre mod   *1150*
forhabban in hreþre. Ða wæs heal roden
feonda feorum, swilce Fin slægen,
cyning on corþre, ond seo cwen numen.
Sceotend Scyldinga to scypon feredon
eal ingesteald eorðcyninges,   *1155*
swylce hie æt Finnes ham findan meahton
sigla, searogimma. Hie on sælade
drihtlice wif to Denum feredon,
læddon to leodum.
            Leoð wæs asungen,
gleomannes gyd. Gamen eft astah,   *1160*
beorhtode bencsweg, byrelas sealdon
win of wunderfatum. Þa cwom Wealhþeo forð
gan under gyldnum beage, þær þa godan twegen

whom war had carried off; their glory was gone.

17 Bereft of friends, the fighting men then went to seek out their
dwellings, to see the Frisian land, their homes and great stronghold.
But Hengest remained with Finn through the slaughter-stained
winter—quite disastrously. He remembered his homeland, though
he could not drive curved prow onto the water. The sea surged
with storms, fought against the wind; winter locked the waves in
fetters of ice until another year came to the courts of men, just as it
still does now—those periods of gloriously bright weather that
always observe their due season.

Then winter was gone, the bosom of the earth beautiful. The
exile, the guest, longed to be quit of these courts; he thought more
particularly of avenging his wrongs than of the sea-voyage—
whether he could contrive some occasion for violence, for he brooded inwardly about the children of the Jutes. So he did not hinder
the way of the world when Hunlaf's son placed Battle-flame, the
best of swords, in his lap; its edges were well known to the Jutes.

So also a cruel death by the sword befell in turn the bold-
hearted Finn in his own home, after Guthlaf and Oslaf bewailed
the grim attack, sorrow following their sea-journey, blamed him
for their share of woes; the restless heart could not be restrained
in the breast. Then the hall was reddened with the life-blood of
foes, Finn killed too, the king among his bodyguard, and the queen
taken. The Scylding marksmen carried away to their ships all the
household property of the king of that country, whatever jewels,
skilfully-wrought gems, they could find in the home of Finn. With
a sea-voyage they carried the noble woman away to the Danes, led
her to her people.

The song, the minstrel's lay, was sung. Once again mirth arose,
the sound from the benches rang out clearly, cup-bearers served
wine in wondrous vessels. Then Wealhtheow came forth, wearing a
golden circlet, and went to where those two fine men, uncle and

sæton suhtergefæderan;   þa gyt wæs hiera sib ætgædere,
æghwylc oðrum trywe.   Swylce þær Unferþ þyle   *1165*
æt fotum sæt frean Scyldinga;
          gehwylc hiora his ferhþe treowde,
þæt he hæfde mod micel,   þeah þe he his magum nære
arfæst æt ecga gelacum.
              Spræc ða ides Scyldinga:
'Onfoh þissum fulle,   freodrihten min,
sinces brytta.   Þu on sælum wes,   *1170*
goldwine gumena,   ond to Geatum spræc
mildum wordum,   swa sceal man don.
Beo wið Geatas glæd,   geofena gemyndig,
nean ond feorran   þu nu hafast.
Me man sægde   þæt þu ðe for sunu wolde   *1175*
hererinc habban.   Heorot is gefælsod,
beahsele beorhta.   Bruc, þenden þu mote,
manigra medo,   ond þinum magum læf
folc ond rice,   þonne ðu forð scyle,
metodsceaft seon.   Ic minne can   *1180*
glædne Hroþulf,   þæt he þa geogoðe wile
arum healdan,   gyf þu ær þonne he,
wine Scildinga,   worold oflætest;
wene ic þæt he mid gode   gyldan wille
uncran eaferan,   gif he þæt eal gemon,   *1185*
hwæt wit to willan   ond to worðmyndum
umborwesendum ær   arna gefremedon.'
     Hwearf þa bi bence   þær hyre byre wæron,
Hreðric ond Hroðmund,   ond hæleþa bearn,
giogoð ætgædere;   þær se goda sæt,   *1190*
Beowulf Geata   be þæm gebroðrum twæm.

XVIII   Him wæs ful boren   ond freondlaþu
wordum bewægned,   ond wunden gold
estum geeawed: earmreade twa,
hrægl ond hringas,   healsbeaga mæst   *1195*
þara þe ic on foldan   gefrægen hæbbe.
Nænigne ic under swegle   selran hyrde
hordmaððum hæleþa,   syþðan Hama ætwæg
to þere byrhtan byrig   Brosinga mene,
sigle ond sincfæt;   searoniðas fleah   *1200*
Eormenrices,   geceas ecne ræd.
Þone hring hæfde   Higelac Geata,
nefa Swertinges,   nyhstan siðe,

nephew, sat; as yet there was friendship between them, each trusting the other. There also the spokesman Unferth sat at the feet of the lord of the Scyldings; both of them trusted his spirit, believed that he had great courage, although he had not been honourable towards his kinsmen in the play of swords.

Then the lady of the Scyldings spoke: 'Take this goblet, my noble prince, distributor of treasure. Be glad, gold-friend of warriors, and speak to the Geats with kindly words, as a man ought to do. Be gracious towards the Geats, mindful of the gifts you now possess from far and near. They told me that you wish to take the warrior to be a son to you. Heorot, the fair ring-hall, is cleansed. Rejoice, while you may, in many rewards, and when you must go forth to face the decree of destiny, bequeath people and kingdom to your kinsmen. I know my gracious Hrothulf—that he will treat these youths honourably if you, friend of the Scyldings, should leave the world before him; I think that he will repay our offspring well, if he remembers all the favours we both bestowed on him for his pleasure and his honour while he was still a child.'

Then she turned to the bench where her boys, Hrethric and Hrothmund, and the sons of the warriors were, young men together; there sat the great man, Beowulf of the Geats, beside the two brothers.

18   A goblet was carried to him and a toast offered in words, and twisted gold was presented with good will: two bracelets, dress and rings, and the greatest necklace of those I have heard spoken of on earth. I have learned of no better treasure-hoard of heroes beneath the heavens since Hama carried off to his fair stronghold the collar of the Brosings,* jewel and rich setting; he fled from Eormanric's treacherous hatred, chose eternal gain. Hygelac of the Geats, grandson of Swerting, had that circlet with him on his last venture

siðþan he under segne   sinc ealgode,
wælreaf werede.   Hyne wyrd fornam,   *1205*
syþðan he for wlenco   wean ahsode,
fæhðe to Frysum.   He þa frætwe wæg,
eorclanstanas   ofer yða ful,
rice þeoden;   he under rande gecranc.
Gehwearf þa in Francna fæþm   feorh cyninges,   *1210*
breostgewædu   ond se beah somod;
wyrsan wigfrecan   wæl reafeden
æfter guðsceare;   Geata leode
hreawic heoldon.
                 Heal swege onfeng.
Wealhðeo maþelode,   heo fore þæm werede spræc: *1215*
'Bruc ðisses beages,   Beowulf leofa,
hyse, mid hæle,   ond þisses hrægles neot,
þeodgestreona,   ond geþeoh tela.
Cen þec mid cræfte,   ond þyssum cnyhtum wes
lara liðe;   ic þe þæs lean geman.   *1220*
Hafast þu gefered   þæt ðe feor ond neah
ealne wideferhþ   weras ehtigað,
efne swa side   swa sæ bebugeð
windgeard weallas.   Wes, þenden þu lifige,
æþeling, eadig!   Ic þe an tela   *1225*
sincgestreona.   Beo þu suna minum
dædum gedefe,   dreamhealdende!
Her is æghwylc eorl   oþrum getrywe,
modes milde,   mandrihtne hold;
þegnas syndon geþwære,   þeod ealgearo,   *1230*
druncne dryhtguman   doð swa ic bidde.'
    Eode þa to setle.   þær wæs symbla cyst;
druncon win weras.   Wyrd ne cuþon,
geosceaft grimme,   swa hit agangen wearð
eorla manegum,   syþðan æfen cwom,   *1235*
ond him Hroþgar gewat   to hofe sinum,
rice to ræste.   Reced weardode
unrim eorla,   swa hie oft ær dydon;
bencþelu beredon;   hit geondbræded wearð
beddum ond bolstrum.   Beorscealca sum   *1240*
fus ond fæge   fletræste gebeag.
Setton him to heafdon   hilderandas,
bordwudu beorhtan.   þær on bence wæs
ofer æþelinge   yþgesene
heaþosteapa helm,   hringed byrne,   *1245*

when beneath the banner he defended treasure, guarded the spoils of slaughter. Fate carried him off when, out of pride, he went looking for trouble, a feud with the Frisians.* The powerful prince wore that ornament, the precious stones, across the bowl of the waves; he fell dead beneath his shield. The body of the king then fell into the hands of the Franks, his breast-armour and the collar together; lesser fighting-men plundered the slain after the battle-shearing; men of the Geats remained on the field of corpses.

The hall resounded with noise. Wealhtheow spoke; before the company she said: 'Beloved Beowulf, enjoy this collar with good fortune, young man, and make good use of this garment, national treasures, and prosper well. Prove yourself with your might, and show kindness to these boys with counsel; I shall remember to reward you for that. You have brought it about that down the ages men far and near will respect you as widely as the sea, the home of the winds, encircles the cliffs. May you be fortunate, prince, for as long as you live! I wish you well of your rich treasures. Be kind in your deeds to my son, you who are possessed of joy! Here every warrior is true to the other, gentle of heart, faithful to the leader of men; the thanes are united, the nation quite prepared, the noble men, having drunk, will do as I ask.'

Then she went to her seat. There was the finest of banquets; men drank wine. They did not know the fate, the grim destiny ordered of old, as it came to pass for many a warrior after evening had come and Hrothgar had gone to his chamber, the powerful man to his couch. Countless warriors guarded the building, as earlier they often did; they cleared the bench-board; it was spread over with bedding and pillows. One among the beer-drinkers, ripe and doomed to die, stooped to his couch in the hall. They set at their heads their war-discs, shields of bright wood. There on the bench above each prince was easily to be seen a towering battle-

1218 þeodgestreona: MS þeogestreona   1229 hold: MS hol *altered from* heol
1234 grimme: MS grimne

þrecwudu þrymlic. Wæs þeaw hyra,
þæt hie oft wæron anwiggearwe,
ge æt ham ge on herge, ge gehwæþer þara
efne swylce mæla, swylce hira mandryhtne
þearf gesælde; wæs seo þeod tilu.   *1250*

XVIIII   Sigon þa to slæpe. Sum sare angeald
æfenræste, swa him ful oft gelamp
siþðan goldsele Grendel warode,
unriht æfnde oþþæt ende becwom,
swylt æfter synnum. Þæt gesyne wearþ,   *1255*
widcuþ werum, þætte wrecend þa gyt
lifde æfter laþum, lange þrage
æfter guðceare.
              Grendles modor,
ides, aglæcwif yrmþe gemunde,
se þe wæteregesan wunian scolde,   *1260*
cealde streamas, siþðan Cain wearð
to ecgbanan angan breþer,
fæderenmæge; he þa fag gewat,
morþre gemearcod, mandream fleon,
westen warode. Þanon woc fela   *1265*
geosceaftgasta; wæs þæra Grendel sum
heorowearh hetelic, se æt Heorote fand
wæccendne wer wiges bidan.
Þær him aglæca ætgræpe wearð;
hwæþre he gemunde mægenes strenge,   *1270*
gimfæste gife ðe him God sealde,
ond him to Anwaldan are gelyfde,
frofre ond fultum; ðy he þone feond ofercwom,
gehnægde hellegast. Þa he hean gewat,
dreame bedæled deaþwic seon,   *1275*
mancynnes feond. Ond his modor þa gyt
gifre ond galgmod gegan wolde
sorhfulne sið, sunu deoð wrecan.
    Com þa to Heorote, ðær Hring-Dene
geond þæt sæld swæfun. Þa ðær sona wearð   *1280*
edhwyrft eorlum siþðan inne fealh
Grendles modor. Wæs se gryre læssa
efne swa micle swa bið mægþa cræft,
wiggryre wifes, be wæpnedmen
þonne heoru bunden, hamere geþuren,   *1285*
sweord swate fah swin ofer helme,
ecgum dyhttig, andweard scireð.

helmet, ringed mail, a magnificent strong shaft. It was their custom always to be ready for war both at home and on an expedition, in case at any time such need befell their leader; they were a fine nation.

19 Then they sank into sleep. One among them paid sorely for his night's rest, as had so often befallen them since Grendel occupied the gold-hall, perpetrated misdeeds until his end came, death in consequence of sins. It came to be seen, widely known among men, that there was still an avenger who survived the loathsome creature for a long while after the conflict.

Grendel's mother, a woman, she-monster, brooded on her misery, she who had to dwell in dreadful waters, cold currents, after Cain killed his only brother, his father's son, by the sword; stained he then went out, marked by murder, to flee the joys of mankind, and occupied the wilderness. Thence sprang many a fated demon; one of these was Grendel, the hateful savage outcast who at Heorot had found one man watchful, awaiting the conflict. There the monster came to grips with him; however, he remembered the power of his strength, the ample gift that God had given him, and counted on the Almighty for help, comfort and support; by that he overcame the fiend, laid low the hellish demon. Then humiliated he went off, the foe of mankind, bereft of joy, to seek out the mansion of death. And his mother, still ravenous and gloomy at heart, purposed to go on a sorry journey to avenge the death of her son.

She came then to Heorot where the Ring-Danes slept all around the hall. Immediately then there came a reverse for the warriors, once Grendel's mother made her way in. The terror was the less dreadful by just so much as the power of women, the war-terror of a female, is that of an armed man when the patterned blade of a hammer-forged sword, stained with blood, mighty of edge, shears through the boar-crest above opposing helmets.

1261 Cain: MS camp   1278 deoð: MS þeod

Ða wæs on healle   heardecg togen,
sweord ofer setlum,   sidrand manig
hafen handa fæst;   helm ne gemunde,   *1290*
byrnan side,   þa hine se broga angeat.
Heo wæs on ofste,   wolde ut þanon,
feore beorgan,   þa heo onfunden wæs.
Hraðe heo æþelinga   anne hæfde
fæste befangen,   þa heo to fenne gang.   *1295*
Se wæs Hroþgare   hæleþa leofost
on gesiðes had   be sæm tweonum,
rice randwiga,   þone ðe heo on ræste abreat,
blædfæstne beorn.   Næs Beowulf ðær,
ac wæs oþer in   ær geteohhod   *1300*
æfter maþðumgife   mærum Geate.
Hream wearð in Heorote;   heo under heolfre genam
cuþe folme;   cearu wæs geniwod,
geworden in wicun.   Ne wæs þæt gewrixle til,
þæt hie on ba healfa   bicgan scoldon   *1305*
freonda feorum!   Þa wæs frod cyning,
har hilderinc,   on hreon mode,
syðþan he aldorþegn   unlyfigendne,
þone deorestan   deadne wisse.

Hraþe wæs to bure   Beowulf fetod,   *1310*
sigoreadig secg.   Samod ærdæge
eode eorla sum,   æþele cempa,
self mid gesiðum,   þær se snotera bad,
hwæþre him Alwalda   æfre wille
æfter weaspelle   wyrpe gefremman.   *1315*
Gang ða æfter flore   fyrdwyrðe man
mid his handscale   —healwudu dynede—
þæt he þone wisan   wordum nægde,
frean Ingwina;   frægn gif him wære,
æfter neodlaðe,   niht getæse.   *1320*

xx   Hroðgar maþelode,   helm Scyldinga:
'Ne frin þu æfter sælum!   Sorh is geniwod
Denigea leodum.   Dead is Æschere,
Yrmenlafes   yldra broþor,
min runwita   ond min rædbora,   *1325*
eaxlgestealla   ðonne we on orlege
hafelan weredon,   þonne hniton feþan,
eoferas cnysedan.   Swylc scolde eorl wesan,
æþeling ærgod,   swylc Æschere wæs!

Then in the hall the hard-edged sword was drawn, from above
the seats many a broad disc lifted firmly by the hand; none thought
of helmet, of broad mail when the horror came upon him. She was
in a hurry, wanted to be gone from there, to save her life now she
was discovered. Swiftly she had taken firm grasp of one of the
princes as she went towards the swamp. He whom she destroyed
on his couch was to Hrothgar the most beloved of heroes between
the seas, having the rank of companion, a powerful shield-fighter,
a man of great renown. Beowulf was not there, for earlier, after
the treasure-giving, a separate lodging had been assigned to the
famous Geat. There was uproar in Heorot; she had taken, covered
in gore, the hand she knew; grief was renewed, come again to the
dwellings. That was not a good bargain, where those on both sides
had to pay with the lives of friends! Then the wise king, grizzled
warrior, was troubled at heart when he knew his chief thane to be
lifeless, the dearest man to be dead.

Swiftly Beowulf, the man blessed with victory, was fetched to
the chamber. At daybreak he went together with his warriors, the
princely champion himself with his companions, to where the wise
man waited to see whether, after tidings of woe, the Almighty
would ever bring about some change on his behalf. The man who
was distinguished in war strode across the floor with his bodyguard
—the hall timbers resounded—so that he might address the wise
lord of the Friends of Ing with words; he asked if the night had been
pleasant, according to his desires.

20 Hrothgar spoke, protector of the Scyldings: 'Do not ask for good
tidings! Sorrow is come again to the people of the Danes. Æschere
is dead—the eldest brother of Yrmenlaf, my confidant and my
councillor, closest comrade when we defended our heads in the
fray, when troops clashed, struck against boar-crests. Whatever a
warrior should be, a prince of proven merit, that Æschere was!

1314 Alwalda: MS alfwalda   1318 nægde: MS hnæg . .   Thorkelin A and B
hnægde   1320 neodlaðe: MS neod laðu   1328 Swylc scolde: MS . . . . olde;
Thorkelin A and B swy . . scolde   1329 æþeling *supplied*

Wearð him on Heorote   to handbanan   *1330*
wælgæst wæfre.   Ic ne wat hwæder
atol æse wlanc   eftsiðas teah,
fylle gefrægnod.   Heo þa fæhðe wræc,
þe þu gystran niht   Grendel cwealdest
þurh hæstne had   heardum clammum,   *1335*
forþan he to lange   leode mine
wanode ond wyrde.   He æt wige gecrang
ealdres scyldig;   ond nu oþer cwom
mihtig manscaða,   wolde hyre mæg wrecan,
ge feor hafað   fæhðe gestæled,   *1340*
þæs þe þincean mæg   þegne monegum,
se þe æfter sincgyfan   on sefan greoteþ,
hreþerbealo hearde.   Nu seo hand ligeð,
se þe eow welhwylcra   wilna dohte.

   Ic þæt londbuend,   leode mine,   *1345*
selerædende   secgan hyrde,
þæt hie gesawon   swylce twegen
micle mearcstapan   moras healdan,
ellorgæstas.   Ðæra oðer wæs,
þæs þe hie gewislicost   gewitan meahton,   *1350*
idese onlicnes;   oðer earmsceapen
on weres wæstmum   wræclastas træd,
næfne he wæs mara   þonne ænig man oðer;
þone on geardagum   Grendel nemdon
foldbuende;   no hie fæder cunnon,   *1355*
hwæþer him ænig wæs   ær acenned
dyrnra gasta.   Hie dygel lond
warigeað, wulfhleoþu,   windige næssas,
frecne fengelad,   ðær fyrgenstream
under næssa genipu   niþer gewiteð,   *1360*
flod under foldan.   Nis þæt feor heonon
milgemearces,   þæt se mere standeð;
ofer þæm hongiað   hrinde bearwas,
wudu wyrtum fæst   wæter oferhelmað.
Þær mæg nihta gehwæm   niðwundor seon,   *1365*
fyr on flode.   No þæs frod leofað
gumena bearna   þæt þone grund wite.
Ðeah þe hæðstapa   hundum geswenced,
heorot hornum trum   holtwudu sece,
feorran geflymed,   ær he feorh seleð,   *1370*
aldor on ofre,   ær he in wille,
hafelan hydan.   Nis þæt heoru stow!

Now a restless murderous demon has slain him in Heorot with her hands. I do not know which way the dreadful creature took her journey back, exulting over the carcass, made infamous by the glut. She has taken vengeance for the quarrel—that last night you killed Grendel in a savage manner with fierce grips because for too long he had diminished and destroyed my people. He fell in the fight, his life forfeit; and now another mighty, wicked ravager has come, wishing to avenge her kinsman, and has gone far in pursuing vengeance for the quarrel—so it may seem to many a thane whose heart weeps for his treasure-giver, a bitter affliction in the breast. Now the hand lies low that was willing to fulfill your every desire.

I have heard that those who dwell in the land, my people, hall-councillors, say this—that they have seen two such huge prowlers in the border regions, alien visitants holding the wastelands. One of these, so far as they could best tell, took the likeness of a woman; the other wretched creature trod the paths of exile in the form of a man, save that he was bigger than any other human; from days of old those who dwell on the earth have called him 'Grendel'; they know of no father, whether any such dark demon was begotten before them. They occupy a secret land,* wolf-haunted slopes, windswept crags, dangerous swamp tracks where the mountain stream passes downwards under the darkness of the crags, water under the earth. It is not far from here, measured in miles, that the lake stands; over it hang frost-covered groves, trees held fast by their roots overshadow the water. There each night may be seen a fearful wonder—fire on the flood. No one alive among the children of men is wise enough to know the bottom. Although the strong-antlered stag, roaming the heath, may seek out the forest when driven from afar, hard pressed by hounds, he will sooner yield up life and spirit on the bank than hide his head there. That is not a pleasant place! From it a surging wave rises up

1331 hwæder: MS hwæþer   1351 onlicnes: MS onlicnæs   1354 nemdon: MS nem . . ; Thorkelin A and B nemdod   1362 standeð: MS stanðeð   1372 hydan *supplied*

Þonon yðgeblond   up astigeð
won to wolcnum,   þonne wind styreþ
lað gewidru,   oðþæt lyft ðrysmaþ,   *1375*
roderas reotað.
                Nu is se ræd gelang
eft æt þe anum.   Eard git ne const,
frecne stowe   ðær þu findan miht
felasinnigne secg;   sec gif þu dyrre!
Ic þe þa fæhðe   feo leanige,   *1380*
ealdgestreonum,   swa ic ær dyde,
wundini golde,   gyf þu on weg cymest.'

XXI   Beowulf maþelode,   bearn Ecgþeowes:
'Ne sorga, snotor guma!   Selre bið æghwæm
þæt he his freond wrece,   þonne he fela murne.   *1385*
Ure æghwylc sceal   ende gebidan
worolde lifes;   wyrce se þe mote
domes ær deaþe;   þæt bið drihtguman
unlifgendum   æfter selest.
Aris, rices weard;   uton hraþe feran   *1390*
Grendles magan   gang sceawigan.
Ic hit þe gehate: no he on helm losaþ,
ne on foldan fæþm,   ne on fyrgenholt,
ne on gyfenes grund,   ga þær he wille.
Ðys dogor þu   geþyld hafa   *1395*
weana gehwylces,   swa ic þe wene to.'
    Ahleop ða se gomela,   Gode þancode,
mihtigan Drihtne,   þæs se man gespræc.
Þa wæs Hroðgare   hors gebæted,
wicg wundenfeax.   Wisa fengel   *1400*
geatolic gende;   gumfeþa stop
lindhæbbendra.   Lastas wæron
æfter waldswaþum   wide gesyne,
gang ofer grundas   þær heo gegnum for
ofer myrcan mor,   magoþegna bær   *1405*
þone selestan   sawolleasne,
þara þe mid Hroðgare   ham eahtode.
Ofereode þa   æþelinga bearn
steap stanhliðo,   stige nearwe,
enge anpaðas,   uncuð gelad,   *1410*
neowle næssas,   nicorhusa fela.
He feara sum   beforan gengde
wisra monna   wong sceawian,

black to the clouds when the wind stirs up hostile storms, till the air grows dim, the skies weep.

Now once again help depends on you alone. You do not yet know the region, the dangerous place where you might find the deeply sinful creature; seek it out if you dare! I will recompense you for the quarrel with money as I did before, with ancient treasures, twisted gold, if you make your way back again.'

21 Beowulf spoke, the son of Ecgtheow: 'Do not be sorrowful, wise man! It is better for anyone that he should avenge his friend, rather than mourn greatly. Each of us must await the end of life in this world; let him who can, achieve glory before death; afterwards, when lifeless, that will be best for a noble man. Rise up, guardian of the kingdom; let us go swiftly to examine the trail of Grendel's relative. I promise you this: she will not escape under cover, neither in the bosom of the earth, nor in the mountain forest, nor at the bottom of the ocean, go where she will. For today, have patience in every affliction, as I expect you to.'

The old man then leapt up, thanked God, the mighty Lord, for what the hero had said. Then a horse was bridled for Hrothgar, a steed with braided mane. The wise ruler moved off in state; the troop of shield-bearers marched forth. The tracks could be widely seen along the forest paths, the trail over the ground where she went straight on over the murky wasteland, carrying a lifeless young thane, the best of those who watched over their home with Hrothgar. Then the son of princes advanced over steep rocky slopes by a narrow path, a constricted route where only one could pass at a time, an unfamiliar way, precipitous crags, many a lair of water-monsters. He went in front with a few knowledgeable men to

1375 ðrysmaþ: MS drysmaþ   1404 þær heo *supplied*

oþþæt he færinga   fyrgenbeamas
ofer harne stan   hleonian funde,   *1415*
wynleasne wudu;   wæter under stod
dreorig ond gedrefed.   Denum eallum wæs,
winum Scyldinga,   weorce on mode
to geþolianne,   ðegne monegum,
oncyð eorla gehwæm,   syðþan Æscheres   *1420*
on þam holmclife   hafelan metton.
    Flod blode weol   —folc to sægon—
hatan heolfre.   Horn stundum song
fuslic fyrdleoð.   Feþa eal gesæt;
gesawon ða æfter wætere   wyrmcynnes fela,   *1425*
sellice sædracan   sund cunnian,
swylce on næshleoðum   nicras licgean,
ða on undernmæl   oft bewitigað
sorhfulne sið   on seglrade,
wyrmas ond wildeor.   Hie on weg hruron   *1430*
bitere ond gebolgne;   bearhtm ongeaton,
guðhorn galan.   Sumne Geata leod
of flanbogan   feores getwæfde,
yðgewinnes,   þæt him on aldre stod
herestræl hearda;   he on holme wæs   *1435*
sundes þe sænra,   ðe hyne swylt fornam.
Hræþe wearð on yðum   mid eoferspreotum
heorohocyhtum   hearde genearwod,
niða genæged   ond on næs togen
wundorlic wægbora;   weras sceawedon   *1440*
gryrelicne gist.
                    Gyrede hine Beowulf
eorlgewædum,   nalles for ealdre mearn.
Scolde herebyrne   hondum gebroden,
sid ond searofah,   sund cunnian,
seo ðe bancofan   beorgan cuþe,   *1445*
þæt him hildegrap   hreþre ne mihte,
eorres inwitfeng   aldre gesceþðan.
Ac se hwita helm   hafelan werede,
se þe meregrundas   mengan scolde,
secan sundgebland,   since geweorðad,   *1450*
befongen freawrasnum,   swa hine fyrndagum
worhte wæpna smið,   wundrum teode,
besette swinlicum,   þæt hine syðþan no
brond ne beadomecas   bitan ne meahton.
    Næs þæt þonne mætost   mægenfultuma,   *1455*

examine the ground, until suddenly he found mountain trees leaning out over a grey rock, a cheerless wood; below lay the water, gory and turbid. There was anguish at heart for all the Danes, for the Scyldings' friends, for many a thane to suffer, distress for each of the warriors, when on the cliff above the water they came upon Æschere's head.

The flood welled with blood, with hot gore—the people gazed at it. From time to time a horn sang out its eager battle-call. The troop all sat down; they saw then upon the water many of the serpent race, strange sea-dragons exploring the deep, also water-monsters lying on the slopes of the crags, such as those that in the morning-time often attend a miserable journey on the sail-way, serpents and wild beasts. They fell away, fierce and swollen with rage; they understood the clear sound, the war-horn ringing. With an arrow from his bow the prince of the Geats parted one of them from life, from its battle with the waves, when a hard warshaft stuck in its vitals; it was slower in swimming on the water when death carried it off. Swiftly the water's strange offspring was hard-pressed in the waves with savagely-barbed boar-spears, violently assailed and dragged on to the crag; men examined the terrifying visitant.

Beowulf dressed himself in warrior's clothing, had no fear at all for his life. The hand-woven war-mail, broad and cunningly adorned, would have to explore the deep—it was able to protect his frame so that no warlike grip, no malicious grasp of any hostile creature, might injure his breast, his life. And a shining helmet guarded the head that would have to disturb the lake bottom, seek out the turbid depths—it was decorated with rich ornament, encircled with a chain-mail guard, just as the weapon-smith had wrought it in days of old, wonderfully formed it, set about with boar-images so that thereafter no sword or battle-blade might bite into it.

Not least among the mighty aids was that which Hrothgar's

[1424] fyrdleoð: MS . . . . leoð; Thorkelin B f . . . leoð

þæt him on ðearfe lah   ðyle Hroðgares;
wæs þæm hæftmece   Hrunting nama;
þæt wæs an foran   ealdgestreona;
ecg wæs iren,   atertanum fah,
ahyrded heaþoswate.   Næfre hit æt hilde ne swac   *1460*
manna ængum,   þara þe hit mid mundum bewand,
se ðe gryresiðas   gegan dorste,
folcstede fara.   Næs þæt forma sið
þæt hit ellenweorc   æfnan scolde.
Huru ne gemunde   mago Ecglafes   *1465*
eafoþes cræftig,   þæt he ær gespræc
wine druncen,   þa he þæs wæpnes onlah
selran sweordfrecan.   Selfa ne dorste
under yða gewin   aldre geneþan,
drihtscype dreogan;   þær he dome forleas,   *1470*
ellenmærðum.   Ne wæs þæm oðrum swa,
syðþan he hine to guðe   gegyred hæfde.

XXII   Beowulf maþelode,   bearn Ecgþeowes:
'Geþenc nu, se mæra   maga Healfdenes,
snottra fengel,   nu ic eom siðes fus,   *1475*
goldwine gumena,   hwæt wit geo spræcon,
gif ic æt þearfe   þinre scolde
aldre linnan,   þæt ðu me a wære
forðgewitenum   on fæder stæle.
Wes þu mundbora   minum magoþegnum,   *1480*
hondgesellum,   gif mec hild nime.
Swylce þu ða madmas,   þe þu me sealdest,
Hroðgar leofa,   Higelace onsend.
Mæg þonne on þæm golde ongitan   Geata dryhten,
geseon sunu Hrædles,   þonne he on þæt sinc starað,   *1485*
þæt ic gumcystum   godne funde
beaga bryttan,   breac þonne moste.
Ond þu Unferð læt   ealde lafe,
wrætlic wægsweord,   widcuðne man
heardecg habban;   ic me mid Hruntinge   *1490*
dom gewyrce,   oþðe mec deað nimeð.'
     Æfter þæm wordum   Weder-Geata leod
efste mid elne,   nalas andsware
bidan wolde;   brimwylm onfeng
hilderince.   Ða wæs hwil dæges   *1495*
ær he þone grundwong   ongytan mehte.
     Sona þæt onfunde,   se ðe floda begong

spokesman lent him in his need—a hafted blade* called Hrunting;
it was foremost among ancient treasures; the edge was iron,
marked with poisoned stripes, hardened in the gore of battle. In
combat it had never failed any of those who grasped it in their
hands when daring to set out on perilous journeys to the meeting-
place of foes. That was not the first time it would have to accomplish a deed of courage. When he lent the weapon to the better
fighter, surely the son of Ecglaf, skilled in strength, did not remember what he had said previously when drunk with wine. He
himself did not dare risk his life, perform noble deeds of valour
beneath the turmoil of waves; there he forfeited glory, his reputation for courage. It was not so with the other man, once he had
dressed himself for war.

22   Beowulf spoke, the son of Ecgtheow: 'Now, famous son of Healfdene, wise ruler, gold-friend of men, now that I am ready to set
out on this venture, consider what we two talked about earlier—
that if I should relinquish life in your cause, you would always
take the role of my father when I passed away. If battle should take
me, be the guardian of my young thanes, my close companions.
Also, beloved Hrothgar, send to Hygelac the precious things you
bestowed on me. Then, when he gazes on that treasure, the leader
of the Geats, Hrethel's son, may understand from the gold that I
found a generous distributor of rings, enjoyed him while I could.
And let Unferth, a man widely known, have this old heirloom, my
beautiful wave-patterned sword, hard of edge; I shall achieve fame
for myself with Hrunting, or else death will take me.'
      With these words the prince of the Weder-Geats turned away
boldly, would wait for no reply at all; the water's surge received the
warrior. It was part of a day before he could catch sight of the level
bottom.
      Straight away she who for a hundred seasons had kept watch on

---

1471 ellenmærðum: MS ellen . . . . um; Thorkelin A and B ellenmærdam
1488 Unferð: MS hunferð

heorogifre beheold   hund missera,
grim ond grædig,   þæt þær gumena sum
ælwihta eard   ufan cunnode.   1500
Grap þa togeanes,   guðrinc gefeng
atolan clommum;   no þy ær in gescod
halan lice;   hring utan ymbbearh,
þæt heo þone fyrdhom   ðurhfon ne mihte,
locene leoðosyrcan   laþan fingrum.   1505
Bær þa seo brimwylf,   þa heo to botme com,
hringa þengel   to hofe sinum,
swa he ne mihte,   no he þæs modig wæs,
wæpna gewealdan;   ac hine wundra þæs fela
swencte on sunde,   sædeor monig   1510
hildetuxum   heresyrcan bræc,
ehton aglæcan.   Ða se eorl ongeat
þæt he in niðsele   nathwylcum wæs,
þær him nænig wæter   wihte ne sceþede,
ne him for hrofsele   hrinan ne mehte   1515
færgripe flodes.   Fyrleoht geseah,
blacne leoman   beorhte scinan.
    Ongeat þa se goda   grundwyrgenne,
merewif mihtig.   Mægenræs forgeaf
hildebille,   hond sweng ne ofteah,   1520
þæt hire on hafelan   hringmæl agol
grædig guðleoð.   Ða se gist onfand
þæt se beadoleoma   bitan nolde,
aldre sceþðan,   ac seo ecg geswac
ðeodne æt þearfe.   Ðolode ær fela   1525
hondgemota,   helm oft gescær,
fæges fyrdhrægl;   ða wæs forma sið
deorum madme,   þæt his dom alæg.
    Eft wæs anræd,   nalas elnes læt,
mærða gemyndig   mæg Hyglaces.   1530
Wearp ða wundenmæl   wrættum gebunden
yrre oretta,   þæt hit on eorðan læg,
stið ond stylecg;   strenge getruwode,
mundgripe mægenes.   Swa sceal man don,
þonne he æt guðe   gegan þenceð   1535
longsumne lof;   na ymb his lif cearað.
    Gefeng þa be eaxle   —nalas for fæhðe mearn—
Guð-Geata leod   Grendles modor.
Brægd þa beadwe heard,   þa he gebolgen wæs,
feorhgeniðlan,   þæt heo on flet gebeah.   1540

the flood's expanse, grim and greedy, fiercely ravenous, discovered that some man from up above was exploring the dwelling-place of monsters. Then she clutched at him, seized the warrior in a dreadful grip; yet for all that, she failed to injure the healthy body; ring-mail shielded him externally so that she could not thrust her hateful fingers through the war-dress, the interlocked shirt on his limbs. Then, when she came to the bottom, the water-wolf carried the commander of rings into her lair, so that—no matter how resolute he might be—he was unable to wield his weapons; and a host of weird creatures harried him in the deep; many a sea-beast tore at his battle-shirt; monsters pursued him. Then the hero realised that he was in some sort of enemy hall, where no water could harm him at all, nor could the flood's sudden grip touch him because of the vaulted hall. He saw fire-light, a pale gleam shining brightly.

Then the great man perceived the accursed creature of the depths, the powerful lake-wife. He made a mighty onslaught with his war-sword, his hand not withholding the blow, so that the ring-adorned thing sang a greedy war-song on her head. Then the newcomer discovered that the battle-brand would not bite, harm her life, but the edge failed the prince in his need. It had endured many hand-to-hand encounters before, often sheared through helmet, war-coat of a doomed man; it was the first occasion for this precious treasure that its glory failed.

Again Hygelac's kinsman was resolute, in no way slack in courage, remembering famous deeds. Then the angry champion threw down the patterned blade, inlaid with ornament, so that it lay on the ground, rigid and steel-edged; he put his trust in strength, his mighty hand-grip. So ought a man to do when he means to gain long-lasting praise in battle; he cares nothing for his life.

Then the prince of the War-Geats seized Grendel's mother by the shoulder—he felt no remorse for the quarrel. Now swollen with rage, battle-hardened, he dragged his mortal enemy so that

1506 brimwylf: MS brimwyl   1508 þæs: MS þæm   1510 swencte: MS swecte
1513 in restored   1520 hond sweng: MS hord swenge   1530 Hyglaces: MS hylaces
1531 wundenmæl: MS wundelmæg

Heo him eft hraþe   andlean forgeald
grimman grapum,   ond him togeanes feng.
Oferwearp þa werigmod   wigena strengest,
feþecempa,   þæt he on fylle wearð.

Ofsæt þa þone selegyst   ond hyre seax geteah,   *1545*
brad ond brunecg;   wolde hire bearn wrecan,
angan eaferan.   Him on eaxle læg
breostnet broden;   þæt gebearh feore,
wið ord ond wið ecge   ingang forstod.
Hæfde ða forsiðod   sunu Ecgþeowes   *1550*
under gynne grund,   Geata cempa,
nemne him heaðobyrne   helpe gefremede,
herenet hearde,   ond halig God
geweold wigsigor.   Witig Drihten,
rodera Rædend,   hit on ryht gesced   *1555*
yðelice,   syþðan he eft astod.

XXIII   Geseah ða on searwum   sigeeadig bil,
ealdsweord eotenisc   ecgum þyhtig,
wigena weorðmynd;   þæt wæs wæpna cyst,
buton hit wæs mare   ðonne ænig mon oðer   *1560*
to beadulace   ætberan meahte,
god ond geatolic,   giganta geweorc.
He gefeng þa fetelhilt,   freca Scyldinga,
hreoh ond heorogrim,   hringmæl gebrægd;
aldres orwena,   yrringa sloh,   *1565*
þæt hire wið halse   heard grapode,
banhringas bræc;   bil eal ðurhwod
fægne flæschoman.   Heo on flet gecrong;
sweord wæs swatig;   secg weorce gefeh.

Lixte se leoma,   leoht inne stod,   *1570*
efne swa of hefene   hadre scineð
rodores candel.   He æfter recede wlat,
hwearf þa be wealle;   wæpen hafenade
heard be hiltum   Higelaces ðegn,
yrre ond anræd.   Næs seo ecg fracod   *1575*
hilderince,   ac he hraþe wolde
Grendle forgyldan   guðræsa fela,
ðara þe he geworhte   to West-Denum—
oftor micle   ðonne on ænne sið
þonne he Hroðgares   heorðgeneatas   *1580*
sloh on sweofote,   slæpende fræt
folces Denigea   fyftyne men,

she fell to the floor. Swiftly she paid him back again with fierce grips, and clutched at him. Weary at heart, the strongest of fighters, of foot-soldiers, then stumbled so that he took a fall.

Then she sat upon the visitor to the hall and drew her knife, broad and bright-edged; she wished to avenge her son, her sole offspring. On his shoulder lay a woven breast-net; that protected his life, prevented entry by point and by edge. Ecgtheow's son, the champion of the Geats, would have fared badly beneath the wide ground then, had the war-mail, hard war-net, not afforded help, and holy God brought about victory in battle. Once he stood up again, the wise Lord, Ruler of the Heavens, easily decided it with justice.

23   Then he saw among the armour a victory-blessed blade, an ancient sword made by ogres, firm in its edges, the pride of fighters; it was the choicest of weapons, save that it was larger than any other man might carry out to battle-play—fine and splendid, the work of giants. He seized the belted hilt, the Scyldings' daring champion, savage and deadly grim, drew the patterned blade; despairing of life, he struck angrily so that it bit her hard on the neck, broke the bone-rings; the sword passed straight through the doomed body. She fell dead on the floor; the sword was bloody; the man rejoiced in his work.

Light shone, brightness gleamed within, just as the candle of the sky shines clearly from heaven. He looked about the building, then turned by the wall; angry and resolute, Hygelac's thane raised his weapon firmly by the hilt. The edge was not useless to the warrior, for he wished swiftly to repay Grendel for those many onslaughts he had made on the West Danes—much more frequent than that one occasion when he slew the companions of Hrothgar's hearth in their sleep, devoured fifteen men of the Danish nation while they

---

1541 andlean: MS handlean   1545 seax: MS seaxe   1546 ond *supplied*   1559 wæs
supplied

ond oðer swylc   ut offerede,
laðlicu lac. He him þæs lean forgeald,
reþe cempa, to ðæs þe he on ræste geseah   *1585*
guðwerigne   Grendel licgan,
aldorleasne,   swa him ær gescod
hild æt Heorote. Hra wide sprong,
syþðan he æfter deaðe   drepe þrowade,
heorosweng heardne,   ond hine þa heafde becearf.   *1590*
    Sona þæt gesawon   snottre ceorlas,
þa ðe mid Hroðgare   on holm wliton,
þæt wæs yðgeblond   eal gemenged,
brim blode fah. Blondenfeaxe,
gomele ymb godne   ongeador spræcon,   *1595*
þæt hig þæs æðelinges   eft ne wendon
þæt he sigehreðig   secean come
mærne þeoden; þa ðæs monige gewearð
þæt hine seo brimwylf   abroten hæfde.
Ða com non dæges. Næs ofgeafon   *1600*
hwate Scyldingas; gewat him ham þonon
goldwine gumena. Gistas setan
modes seoce,   ond on mere staredon;
wiston ond ne wendon,   þæt hie heora winedrihten
selfne gesawon.
                  þa þæt sweord ongan   *1605*
æfter heaþoswate   hildegicelum,
wigbil wanian. Þæt wæs wundra sum,
þæt hit eal gemealt   ise gelicost,
ðonne forstes bend   Fæder onlæteð,
onwindeð wælrapas,   se geweald hafað   *1610*
sæla ond mæla; þæt is soð Metod.
Ne nom he in þæm wicum,   Weder-Geata leod,
maðmæhta ma,   þeh he þær monige geseah,
buton þone hafelan   ond þa hilt somod,
since fage; sweord ær gemealt,   *1615*
forbarn brodenmæl; wæs þæt blod to þæs hat,
ættren ellorgæst,   se þær inne swealt.
Sona wæs on sunde,   se þe ær at sæcce gebad
wighryre wraðra,   wæter up þurhdeaf.
Wæron yðgebland   eal gefælsod,   *1620*
eacne eardas,   þa se ellorgast
oflet lifdagas   ond þas lænan gesceaft.
    Com þa to lande   lidmanna helm
swiðmod swymman; sælace gefeah,

slept, and as many others carried away, loathsome plunder. He had paid him his reward for that, the fierce champion, to the effect that he now saw Grendel lying on his couch, sated with war, lifeless, so much had he been injured earlier in the battle at Heorot. The corpse split open when, after death, it suffered a blow, a hard sword-stroke, and thus he cut off his head.

Straight away the wise men who were gazing at the water with Hrothgar saw that the surging waves were all troubled, the sea stained with blood. The aged men, grey-haired, spoke together of the great man, saying that they did not expect to see the prince return, exulting in victory, to seek out the famous king; to many it seemed certain that the sea-wolf had destroyed him. The ninth hour of the day had come. The bold Scyldings forsook the crag; the gold-friend of men went back to his home. The visitors sat on, sick at heart, and stared at the lake; they wished—and did not expect—that they might see their friend and leader himself.

Then, because of the battle-gore, that sword, the fighting blade, began to dwindle into icicles of war. It was a marvel of marvels how it all melted away, just like the ice when the Father, he who has power over times and seasons, loosens the fetters of frost, unbinds the water's bonds; that is true Providence. The prince of the Weder-Geats took no more precious possessions from that dwelling, although he saw many there, but only the head together with the hilt, shining with treasure; the sword itself had already melted, the patterned blade burned away: the blood was too hot for it, the alien demon that had died there too poisonous. He who in the conflict had survived the battle-fall of foes, straight away took to swimming, plunged upwards through the water. The currents, vast tracts, were all cleansed when the alien demon gave up the days of her life and this transitory state.

Then the protector of seafarers, swimming with a brave heart, came to land; he rejoiced in the sea-plunder, the great burden he

mægenbyrþenne þara þe he him mid hæfde.   1625
Eodon him þa togeanes,   Gode þancodon,
ðryðlic þegna heap,   þeodnes gefegon,
þæs þe hi hyne gesundne   geseon moston.
Ða wæs of þæm hroran   helm ond byrne
lungre alysed.   Lagu drusade,   1630
wæter under wolcnum,   wældreore fag.
  Ferdon forð þonon   feþelastum,
ferhþum fægne,   foldweg mæton,
cuþe stræte.   Cyningbalde men
from þæm holmclife   hafelan bæron   1635
earfoðlice   heora æghwæþrum
felamodigra.   Feower scoldon
on þæm wælstenge   weorcum geferian
to þæm goldsele   Grendles heafod,
oþðæt semninga   to sele comon   1640
frome, fyrdhwate   feowertyne
Geata gongan;   gumdryhten mid
modig on gemonge   meodowongas træd.
Ða com in gan   ealdor ðegna,
dædcene mon   dome gewurþad,   1645
hæle hildedeor,   Hroðgar gretan.
Þa wæs be feaxe   on flet boren
Grendles heafod,   þær guman druncon,
egeslic for eorlum   ond þære idese mid,
wliteseon wrætlic;   weras on sawon.   1650

XXIIII   Beowulf maþelode,   bearn Ecgþeowes:
'Hwæt, we þe þas sælac,   sunu Healfdenes,
leod Scyldinga,   lustum brohton,
tires to tacne,   þe þu her to locast.
Ic þæt unsoft   ealdre gedigde,   1655
wigge under wætere,   weorc geneþde
earfoðlice.   Ætrihte wæs
guð getwæfed,   nymðe mec God scylde.
Ne meahte ic æt hilde   mid Hruntinge
wiht gewyrcan,   þeah þæt wæpen duge.   1660
Ac me geuðe   ylda Waldend
þæt ic on wage geseah   wlitig hangian
ealdsweord eacen   —oftost wisode
winigea leasum—   þæt ic ðy wæpne gebræd.
Ofsloh ða æt þære sæcce,   þa me sæl ageald,   1665
huses hyrdas.   Þa þæt hildebil

had with him. A splendid band of thanes went to meet him, thanked God, rejoiced in their prince—that they were allowed to see him safe. Then helmet and mail-coat were quickly loosened from the strong man. The lake grew still, the waters beneath the clouds, stained with the gore of slaughter.

They journeyed forth from there with joyful hearts, retracing their footsteps, measured the path, the familiar road. Men brave as kings carried the head from the cliff by the water—difficult for any two of the great-hearted men. Four had laboriously to convey Grendel's head on the corpse-stake to the gold-hall, until presently they came striding to the hall, fourteen brave Geats, bold in war; among them the leader of men, proud in their midst, trod the fields by the mead-hall. Then the chief of thanes, a man bold in his deeds, enriched by glory, a hero brave in battle, came striding in to greet Hrothgar. The head of Grendel was carried in by the hair on to the hall floor where people were drinking—an object of horror to the warriors and the lady with them, a marvellous spectacle; men looked at it.

24 Beowulf spoke, the son of Ecgtheow: 'Well, son of Healfdene, prince of Scyldings, we have gladly brought you this sea-plunder which you look on here, as a token of success. I hardly came through it alive, the underwater conflict, engaged in the business not without difficulty. The battle would have ended at once had God not shielded me. I could accomplish nothing with Hrunting in the fight, fine though that weapon may be. But the Ruler of men granted me that I should see hanging, beautiful on the wall, an enormous ancient sword—he has often guided the friendless thus— so that I might wield that weapon. Then in the conflict, when my opportunity came, I struck down the guardians of that house. Then that war-sword, the patterned blade, burned away as the

forbarn, brogdenmæl,   swa þæt blod gesprang,
hatost heaþoswata.   Ic þæt hilt þanan
feondum ætferede,   fyrendæda wræc,
deaðcwealm Denigea,   swa hit gedefe wæs.   *1670*
Ic hit þe þonne gehate   þæt þu on Heorote most
sorhleas swefan   mid þinra secga gedryht
ond þegna gehwylc   þinra leoda,
duguðe ond iogoþe,   þæt þu him ondrædan ne þearft,
þeoden Scyldinga,   on þa healfe,   *1675*
aldorbealu eorlum,   swa þu ær dydest.'
    Ða wæs gylden hilt   gamelum rince,
harum hildfruman   on hand gyfen,
enta ærgeweorc.   Hit on æht gehwearf
æfter deofla hryre   Denigea frean,   *1680*
wundorsmiþa geweorc;   ond þa þas worold ofgeaf
gromheort guma,   Godes andsaca,
morðres scyldig,   ond his modor eac,
on geweald gehwearf   woroldcyninga
ðæm selestan   be sæm tweonum,   *1685*
ðara þe on Scedenigge   sceattas dælde.
    Hroðgar maðelode,   hylt sceawode,
ealde lafe.   On ðæm wæs or writen
fyrngewinnes,   syðþan flod ofsloh,
gifen geotende,   giganta cyn;   *1690*
frecne geferdon.   Þæt wæs fremde þeod
ecean Dryhtne;   him þæs endelean
þurh wæteres wylm   Waldend sealde.
Swa wæs on ðæm scennum   sciran goldes
þurh runstafas   rihte gemearcod,   *1695*
geseted ond gesæd,   hwam þæt sweord geworht,
irena cyst,   ærest wære,
wreoþenhilt ond wyrmfah.   Ða se wisa spræc,
sunu Healfdenes   —swigedon ealle—
'Þæt la mæg secgan,   se þe soð ond riht   *1700*
fremeð on folce,   feor eal gemon,
eald eðelweard,   þæt ðes eorl wære
geboren betera!   Blæd is aræred
geond widwegas,   wine min Beowulf,
ðin ofer þeoda gehwylce.   Eal þu hit geþyldum healdest, *1705*
mægen mid modes snyttrum.   Ic þe sceal mine gelæstan
freode, swa wit furðum spræcon.
                    Ðu scealt to frofre weorþan

blood gushed out, the hottest of battle-gore. I have brought back that hilt from the foes, avenged the evil deeds, the slaughter of Danes, as was fitting. I promise you, then, that you may sleep in Heorot free from care, with your band of men and every thane of your people, tried warriors and youths—that you need not fear deadly injury to your soldiers from that quarter, as you did before, prince of Scyldings!'

Then the golden hilt, the ancient work of giants, was given into the hand of the old hero, the grizzled war-leader. After the fall of the devils it passed, the work of marvellous smiths, into the possession of the lord of the Danes; and when the angry-hearted creature, the enemy of God, forsook this world—and his mother too—it passed into the power of the best of earthly kings between the seas, of those who distributed wealth in the Danish realm.

Hrothgar spoke, examining the hilt, ancient heirloom. On it there was engraved the origin of the ancient strife, when the flood, the gushing ocean, slew the race of giants—they suffered fearfully.* That was a nation estranged from the eternal Lord; therefore the Ruler gave them their final reward through the surge of water. On the plates of shining gold was thus correctly marked in runic lettering, set down and told, for whom that sword, the choicest of irons, with twisted hilt and serpentine patterns, had first been wrought.

Then the wise man, the son of Healfdene, spoke (everyone was silent): 'Well, one who furthers truth and justice among the people, an old guardian of the homeland who remembers all that has passed, may say that this warrior was born the better man. Your glory, Beowulf my friend, will be exalted among every nation, throughout distant regions. You carry all this power of yours with patience and prudence of mind. I shall fulfil my friendship towards you, just as we spoke together a short time ago. You shall

eal langtwidig   leodum þinum
hæleðum to helpe.
                Ne wearð Heremod swa
eaforum Ecgwelan,   Ar-Scyldingum;   *1710*
ne geweox he him to willan,   ac to wælfealle
ond to deaðcwalum   Deniga leodum.
Breat bolgenmod   beodgeneatas,
eaxlgesteallan,   oþþæt he ana hwearf,
mære þeoden,   mondreamum from.   *1715*
Ðeah þe hine mihtig God   mægenes wynnum,
eafeþum stepte,   ofer ealle men
forð gefremede,   hwæþere him on ferhþe greow
breosthord blodreow;   nallas beagas geaf
Denum æfter dome.   Dreamleas gebad,   *1720*
þæt he þæs gewinnes   weorc þrowade,
leodbealo longsum.   Ðu þe lær be þon,
gumcyste ongit!   Ic þis gid be þe
awræc wintrum frod.
                Wundor is to secganne
hu mihtig God   manna cynne   *1725*
þurh sidne sefan   snyttru bryttað,
eard ond eorlscipe;   he ah ealra geweald.
Hwilum he on lufan   læteð hworfan
monnes modgeþonc   mæran cynnes,
seleð him on eþle   eorþan wynne   *1730*
to healdanne,   hleoburh wera,
gedeð him swa gewealdene   worolde dælas,
side rice,   þæt he his selfa ne mæg
for his unsnyttrum   ende geþencean.
Wunað he on wiste;   no hine wiht dweleð   *1735*
adl ne yldo,   ne him inwitsorh
on sefan sweorceð,   ne gesacu ohwær
ecghete eoweð,   ac him eal worold
wendeð on willan.   He þæt wyrse ne con—

xxv   —oðþæt him on innan   oferhygda dæl   *1740*
weaxeð ond wridað;   þonne se weard swefeð,
sawele hyrde;   bið se slæp to fæst,
bisgum gebunden—   bona swiðe neah,
se þe of flanbogan   fyrenum sceoteð.
Þonne bið on hreþre   under helm drepen   *1745*
biteran stræle   —him bebeorgan ne con—
wom wundorbebodum   wergan gastes.
Þinceð him to lytel   þæt he to lange heold;

become a comfort to your people, a help to heroes, given to endure for a very long time.

Heremod, the offspring of Ecgwela, was not thus to the Honoured-Scyldings; he did not grow to be a delight to them, but to bring slaughter and deadly injury to the Danish people. His heart swollen with rage, he destroyed the companions of his table, close comrades, until alone, he, the famous prince, turned away from the joys of men. Although mighty God had raised him up in strength, had advanced him above all men in the pleasures of power, nevertheless within his breast the secrets of his heart grew blood-thirsty; in no way did he give rings to the Danes for the sake of glory. Joyless he survived to suffer the pain of that strife, a lasting injury to the people. Teach yourself from this, understand nobility! Wise with the passing winters, I have recited this story for your benefit.

It is a marvel to tell how mighty God in his ample spirit distributes to mankind wisdom, homeland and heroism. He has power over all things. Sometimes he allows the thoughts of the heart of a man of famous race to follow his desire, grants him the joy of land in his own country, a safe stronghold of men to rule over, makes regions of the world subject to him thus, an ample kingdom, so that in his unwisdom he himself cannot conceive an end to it. He lives in abundance; neither sickness nor old age afflict him at all, no evil sorrow darkens his spirit, no enmity anywhere reveals violent hatred, but the whole world turns at his will. He knows nothing worse—

25 —until within him great arrogance grows and flourishes; then the watchman, the guardian of the soul slumbers; bound in cares, that sleep will be too deep, the slayer very near who wickedly shoots with an arrow from his bow.* Then he who knows not how to protect himself will be stricken beneath his helmet in the breast with a bitter shaft, with the crooked mysterious promptings of the evil demon. That which he has held so long seems too little for

1737 sefan: MS sefa.

gytsað gromhydig,   nallas on gylp seleð
fætte beagas.   Ond he þa forðgesceaft   1750
forgyteð ond forgymeð,   þæs þe him ær God sealde,
wuldres Waldend,   weorðmynda dæl.
Hit on endestæf   eft gelimpeð,
þæt se lichoma   læne gedreoseð,
fæge gefealleð;   fehð oþer to,   1755
se þe unmurnlice   madmas dæleþ,
eorles ærgestreon,   egesan ne gymeð.
   Bebeorh þe ðone bealonið,   Beowulf leofa,
secg betsta,   ond þe þæt selre geceos,
ece rædas;   oferhyda ne gym,   1760
mære cempa!   Nu is þines mægnes blæd
ane hwile;   eft sona bið
þæt þec adl oððe ecg   eafoþes getwæfeð,
oððe fyres feng,   oððe flodes wylm,
oððe gripe meces,   oððe gares fliht,   1765
oððe atol yldo;   oððe eagena bearhtm
forsiteð ond forsworceð;   semninga bið,
þæt ðec, dryhtguma,   deað oferswyðeð.
   Swa ic Hring-Dena   hund missera
weold under wolcnum,   ond hig wigge beleac   1770
manigum mægþa   geond þysne middangeard,
æscum ond ecgum,   þæt ic me ænigne
under swegles begong   gesacan ne tealde.
Hwæt, me þæs on eþle   edwenden cwom,
gyrn æfter gomene,   seoþðan Grendel wearð,   1775
ealdgewinna,   ingenga min.
Ic þære socne   singales wæg
modceare micle.   Þæs sig Metode þanc,
ecean Dryhtne,   þæs ðe ic on aldre gebad,
þæt ic on þone hafelan   heorodreorigne   1780
ofer eald gewin   eagum starige!
Ga nu to setle,   symbelwynne dreoh,
wiggeweorþad.   Unc sceal worn fela
maþma gemænra,   siþðan morgen bið.’
   Geat wæs glædmod,   geong sona to   1785
setles neosan,   swa se snottra heht.
Þa wæs eft swa ær   ellenrofum,
fletsittendum   fægere gereorded
niowan stefne.   Nihthelm geswearc
deorc ofer dryhtgumum.   Duguð eal aras;   1790
wolde blondenfeax   beddes neosan,

him; angry-minded, he covets, never giving away plated rings in display. And because of the great honours which God, the Ruler of Glory, had earlier bestowed on him, he forgets and neglects what is ordained for the future. In the end it happens as a matter of course that the transitory flesh declines, falls doomed; another man takes over who, not obsessed by fear, will distribute the treasures, the warrior's former wealth, without reluctance.

Guard yourself against that pernicious wickedness, beloved Beowulf, best of men, and choose for yourself the better part—eternal gains; do not be obsessed by arrogance, famous champion! Now for a time there is glory in your strength; yet soon it shall be that sickness or sword-edge will part you from your power—or the fire's embrace, or the flood's surge, or blade's attack, or spear's flight, or dreadful old age; or else the brightness of the eyes will fade and grow dim; presently it will come about that death shall overpower you, noble man.

Thus for a hundred seasons I ruled the Ring-Danes beneath the skies, and secured them from war by spear and sword-edge against many nations throughout the world, so that I did not reckon on any opponent beneath the expanse of heaven. Well, there came a set-back to me in my own country, misery following merriment, when Grendel, the old enemy, became my invader. Because of that persecution I have constantly borne great anxiety of mind. Thanks be to Providence, the eternal Lord, that after ancient tribulation I have lived long enough to gaze with my eyes on that blood-stained head! Distinguished in battle, go now to your seat, join in the joy of the banquet. When morning comes, a great many treasures shall be shared between us.'

The Geat was glad at heart, went at once to take his seat as the wise man bade. Then once again, as before, a feast was agreeably spread for those men renowned for courage who sat in the hall. The cover of night grew dark, black over the noble men. The band of companions all rose; the grey-haired man, the old Scylding,

---

¹⁷⁵⁰ fætte: MS fædde   ¹⁷⁷⁴ edwenden: MS edwendan

gamela Scylding.   Geat unigmetes wel,
rofne randwigan,   restan lyste.
Sona him seleþegn   siðes wergum,
feorrancundum   forð wisade,   1795
se for andrysnum   ealle beweotede
þegnes þearfe,   swylce þy dogore
heaþoliðende   habban scoldon.
   Reste hine þa rumheort.   Reced hliuade
geap ond goldfah;   gæst inne swæf,   1800
oþþæt hrefn blaca   heofones wynne
bliðheort bodode.   Ða com beorht scacan
scima æfter sceadwe.   Scaþan onetton,
wæron æþelingas   eft to leodum
fuse to farenne;   wolde feor þanon   1805
cuma collenferhð   ceoles neosan.
   Heht þa se hearda   Hrunting beran
sunu Ecglafes,   heht his sweord niman,
leoflic iren;   sægde him þæs leanes þanc,
cwæð, he þone guðwine   godne tealde,   1810
wigcræftigne,   nales wordum log
meces ecge: þæt wæs modig secg.
Ond þa siðfrome,   searwum gearwe
wigend wæron.   Eode weorð Denum
æþeling to yppan,   þær se oþer wæs;   1815
hæle hildedeor   Hroðgar grette.

XXVI   Beowulf maþelode,   bearn Ecgþeowes:
'Nu we sæliðend   secgan wyllað,
feorran cumene,   þæt we fundiaþ
Higelac secan.   Wæron her tela,   1820
willum bewenede;   þu us wel dohtest.
gif ic þonne on eorþan   owihte mæg
þinre modlufan   maran tilian,
gumena dryhten,   ðonne ic gyt dyde,
guðgeweorca,   ic beo gearo sona.   1825
Gif ic þæt gefricge   ofer floda begang,
þæt þec ymbsittend   egesan þywað,
swa þec hetende   hwilum dydon,
ic ðe þusenda   þegna bringe,
hæleþa to helpe.   Ic on Higelace wat,   1830
Geata dryhten,   þeah ðe he geong sy,
folces hyrde,   þæt he mec fremman wile
wordum ond weorcum,   þæt ic þe wel herige

wished to seek out his bed. The Geat, renowned shield-fighter, was particularly well pleased to rest. Straight away a hall-thane who out of courtesy attended to all the needs of a thane—such as a seafaring warrior had to have in those days—led him forth, weary from his exploit, having come from afar.

Then the great-hearted man took his rest. The building towered up, gabled and decked with gold; within it the guest slept, until the black raven, cheerful at heart, announced the joy of the sky.* Then came brightness advancing, radiance following shadows. The soldiers made haste, the princes were eager to journey back to their people. Bold in spirit, the visitor wished to seek out his ship, far from there.

Then the brave man commanded Hrunting to be carried to the son of Ecglaf, commanded him to take his sword, the precious iron; he gave him thanks for the loan of it, said that he reckoned it a good friend in war, strong in battle, by none of his words disparaged the edge of the blade: that was a gallant man. And then the fighting-men, eager for the journey, were ready in their armour. The prince, precious to the Danes, went to the dais where the other was; the hero brave in battle addressed Hrothgar.

26 Beowulf spoke, the son of Ecgtheow: 'Now we seafarers, come from afar, wish to say that we are anxious to seek out Hygelac. We have been properly, delightfully entertained here; you have treated us well. If while on earth I might in any way earn more of the love of your heart than I have yet done, by warlike deeds, I shall be ready at once, leader of men. If over the expanse of the flood I learn that those dwelling round about threaten you with terrible things, as those hating you have sometimes done, I will bring a thousand thanes, heroes to your aid. As for Hygelac, leader of the Geats, guardian of the nation, I know that, young though he may be, he would be willing to assist me by words and deeds, so

ond þe to geoce   garholt bere,
mægenes fultum,   þær ðe bið manna þearf.   *1835*
Gif him þonne Hreþric   to hofum Geata
geþingeð, þeodnes bearn,   he mæg þær fela
freonda findan;   feorcyþðe beoð
selran gesohte   þæm þe him selfa deah.'
   Hroðgar maþelode   him on andsware: *1840*
'Þe þa wordcwydas   wigtig Drihten
on sefan sende;   ne hyrde ic snotorlicor
on swa geongum feore   guman þingian.
Þu eart mægenes strang   ond on mode frod,
wis wordcwida.   Wen ic talige,   *1845*
gif þæt gegangeð,   þæt ðe gar nymeð,
hild heorugrimme   Hreþles eaferan,
adl oþðe iren   ealdor ðinne,
folces hyrde,   ond þu þin feorh hafast,
þæt þe Sæ-Geatas   selran næbben   *1850*
to geceosenne   cyning ænigne,
hordweard hæleþa,   gyf þu healdan wylt
maga rice.   Me þin modsefa
licað leng swa wel,   leofa Beowulf.
Hafast þu gefered   þæt þam folcum sceal,   *1855*
Geata leodum   ond Gar-Denum,
sib gemæne   ond sacu restan,
inwitniþas,   þe hie ær drugon;
wesan, þenden ic wealde   widan rices,
maþmas gemæne,   manig oþerne   *1860*
godum gegrettan   ofer ganotes bæð;
sceal hringnaca   ofer heafu bringan
lac ond luftacen.   Ic þa leode wat
ge wið feond ge wið freond   fæste geworhte,
æghwæs untæle   ealde wisan.'   *1865*
   Ða git him eorla hleo   inne gesealde,
mago Healfdenes   maþmas twelfe,
het hine mid þæm lacum   leode swæse
secean on gesyntum,   snude eft cuman.
Gecyste þa   cyning æþelum god,   *1870*
þeoden Scyldinga   ðegn betstan
ond be healse genam;   hruron him tearas,
blondenfeaxum.   Him wæs bega wen,
ealdum, infrodum,   oþres swiðor,
þæt hie seoððan no   geseon mostan,   *1875*
modige on meþle.   Wæs him se man to þon leof,

that I might show my esteem for you and carry a forest of spears to help you, the support of strength where you have need of men. If then Hrethric, the prince's son, decides to come to the courts of the Geats, he will be able to find many friends there; distant countries are well sought by one who is himself strong.'

Hrothgar spoke to him in reply: 'The wise Lord sent that speech into your mind; I have never heard a man of so young an age talk more sagaciously. You are mighty in strength and prudent in spirit, sensible in speech. I think it likely, if it comes about that the spear, sword-grim war, sickness or iron, take Hrethel's offspring, your chief, the guardian of the nation, and you are still living, that the Sea-Geats would have no better man to choose as king and guardian of the treasure-hoard of heroes, if you wish to hold your kinsman's kingdom. The longer I know them, the better your mind and spirit please me, beloved Beowulf. You have brought it about that there shall be mutual friendship between the nations, the people of the Geats and the Spear-Danes, and conflict, the acts of malice in which they previously engaged, shall rest; for as long as I rule the broad kingdom there shall be treasures in common— many a man greet another with great gifts across the gannet's bath; the curved vessel shall bring presents and tokens of love across the sea. I know the people to be steadfast both towards foe and towards friend, blameless in every respect in the ancient manner.'

Then moreover the defence of warriors, Healfdene's kinsman, gave him in the hall twelve treasures, bade him seek out his own dear people in safety with these presents, come back again quickly. Then the prince of the Scyldings, a king great in nobility, kissed the best of thanes, and clasped him by the neck; tears fell from the grey-haired man. Being old and very wise, two things might be expected, the second more strongly—that they would not see one another again, brave in the council. That man was so loved by him

þæt he þone breostwylm   forberan ne mehte;
ac him on hreþre   hygebendum fæst
æfter deorum men   dyrne langað
beorn wið blode.

       Him Beowulf þanan,   *1880*
guðrinc goldwlanc,   græsmoldan træd,
since hremig.   Sægenga bad
agendfrean,   se þe on ancre rad.
Þa wæs on gange   gifu Hroðgares
oft geæhted.   Þæt wæs an cyning,   *1885*
æghwæs orleahtre,   oþþæt hine yldo benam
mægenes wynnum,   se þe oft manegum scod.

XXVII   Cwom þa to flode   felamodigra
hægstealdra heap;   hringnet bæron,
locene leoðosyrcan.   Landweard onfand   *1890*
eftsið eorla,   swa he ær dyde.
No he mid hearme   of hliðes nosan
gæstas grette,   ac him togeanes rad,
cwæð þæt wilcuman   Wedera leodum
scaþan scirhame   to scipe foron.   *1895*
Þa wæs on sande   sægeap naca
hladen herewædum,   hringedstefna
mearum ond maðmum;   mæst hlifade
ofer Hroðgares   hordgestreonum.
He þæm batwearde   bunden golde   *1900*
swurd gesealde,   þæt he syðþan wæs
on meodubence   maþme þy weorþra,
yrfelafe.
       Gewat him on naca
drefan deop wæter,   Dena land ofgeaf.
Þa wæs be mæste   merehrægla sum,   *1905*
segl sale fæst;   sundwudu þunede.
No þær wegflotan   wind ofer yðum
siðes getwæfde.   Sægenga for,
fleat famigheals   forð ofer yðe,
bundenstefna   ofer brimstreamas,   *1910*
þæt hie Geata clifu   ongitan meahton,
cuþe næssas.   Ceol up geþrang
lyftgeswenced,   on lande stod.
    Hraþe wæs æt holme   hyðweard geara,
se þe ær lange tid   leofra manna   *1915*
fus æt faroðe   feor wlatode.

that he could not restrain the breast's surging; but a hidden yearning for the beloved man burned in the blood, fixed in the heart-strings.

Beowulf departed, trod the grassy earth, a warrior proud in the gold, exulting in treasure. The sea-traveller, which rode at anchor, awaited its master. Then on the journey Hrothgar's gift was often praised. That was a peerless king, faultless in every respect, until old age, which has often ruined many, took from him the joys of strength.

27   Then the band of great-hearted young men came to the flood; they wore ring-mail, an interlocked shirt on their limbs. The guard at the coast noticed the return of the warriors, as he had done before. He did not greet the guests with defiance from the top of the cliff, but rode to meet them, declared that the soldiers in shining armour going down to the ship would be welcome to the people of the Weders. Then on the sand the broad seagoing vessel, the curved prow, was loaded with battle-dress, steeds and treasures; the mast towered up over wealth from Hrothgar's hoard. He gave the boat-guard a gold-inlaid sword, so that thereafter he was the more honoured on the mead-bench on account of that treasure, the heirloom.

The vessel forsook the land of the Danes, moved out to stir the deep water. Then at the mast the sail was made fast by a rope, a fine sea-dress; the water-borne timbers creaked. The wind over the billows did not hinder the wave-floater from its journey. The sea-traveller advanced, floated foamy-necked over the waves, the clamped prow over the ocean currents, until they could descry the Geatish cliffs, familiar headlands. Driven by the breeze, the craft pressed forward, grounded on land.

Swiftly the landing-guard, he who, eager for the beloved men, had for a long time before gazed far out across the currents, was

1883 agendfrean: MS agedfrean   1889 heap *supplied*   1893 gæstas: MS *word lost at edge*; Thorkelin A gæs.   1902ᵇ MS maþma þy weorþre   1903 naca: MS nacan

Sælde to sande   sidfæþme scip
oncerbendum fæst,   þy læs hym yþa ðrym
wudu wynsuman   forwrecan meahte.
Het þa up beran   æþelinga gestreon,   *1920*
frætwe ond fætgold;   næs him feor þanon
to gesecanne   sinces bryttan,
Higelac Hreþling   þær æt ham wunað
selfa mid gesiðum   sæwealle neah.
 Bold wæs betlic,   bregorof cyning,   *1925*
heah in healle,   Hygd swiðe geong,
wis, welþungen,   þeah ðe wintra lyt
under burhlocan   gebiden hæbbe,
Hæreþes dohtor;   næs hio hnah swa þeah,
ne to gneað gifa   Geata leodum   *1930*
maþmgestreona.   Mod Þryðo wæg,
fremu folces cwen,   firen ondrysne.
Nænig þæt dorste   deor geneþan
swæsra gesiða,   nefne sinfrea,
þæt hire an dæges   eagum starede;   *1935*
ac him wælbende   weotode tealde,
handgewriþene;   hraþe seoþðan wæs
æfter mundgripe   mece geþinged,
þæt hit sceadenmæl   scyran moste,
cwealmbealu cyðan.   Ne bið swylc cwenlic þeaw   *1940*
idese to efnanne,   þeah ðe hio ænlicu sy,
þætte freoðuwebbe   feores onsæce
æfter ligetorne   leofne mannan.
 Huru þæt onhohsnode   Hemminges mæg.
Ealodrincende   oðer sædan,   *1945*
þæt hio leodbealewa   læs gefremede,
inwitniða,   syððan ærest wearð
gyfen goldhroden   geongum cempan,
æðelum diore,   syððan hio Offan flet
ofer fealone flod   be fæder lare   *1950*
siðe gesohte.   Ðær hio syððan well
in gumstole,   gode mære,
lifgesceafta   lifigende breac,
hiold heahlufan   wið hæleþa brego,
ealles moncynnes   mine gefræge   *1955*
þone selestan   bi sæm tweonum,
eormencynnes.   Forðam Offa wæs
geofum ond guðum,   garcene man
wide geweorðod;   wisdome heold

ready by the water. He moored the broad-bosomed ship in the sand, fast by its anchor-ropes, lest the force of the waves should drive the superb timbers away. Then he commanded that the princes' wealth, the ornaments and plated gold, be carried up; they would not have to go far from there to seek the distributor of treasure, Hygelac son of Hrethel, where he himself dwelt with his companions, near to the sea-wall.

The building was splendid, the king most renowned, high in the hall—Hæreth's daughter Hygd very young, wise, accomplished, though she had lived few winters within the enclosed stronghold; yet she was not mean, not too niggardly in gifts of treasured wealth to the people of the Geats. Thryth,* imperious queen of the nation, showed haughtiness, a terrible sin. There was no brave man among the dear companions, save for her overlord, who by day dared venture to gaze at her with his eyes; but he might reckon deadly fetters, twisted by hand, assured for him; that after seizure, the sword would be prescribed, the patterned blade should settle it, make known a violent death. Such a thing is no queenly custom for a lady to practise, peerless though she may be—that a 'peace-weaver' should take the life of a beloved man on account of a fancied insult.

However, Hemming's kinsman put a stop to that. Those drinking ale told another tale—that she brought about fewer acts of malice, injuries to the people, as soon as she was given, adorned with gold, to the young champion, the dear prince, when at her father's bidding she sought out Offa's hall in a journey across the yellowish flood. There she subsequently occupied the throne well, famous for virtue, while living made good use of the life destined for her, maintained a profound love for the chief of heroes—the best, as I have heard, of all mankind, of the entire race between the seas. Indeed Offa, a spear-bold man, was widely honoured for gifts and

---

[1918] oncerbendum: MS oncearbendum   [1926] heah in healle: MS hea healle
[1944] onhohsnode Hemminges: MS onhohsnod hemninges   [1956] þone: MS þæs

eðel sinne. Þonon Eomer woc   1960
hæleðum to helpe,   Heminges mæg,
nefa Garmundes,   niða cræftig.

XXVIII   Gewat him ða se hearda   mid his hondscole
sylf æfter sande   sæwong tredan,
wide waroðas.   Woruldcandel scan,   1965
sigel suðan fus.   Hi sið drugon,
elne geeodon,   to ðæs ðe eorla hleo,
bonan Ongenþeoes   burgum in innan,
geongne guðcyning   godne gefrunon
hringas dælan.   Higelace wæs   1970
sið Beowulfes   snude gecyðed,
þæt ðær on worðig   wigendra hleo,
lindgestealla,   lifigende cwom,
heaðolaces hal   to hofe gongan.
Hraðe wæs gerymed,   swa se rica bebead,   1975
feðegestum   flet innanweard.
    Gesæt þa wið sylfne,   se ða sæcce genæs,
mæg wið mæge,   syððan mandryhten
þurh hleoðorcwyde   holdne gegrette
meaglum wordum.   Meoduscencum   1980
hwearf geond þæt side reced   Hæreðes dohtor,
lufode ða leode,   liðwæge bær
Hæðnum to handa.
                    Higelac ongan
sinne geseldan   in sele þam hean
fægre fricgcean;   hyne fyrwet bræc,   1985
hwylce Sæ-Geata   siðas wæron:
'Hu lomp eow on lade,   leofa Biowulf,
þa ðu færinga   feorr gehogodest
sæcce secean   ofer sealt wæter,
hilde to Hiorote?   Ac ðu Hroðgare   1990
widcuðne wean   wihte gebettest,
mærum ðeodne?   Ic ðæs modceare
sorhwylmum seað,   siðe ne truwode
leofes mannes.   Ic ðe lange bæd
þæt ðu þone wælgæst   wihte ne grette,   1995
lete Suð-Dene   sylfe geweorðan
guðe wið Grendel.   Gode ic þanc secge
þæs ðe ic ðe gesundne   geseon moste.'
    Biowulf maðelode,   bearn Ecgðioes:
'Þæt is undyrne,   dryhten Higelac,   2000

battles; he held his homeland with wisdom. Thence sprang Eomer, to be a help to heroes—a kinsman of Hemming, grandson of Garmund, skilful in conflicts.

28 Then the bold man himself went along the sand with his body-guard, treading the beach, the wide shores. The world's candle shone, the sun hastening from the south. They made their way, going eagerly, to where they heard that the defence of warriors, the slayer of Ongentheow,* the great young war-king, was dealing out rings in the stronghold. Beowulf's journey was quickly made known to Hygelac—that there in the precincts the defence of fighting-men, his shield-companion, came walking alive to the court, safe from the game of war. The floor within was swiftly cleared for those who were coming on foot, as the powerful man commanded.

Then he who had come safely through combat sat down facing him, kinsman facing kinsman, after he had greeted the faithful leader of men with ceremonial speech, sincere words. Hæreth's daughter moved through the spacious building with mead-cups, cared for the people, carried flagons of drink to the hands of the Hæthnas.

Hygelac began courteously to question his comrade in that lofty hall; curiosity pricked him as to what the adventures of the Sea-Geats had been: 'How did you fare on the journey, beloved Beowulf, when you suddenly resolved to seek out combat far off across the salt water, battle at Heorot? And did you in any way remedy the widely-known woes of the famous prince, Hrothgar? I have brooded over this with anxiety of mind, surging grief, mistrusting the venture of my beloved man. I long begged you that you should in no way approach that murderous demon, letting the South Danes settle the war against Grendel themselves. I give thanks to God that I was allowed to see you safe.'

Beowulf, the son of Ecgtheow, spoke: 'My leader Hygelac, the

1960 Eomer: MS geomor   1991 widcuðne: MS wiðcuðne

mæru gemeting   monegum fira,
hwylc orleghwil   uncer Grendles
wearð on ðam wange,   þær he worna fela
Sige-Scyldingum   sorge gefremede,
yrmðe to aldre.   Ic ðæt eall gewræc,   2005
swa begylpan ne þearf   Grendeles maga
ænig ofer eorðan   uhthlem þone,
se ðe lengest leofað   laðan cynnes,
facne bifongen.
    Ic ðær furðum cwom
to ðam hringsele   Hroðgar gretan.   2010
Sona me se mæra   mago Healfdenes,
syððan he modsefan   minne cuðe,
wið his sylfes sunu   setl getæhte.
Weorod wæs on wynne;   ne seah ic widan feorh
under heofones hwealf   healsittendra   2015
medudream maran.   Hwilum mæru cwen,
friðusibb folca,   flet eall geondhwearf,
bædde byre geonge;   oft hio beahwriðan
secge sealde,   ær hie to setle geong;
hwilum for duguðe   dohtor Hroðgares   2020
eorlum on ende   ealuwæge bær.
Þa ic Freaware   fletsittende
nemnan hyrde,   þær hio nægled sinc
hæleðum sealde.
    Sio gehaten is
geong, goldhroden,   gladum suna Frodan.   2025
Hafað þæs geworden   wine Scyldinga,
rices hyrde,   ond þæt ræd talað
þæt he mid ðy wife   wælfæhða dæl,
sæcca gesette.   Oft seldan hwær
æfter leodhryre   lytle hwile   2030
bongar bugeð,   þeah seo bryd duge!
  Mæg þæs þonne ofþyncan   ðeodne Heaðobeardna
ond þegna gehwam   þara leoda,
þonne he mid fæmnan   on flett gæð,
dryhtbearn Dena,   duguða biwenede;   2035
on him gladiað   gomelra lafe,
heard ond hringmæl   Heaðabeardna gestreon
þenden hie ðam wæpnum   wealdan moston—

XXIX —oððæt hie forlæddan   to ðam lindplegan
swæse gesiðas   ond hyra sylfra feorh.   2040

famous encounter is openly known to many men—what period of conflict came about between Grendel and me in the place where he brought an abundance of sorrows to the Victorious-Scyldings, constant misery.* I avenged everything, so that none of Grendel's kin on earth—not he who, encompassed by deceit, lives longest of all that loathsome race—will have cause to boast of that pre-dawn clash.

There I first came to the ring-hall to greet Hrothgar. Straight away, when he knew my purpose, the famous kinsman of Healfdene assigned me a seat facing his own sons. The company was joyful; in my whole life I have not seen beneath the vault of heaven a greater rejoicing in mead among those sitting in the hall. At times the famous queen, peace-pledge of the nations, passed through the entire building, encouraged the young warriors; often she presented a twisted circlet to a man before she went to her seat; at times Hrothgar's daughter carried an ale-cup before the tried men, to each of the warriors in turn. I heard those sitting in the hall call her Freawaru, as she presented the studded treasure to heroes.

Young, adorned with gold, she is promised to the gracious son of Froda.* That has been agreed upon by the Scyldings' friend, the guardian of the kingdom, and he considers it good advice that, by means of this woman, he should settle their share of slaughterous feuds, of conflicts. It seldom happens after the fall of a prince that the deadly spear rests for even a little while—worthy though the bride may be!

It may displease the prince of the Heathobards and every thane of those peoples when he goes in the hall with the girl, that the noble sons of the Danes are splendidly entertained; upon them will glisten the heirlooms of ancestors, hard and ring-adorned, the treasure of Heathobards for as long as they could wield those weapons—

29 —until in the play of shields they brought their dear companions and their own lives to destruction.

2001 mæru *restored*   2002 orleghwil: MS . . . . . hwil   2006 ne *supplied*
2007 ænig *restored*   2009 facne: MS f . . . .; Thorkelin A fæ ., Thorkelin B fer . .
2019 sealde *restored*   2020 duguðe: MS . . . . . e; Thorkelin B . uguðe
2023 nægled: MS . . . led; Thorkelin A and B . . gled   2024 is *restored*   2026 hafað:
MS . . fað; Thorkelin A and B iafað   2032 ðeodne: MS ðeoden   2037 Heaðabeardna:
MS heaða bearna   2039 *fitt number supplied*

Þonne cwið æt beore,   se þe beah gesyhð,
eald æscwiga,   se ðe eall geman
garcwealm gumena   —him bið grim sefa—
onginneð geomormod   geongum cempan
þurh hreðra gehygd,   higes cunnian,   *2045*
wigbealu weccean,   ond þæt word acwyð:
'Meaht ðu, min wine,   mece gecnawan
þone þin fæder   to gefeohte bær
under heregriman   hindeman siðe,
dyre iren,   þær hyne Dene slogon,   *2050*
weoldon wælstowe,   syððan Wiðergyld læg,
æfter hæleþa hryre,   hwate Scyldungas?
Nu her þara banena   byre nathwylces
frætwum hremig   on flet gæð,
morðres gylpeð   ond þone maðþum byreð,   *2055*
þone þe ðu mid rihte   rædan sceoldest!'
    Manað swa ond myndgað   mæla gehwylce
sarum wordum,   oððæt sæl cymeð
þæt se fæmnan þegn   fore fæder dædum
æfter billes bite   blodfag swefeð,   *2060*
ealdres scyldig;   him se oðer þonan
losað lifigende,   con him land geare.
Þonne bioð abrocene   on ba healfe
aðsweord eorla;   syððan Ingelde
weallað wælniðas   ond him wiflufan   *2065*
æfter cearwælmum   colran weorðað.
Þy ic Heaðobeardna   hyldo ne telge,
dryhtsibbe dæl   Denum unfæcne,
freondscipe fæstne.
                          Ic sceal forð sprecan
gen ymbe Grendel,   þæt ðu geare cunne,   *2070*
sinces brytta,   to hwan syððan wearð
hondræs hæleða.   Syððan heofones gim
glad ofer grundas,   gæst yrre cwom,
eatol æfengrom,   user neosan,
ðær we gesunde   sæl weardodon.   *2075*
Þær wæs Hondscio   hild onsæge,
feorhbealu fægum;   he fyrmest læg,
gyrded cempa.   Him Grendel wearð,
mærum maguþegne,   to muðbonan,
leofes mannes   lic eall forswealg.   *2080*
No ðy ær ut ða gen   idelhende
bona blodigtoð   bealewa gemyndig,

Then he who sees the ring, an old spear-fighter who remembers all the death of men by darts—grim will be his spirit—will speak over the beer, sad in mind, begin to test the mettle of a young champion, to awaken the violence of war through the thought of his heart, and will speak these words: 'Can you, my friend, recognise the sword, the precious iron which your father beneath his war-visor carried into the fray on his last expedition, where the Danes, the bold Scyldings, slew him, had mastery of the battle-field when, after the fall of heroes, Withergyld lay dead? Now some son or other of those slayers walks in the hall, exulting in the trappings, boasts of the killing and wears the treasure which by rights you should possess!'

On every occasion thus he will provoke and prompt the mind with bitter words, until the moment comes that the girl's thane will sleep stained with blood from the bite of a sword, his life forfeit, because of his father's deeds; the other will escape with his life, knowing the land well. So then the sworn oaths of warriors will be broken on both sides; after that deadly hatred will well up in Ingeld, and because of surging anxiety, his love for his wife will grow cooler. Therefore I do not reckon the faith of the Heatho-bards, their great alliance with the Danes, to be without deceit, a firm friendship.

I shall speak once again about Grendel, so that you may clearly know, distributor of treasure, how the hand-to-hand combat of heroes turned out. After the gem of heaven had glided over the earth, the angry demon came, a dreadful hostility in the dusk, to visit us where, unharmed, we kept watch over the hall. There the battle was fatal to Hondscioh, a deadly injury to the doomed man; he was the first to lie dead, girded champion. Grendel destroyed the famous young thane with his mouth, swallowing the entire body of the beloved man. Nevertheless the bloody-toothed slayer,

---

2042 geman: MS g . . . .; Thorkelin B genam   2044 geongum: MS geon . .; Thorkelin A and B geong . .   2055 gylpeð: MS gyl . . .; Thorkelin B gylped 2062 lifigende: MS . . . . e; Thorkelin A . . figende   2063 abrocene: MS . . . . ocene; Thorkelin A and B orocene   2064 syððan: MS . . . ðan 2067 Heaðobeardna: MS heaðo bearna   2076 hild: MS hilde   2079 maguþegne: MS magū þegne

of ðam goldsele   gongan wolde;
ac he mægnes rof   min costode,
grapode gearofolm.   Glof hangode   *2085*
sid ond syllic,   searobendum fæst;
sio wæs orðoncum   eall gegyrwed,
deofles cræftum   ond dracan fellum.
He mec þær on innan   unsynnigne,
dior dædfruma,   gedon wolde   *2090*
manigra sumne;   hyt ne mihte swa,
syððan ic on yrre   uppriht astod.
   To lang ys to reccenne   hu ic ðam leodsceaðan
yfla gehwylces   ondlean forgeald.
Þær ic, þeoden min,   þine leode   *2095*
weorðode weorcum.   He on weg losade,
lytle hwile   lifwynna breac;
hwæþre him sio swiðre   swaðe weardade
hand on Hiorte,   ond he hean ðonan,
modes geomor   meregrund gefeoll.   *2100*

xxx   Me þone wælræs   wine Scildunga
fættan golde   fela leanode,
manegum maðmum,   syððan mergen com
ond we to symble   geseten hæfdon.
Þær wæs gidd ond gleo.   Gomela Scilding,   *2105*
fela fricgende,   feorran rehte;
hwilum hildedeor   hearpan wynne,
gomenwudu grette,   hwilum gyd awræc
soð ond sarlic,   hwilum syllic spell
reht æfter rihte   rumheort cyning;   *2110*
hwilum eft ongan   eldo gebunden
gomel guðwiga   gioguðe cwiðan,
hildestrengo;   hreðer inne weoll,
þonne he wintrum frod   worn gemunde.
   Swa we þærinne   ondlangne dæg   *2115*
niode naman,   oððæt niht becwom
oðer to yldum.   Þa wæs eft hraðe
gearo gyrnwræce   Grendeles modor,
siðode sorhfull.   Sunu deað fornam,
wighete Wedra.   Wif unhyre   *2120*
hyre bearn gewræc,   beorn acwealde
ellenlice;   þær wæs Æschere,
frodan fyrnwitan,   feorh uðgenge.
Noðer hy hine ne moston,   syððan mergen cwom,

intent on destruction, did not wish to go out of the gold-hall empty-handed; but, renowned for strength, he made trial of me, clutching with an eager hand. A pouch hung there,* wide and wonderful, made fast with cunning clasps; it had been entirely fashioned with ingenuity, the skill of the devil, and dragon-skins. He wished, the bold source of wicked deeds, to put me inside it, guiltless, as one of many; he could not do so, once I stood upright in anger.

It is too long to tell how I paid that scourge of the people back again for every evil deed. By my actions there, my prince, I brought honour to your people. He escaped away, enjoyed the delight of life for a little while; however, his right hand remained behind, a spoor in Heorot, and he went from there humiliated, mournful at heart sank to the bottom of the lake.

30 The Scyldings' friend rewarded me for that deadly onslaught with much plated gold, many treasures, when morning came and we had sat down to the banquet. There was story and song. The old Scylding, who had heard many things, told of times far off; sometimes the battle-brave man plucked the joyful wood, the pleasing harp, sometimes he recited a story, true and sorrowful, sometimes the great-hearted king told aright a strange tale; sometimes, again, the old war-fighter, bowed with age, would lament his youth, his strength in battle; the heart welled within when, wise with winters, he remembered so much.

So all day long we took our pleasure there, until another night came to men. Then in turn Grendel's mother was swiftly ready for the avenging of wrongs, took a sorry journey. Death, the war-hatred of the Weders, had carried off the son. The hideous woman avenged her child, boldly destroyed a warrior; there it was that life departed from Æschere, sage old councillor. Not when morn-

---

2085 gearofolm: MS geareofolm   2093 ic ðam: *restored from* Thorkelin A icdā
2094 ondlean: MS hon . . . .; Thorkelin A hondlean   2097 breac: MS br . . .;
Thorkelin A bræc, B breᵽc   2101 *fitt number supplied* 2108 gomenwudu: MS go
. . . wudu; Thorkelin A and B gomelwudu

deaðwerigne,   Denia leode   2125
bronde forbærnan,   ne on bæl hladan
leofne mannan;   hio þæt lic ætbær
feondes fæðmum   under firgenstream.
Þæt wæs Hroðgare   hreowa tornost,
þara þe leodfruman   lange begeate.   2130
    Þa se ðeoden mec   ðine life
healsode hreohmod,   þæt ic on holma geþring
eorlscipe efnde,   ealdre geneðde,
mærðo fremede;   he me mede gehet.
Ic ða ðæs wælmes,   þe is wide cuð,   2135
grimne gryrelicne   grundhyrde fond.
Þær unc hwile wæs   hand gemæne;
holm heolfre weoll,   ond ic heafde becearf
in ðam guðsele   Grendeles modor
eacnum ecgum.   Unsofte þonan   2140
feorh oðferede;   næs ic fæge þa gyt;
ac me eorla hleo   eft gesealde
maðma menigeo,   maga Healfdenes.

XXXI   Swa se ðeodkyning   þeawum lyfde;
nealles ic ðam leanum   forloren hæfde,   2145
mægnes mede,   ac he me maðmas geaf,
sunu Healfdenes,   on minne sylfes dom;
ða ic ðe, beorncyning,   bringan wylle,
estum geywan.   Gen is eall æt ðe
lissa gelong;   ic lyt hafo   2150
heafodmaga,   nefne Hygelac ðec!'
    Het ða in beran   eafor, heafodsegn,
heaðosteapne helm,   hare byrnan,
guðsweord geatolic,   gyd æfter wræc:
'Me ðis hildesceorp   Hroðgar sealde,   2155
snotra fengel;   sume worde het,
þæt ic his ærest ðe   est gesægde.
Cwæð þæt hyt hæfde   Hiorogar cyning,
leod Scyldunga,   lange hwile;
no ðy ær suna sinum   syllan wolde,   2160
hwatum Heorowearde,   þeah he him hold wære,
breostgewædu.   Bruc ealles well!'
    Hyrde ic þæt þam frætwum   feower mearas
lungre, gelice   last weardode,
æppelfealuwe.   He him est geteah   2165
meara ond maðma.   Swa sceal mæg don,

ing came, could the people of the Danes burn him, sated with war, in the blaze, neither lay the beloved man on the pyre; she had carried the body off in a fiend's embrace beneath a mountain stream. To Hrothgar that was the most grievous of sorrows of those which had long befallen the chieftain of the people.

Then, troubled in mind, the prince implored me that, for your sake, I should display heroism in the tumult of waters, should risk life, should achieve a glorious deed; he promised me reward. Then, as is widely known, I found in the surge a terrible grim guardian of the deep. There for a time we locked, hand-to-hand; the water welled with blood, and in that war-hall I cut off the head of Grendel's mother with a great blade. I hardly got away from there alive— I was not yet doomed to die; but the defence of warriors, Healfdene's kinsman, again bestowed on me many treasures.

31 The king of that nation lived thus in the traditional manner; I lost no reward whatever, the recompense of strength, but Healfdene's son gave me treasures of my own choosing; these I wish to bring to you, warrior king, to present with good will. All favour is still dependent on you; I have few close kinsmen except for you, Hygelac!'

Then he commanded them to carry in the boar-standard, symbol of chieftaincy, towering battle-helmet, the grey mail-coat, the splendid war-sword, and related their story: 'The wise ruler, Hrothgar, presented me with this battle-garb; he commanded me in one speech that I should first tell you about his gracious gift. He said that King Heorogar, the prince of the Scyldings, had it for a long while; nevertheless he would not give it, the breast-armour, to his son, bold Heoroweard, faithful to him though he was. Make good use of it all!'

I heard that four swift steeds, all alike, yellow as apples, followed those adornments. He made over to him the gracious gift of steeds and treasures. So ought a kinsman to act, never weave a web of

---

²¹²⁸ fæðmum under: MS f . . . . der; Thorkelin A fæð . . under   ²¹³⁶ grimne:
MS grimme   ²¹³⁹ gusðele: MS s . . ; Thorkelin A and B sele   ²¹⁴⁶ maðmas:
MS . . . . . s   ²¹⁴⁷ minne: MS . . . ne

nealles inwitnet   oðrum bregdon
dyrnum cræfte,   deað renian
hondgesteallan.   Hygelace wæs,
niða heardum,   nefa swyðe hold,   2170
ond gehwæðer oðrum   hroþra gemyndig.
Hyrde ic þæt he ðone healsbeah   Hygde gesealde,
wrætlicne wundurmaððum,   ðone þe him Wealhðeo geaf
ðeodnes dohtor,   þrio wicg somod
swancor ond sadolbeorht;   hyre syððan wæs   2175
æfter beahðege   breost geweorðod.
   Swa bealdode   bearn Ecgðeowes,
guma guðum cuð,   godum dædum,
dreah æfter dome;   nealles druncne slog
heorðgeneatas;   næs him hreoh sefa,   2180
ac he mancynnes   mæste cræfte,
ginfæstan gife,   þe him God sealde,
heold hildedeor.   Hean wæs lange,
swa hyne Geata bearn   godne ne tealdon,
ne hyne on medobence   micles wyrðne   2185
drihten Wedera   gedon wolde;
swyðe wendon,   þæt he sleac wære,
æðeling unfrom.   Edwenden cwom
tireadigum menn   torna gehwylces.
   Het ða eorla hleo   in gefetian,   2190
heaðorof cyning,   Hreðles lafe,
golde gegyrede;   næs mid Geatum ða
sincmaðþum selra   on sweordes had.
Þæt he on Biowulfes   bearm alegde,
ond him gesealde   seofan þusendo,   2195
bold ond bregostol.   Him wæs bam samod
on ðam leodscipe   lond gecynde,
eard, eðelriht,   oðrum swiðor,
side rice,   þam ðær selra wæs.
   Eft þæt geiode   ufaran dogrum   2200
hildehlæmmum,   syððan Hygelac læg
ond Heardrede   hildemeceas
under bordhreoðan   to bonan wurdon,
ða hyne gesohtan   on sigeþeode
hearde hildfrecan,   Heaðo-Scilfingas,   2205
niða genægdan   nefan Hererices:
syððan Beowulfe   brade rice
on hand gehwearf.
             He geheold tela

malice for the other with secret craft, devise the death of a close comrade. Hygelac's nephew, stern in combats, was very faithful to him, and each was mindful of the other's profit. I heard that he presented to Hygd the neck-ring, the wonderful adorned treasure, that Wealhtheow, a prince's daughter, had given him, together with three horses, graceful and bright with saddles; after receiving the ring her breast was thenceforward honoured.

Thus Ecgtheow's son, a man well known for battles, for great deeds, displayed his bravery, acted with honour; never did he slay the companions of his hearth when drunk; his heart was not savage but, brave in battle, with the greatest strength among mankind, he held the ample gift which God had bestowed on him. He had long been despised, since the children of the Geats did not reckon him a fine man, nor would the leader of the Weders do him great honour on the mead-bench; they firmly believed him to be slothful, a feeble prince.* There came to the man blessed with glory a change from all troubles.

Then the defence of warriors, a king renowned in battle, commanded them to fetch in Hrethel's heirloom, decked with gold; there was not then among the Geats a better treasure in the shape of a sword. He laid that in Beowulf's lap, and bestowed on him seven thousand hides,* a hall and princely throne. Both of them alike owned inherited land in that country, a dwelling, ancestral rights—to the other in particular, whose rank was higher, a wide kingdom.

In clashes of battle in later days—after Hygelac lay dead, and battle-blades beneath the shield's shelter had been the death of Heardred when the War-Scylfings, bold battle-fighters, sought him out among his victorious nation, assailed the nephew of Hereric with enmity—it came to pass that then the broad kingdom came into Beowulf's hand.*

For fifty winters he held it well—he was then a wise king, an old

2168 renian: MS re . . . .; Thorkelin A and B ren .   2174 ðeodnes: MS ðeo . . . .;
Thorkelin A and B ðeod .   2176 breost: MS brost   2186 Wedera: MS wereda
2187 wendon: MS . . . . on; Thorkelin A and B . don   2202 Heardrede: MS hearede
2205 hildfrecan: MS hilde frecan

fiftig wintra —wæs ða frod cyning,
eald eþelweard— oððæt an ongan   2210
deorcum nihtum, draca ricsian
se ðe on heaum hofe hord beweotode,
stanbeorh steapne; stig under læg
eldum uncuð. Þær on innan giong
niða nathwylc, se ðe neh gefeng   2215
hæðnum horde hond wæge nam,
sid since fah. Ne he þæt syððan bemað,
þeah ðe he slæpende besyred wurde
þeofes cræfte; þæt sie ðiod onfand,
bufolc beorna, þæt he gebolgen wæs.   2220

XXXII   Nealles mid gewealdum wyrmhord abræc,
sylfes willum, se ðe him sare gesceod;
ac for þreanedlan þeow nathwylces
hæleða bearna heteswengeas fleoh,
ærnes þearfa, ond ðær inne fealh,   2225
secg synbysig. Sona inwlatode,
þæt . . . . . ðam gyste gryrebroga stod;
hwæðre earmsceapen . . . .
. . . . sceapen
. . . . þa hyne se fær begeat, 2230
sincfæt . . . . Þær wæs swylcra fela
in ðam eorðhuse ærgestreona,
swa hy on geardagum gumena nathwylc,
eormenlafe æþelan cynnes,
þanchycgende þær gehydde,   2235
deore maðmas. Ealle hie deað fornam
ærran mælum, ond se an ða gen
leoda duguðe se ðær lengest hwearf
weard winegeomor wende þæs ylcan
þæt he lytel fæc longgestreona   2240
brucan moste.
                   Beorh eallgearo
wunode on wonge wæteryðum neah,
niwe be næsse, nearocræftum fæst.
Þær on innan bær eorlgestreona
hringa hyrde hordwyrðne dæl,   2245
fættan goldes, fea worda cwæð:
   'Heald þu nu, hruse, nu hæleð ne mostan,
eorla æhte! Hwæt, hyt ær on ðe
gode begeaton. Guðdeað fornam,

guardian of the homeland—until there began to hold sway in the dark nights a certain creature, a dragon, which in a lofty dwelling kept watch over a hoard, a high stone barrow; beneath lay a passage unknown to men. Into this some man or other had gone, who got near to the heathen hoard, whose hand seized a flagon, large, adorned with treasure. Nor did it afterwards conceal the fact, though it had been tricked by a thief's cunning while sleeping; the men of the people dwelling there found that out when it was swollen with rage.

32 He who grievously despoiled it did not break into the serpent's hoard on purpose by his own choice at all; but in sore distress, the slave of one or another hero's son fled from hostile blows, in need of a dwelling, and made his way inside there, a man troubled by sin. As soon as he looked inside, a terrible horror arose in the stranger; however, the poor wretch [escaped the dreadful serpent]. When the sudden attack came upon him [he took with him] a precious cup. There were many such ancient treasures in that earthen house, just as in days gone by some man or other had carefully hidden precious jewels there, the immense legacy of a noble race.* Death had carried off them all in former times, and the one man remaining of the tried warriors of the people, he who lived there longest, a guardian mourning his friends, expected the same fate as theirs—that only for a little while would he be allowed to enjoy the long-accumulated treasures.

A barrow stood all ready on open ground near the sea-waves, new by the headland, secure in its powers of confinement. Into this the keeper of the rings carried a large amount of what was worth hoarding, noble treasures, plated gold, spoke few words:

'Hold now, you earth, the possession of warriors, now that the heroes cannot! Indeed, it was from you that the great men formerly won it. Death in war, fierce mortal havoc, has carried off every man

2211 ricsian: Thorkelin A ricsan   2215-17 se ðe neh . . . wæge nam sid . . . bemað supplied   2218 besyred wurde: MS besyre . . . . . de   2219 onfand supplied 2220 gebolgen: MS gebolge   2221-2 gewealdum wyrmhord abræc: MS geweoldum wyrm horda cræft   2223 þeow: MS þe . .   2225 ærnes supplied   2225 fealh: MS weal corrected from feal; Thorkelin A and B weall   2226 inwlatode: MS mwatide   2237 se: MS si   2239 wende . . . ylcan: MS thus, overwritten rihde . . . yldan   2245 hordwyrðne: MS hardwyrðne   2247 mostan: MS thus, overwritten mæstan

feorhbealo frecne,   fyra gehwylcne   2250
leoda minra,   þara ðe þis lif ofgeaf,
gesawon seledreamas.   Nah hwa sweord wege
oððe feormie   fæted wæge,
dryncfæt deore;   duguð ellor scoc.
Sceal se hearda helm   hyrsted golde   2255
fætum befeallen;   feormynd swefað,
þa ðe beadogriman   bywan sceoldon;
ge swylce seo herepad,   sio æt hilde gebad
ofer borda gebræc   bite irena,
brosnað æfter beorne;   ne mæg byrnan hring   2260
æfter wigfruman   wide feran
hæleðum be healfe.   Næs hearpan wyn,
gomen gleobeames,   ne god hafoc
geond sæl swingeð,   ne se swifta mearh
burhstede beateð.   Bealocwealm hafað   2265
fela feorhcynna   forð onsended!'
     Swa giomormod   giohðo mænde,
an æfter eallum,   unbliðe hwearf
dæges ond nihtes,   oððæt deaðes wylm
hran æt heortan.
                    Hordwynne fond   2270
eald uhtsceaða   opene standan,
se ðe byrnende   biorgas seceð,
nacod niðdraca,   nihtes fleogeð
fyre befangen.   Hyne foldbuend
swiðe ondrædað.   He gesecean sceall   2275
hord on hrusan,   þær he hæðen gold
warað wintrum frod;   ne byð him wihte ðy sel.
     Swa se ðeodsceaða   þreo hund wintra
heold on hrusan   hordærna sum
eacencræftig,   oððæt hyne an abealch   2280
mon on mode;   mandryhtne bær
fæted wæge,   frioðowære bæd
hlaford sinne.   Ða wæs hord rasod,
onboren beaga hord,   bene getiðad
feasceaftum men.   Frea sceawode   2285
fira fyrngeweorc   forman siðe.
     Þa se wyrm onwoc,   wroht wæs geniwad;
stonc ða æfter stane,   stearcheort onfand
feondas fotlast;   he to forð gestop
dyrnan cræfte,   dracan heafde neah.   2290
     Swa mæg unfæge   eaðe gedigan

of my people who forsook this life, saw the last of joys in the hall. I have none who bears the sword or polishes the plated flagon, precious drinking-cup; the company of tried warriors has passed elsewhere. The hard helmet, decorated with gold, must be reft of its plates; the polishers who should burnish the war-visor are asleep; so also the war-coat, which endured the bite of iron over the splintering of shields, falls to pieces along with the warrior; nor can the mail's rings travel far with the war-leader, side-by-side with heroes. There is no delight in the harp, mirth in the singing wood, nor does a fine hawk swoop through the hall, nor the swift steed stamp in the courtyard. Baleful death has despatched many of the human race!'

Thus, sad in mind, the lone survivor lamented his grief, unhappy, moved through day and night until the surge of death touched his heart.

The ancient pre-dawn scourge who, burning, seeks out barrows —the smooth-skinned, malicious dragon who flies by night encircled in fire—found the delightful hoard standing open. Those who dwell on earth greatly fear it. It is its nature to seek out a hoard in the earth where, wise with winters, it guards heathen gold; it is none the better for that.

Thus for three hundred winters the scourge of the nation held a particularly immense treasure-house in the earth, until a certain man enraged its heart; he carried to his leader the plated flagon, asked his lord for peace-conditions. So the hoard was ransacked, the hoard of rings diminished, the wretched man granted his request. The prince examined the ancient work of men for the first time.

Then the serpent awoke, a new grievance arose; it moved rapidly along the rock, ruthless in heart, discovered the enemy's footprint —with stealthy craft he had stepped too far forward near to the dragon's head. Thus a man not fated to die, whom the favour of

2250 feorh bealo: MS *thus, overwritten* reorh bealc; fyra: MS fyrena   2251 þara: MS þana; lif *supplied*   2253 feormie: MS f . . . . . .   2254 duguð: MS dug . . ; scoc: MS seoc   2255 hyrsted: MS . . . sted   2268 hwearf: MS hwe . . . 2275 swiðe ondrædað: MS . . . . da .   2276 hord on: MS . . r . . . . 2279 hrusan: MS hrusam

wean ond wræcsið,   se ðe Waldendes
hyldo gehealdeþ.   Hordweard sohte
georne æfter grunde,   wolde guman findan
þone þe him on sweofote   sare geteode;   *2295*
hat ond hreohmod   hlæw oft ymbehwearf,
ealne utanweardne;   ne ðær ænig mon
on þære westenne;   hwæðre wiges gefeh,
beaduwe weorces;   hwilum on beorh æthwearf,
sincfæt sohte;   he þæt sona onfand   *2300*
ðæt hæfde gumena sum   goldes gefandod,
heahgestreona.
             Hordweard onbad
earfoðlice   oððæt æfen cwom.
Wæs ða gebolgen   beorges hyrde,
wolde se laða   lige forgyldan   *2305*
drincfæt dyre.   Þa wæs dæg sceacen
wyrme on willan;   no on wealle læng
bidan wolde,   ac mid bæle for,
fyre gefysed.   Wæs se fruma egeslic
leodum on lande,   swa hyt lungre wearð   *2310*
on hyra sincgifan   sare geendod.

XXXIII   Ða se gæst ongan   gledum spiwan,
beorht hofu bærnan;   bryneleoma stod
eldum on andan.   No ðær aht cwices
lað lyftfloga   læfan wolde.   *2315*
Wæs þæs wyrmes wig   wide gesyne,
nearofages nið   nean ond feorran,
hu se guðsceaða   Geata leode
hatode ond hynde.   Hord eft gesceat,
dryhtsele dyrnne   ær dæges hwile.   *2320*
Hæfde landwara   lige befangen,
bæle ond bronde;   beorges getruwode,
wiges ond wealles;   him seo wen geleah.
   Þa wæs Biowulfe   broga gecyðed
snude to soðe,   þæt his sylfes ham,   *2325*
bolda selest,   brynewylmum mealt,
gifstol Geata.   Þæt ðam godan wæs
hreow on hreðre,   hygesorga mæst.
Wende se wisa   þæt he Wealdende
ofer ealde riht,   ecean Dryhtne,   *2330*
bitre gebulge;   breost innan weoll
þeostrum geþoncum,   swa him geþywe ne wæs.

the Ruler protects, can survive miseries and banishment with ease. The guardian of the hoard eagerly searched along the ground, wanted to find the man who had treated it cruelly while it slept; hot and savage at heart, it frequently circled all round the mound on the outside; there was no man in that wilderness; however, it rejoiced in anticipation of conflict, an act of war; sometimes it turned back into the barrow, searched for the precious cup; it soon discovered that some man had tampered with the gold, the princely treasure.

With difficulty, the guardian of the hoard waited until evening came. Then the keeper of the barrow was swollen with rage, the loathsome creature wanted to pay them back for the precious drinking-cup with fire. Then to the serpent's gratification, the day had passed; it would not stay longer within the walls, but set out with flame, ready with fire. The beginning was terrible to the people in the land, just as presently it would end with bitterness for their treasure-giver.

33 Then the visitant began to spew forth coals of fire, to burn the bright houses; the light of burning arose, bringing terror upon men. The loathsome creature flying in the air wished to leave nothing there alive. From far and near the serpent's warfare, cruelly hostile malice, was widely evident, how the warlike scourge persecuted and humiliated the people of the Geats. It darted back to the hoard, its secret, splendid hall, before daytime. It had encircled those who dwelt in the land with flame, fire and burning; it put its trust in the barrow, warfare and the rampart; the expectation deceived it.

Then the truth of the horror was quickly made known to Beowulf—that his own home, the finest of buildings, the Geats' throne, source of gifts, had melted away in the burning surges. That was a distress to the spirit of the great man, the greatest of sorrows to the mind. The wise man supposed that he had bitterly offended the Ruler, eternal Lord, by breaking some ancient law; his breast within surged with dark thoughts, which was unusual for him.

2296 hlæw: MS hlǣwū   2298 wiges: MS hilde   2299 beaduwe: MS bea . . . .
2305 se laða: MS fela ða   2307 læng: MS læg   2325 ham: MS him

Hæfde ligdraca   leoda fæsten,
ealond utan,   eorðweard ðone
gledum forgrunden.   Him ðæs guðkyning,   2335
Wedera þioden,   wræce leornode.
Heht him þa gewyrcean   wigendra hleo
eallirenne,   eorla dryhten,
wigbord wrætlic;   wisse he gearwe,
þæt him holtwudu   helpan ne meahte,   2340
lind wið lige.   Sceolde liþend daga,
æþeling ærgod,   ende gebidan,
worulde lifes   —ond se wyrm somod,
þeah ðe hordwelan   heolde lange.
Oferhogode ða   hringa fengel,   2345
þæt he þone widflogan   weorode gesohte,
sidan herge;   no he him þa sæcce ondred,
ne him þæs wyrmes wig   for wiht dyde,
eafoð ond ellen,   forðon he ær fela
nearo neðende   niða gedigde,   2350
hildehlemma,   syððan he Hroðgares,
sigoreadig secg,   sele fælsode
ond æt guðe forgrap   Grendeles mægum
laðan cynnes.
No þæt læsest wæs
hondgemota,   þær mon Hygelac sloh,   2355
syððan Geata cyning   guðe ræsum,
freawine folca   Freslondum on,
Hreðles eafora   hiorodryncum swealt,
bille gebeaten.   Þonan Biowulf com
sylfes cræfte,   sundnytte dreah;   2360
hæfde him on earme   eorla xxx
hildegeatwa,   þa he to holme beag.
Nealles Hetware   hremge þorfton
feðewiges,   þe him foran ongean
linde bæron;   lyt eft becwom   2365
fram þam hildfrecan   hames niosan.
Oferswam ða sioleða bigong   sunu Ecgðeowes,
earm anhaga   eft to leodum.
Þær him Hygd gebead   hord ond rice,
beagas ond bregostol;   bearne ne truwode,   2370
þæt he wið ælfylcum   eþelstolas
healdan cuðe,   ða wæs Hygelac dead.
No ðy ær feasceafte   findan meahton
æt ðam æðelinge   ænige ðinga,

The fiery dragon had utterly crushed with coals of fire the fortress of the people from the seaboard to the interior. The war-king, the prince of the Weders, planned revenge on it for this. The defence of fighting-men, the leader of warriors, commanded to be made for him a wonderful war-shield all of iron; he knew very well that forest wood could not help him—limewood against flame. The seafarer, a prince of proven merit, had to meet the end of his days, his life in the world—and the dragon as well, long though it had held the hoarded wealth.

Then the ruler of rings disdained to seek out the wide-flying creature with a troop, an extensive force; he had no fear for himself in the combat, nor did he make much of the serpent's war-power, strength and courage, because, risking danger, he had previously survived many violent situations, clashes of battle, since he, a man blessed with victory, had cleansed Hrothgar's hall and crushed to death in battle Grendel's kin, of loathsome race.

Not the least of hand-to-hand encounters was that where they slew Hygelac, when the king of the Geats, lord and friend of the people, died by blood-drinking blades in the onslaught of war in Frisia, the offspring of Hrethel beaten down by the sword. Beowulf came away from there by his own strength, engaged in a feat of swimming; he held in his arm the battle-gear of thirty warriors when he turned to the water.* The Hetware had no cause at all for exultation in the conflict of troops when they carried limewood shields against him; few came back from that battle-fighter to seek out their homes.

Then the son of Ecgtheow, a wretched solitary, swam over the expanse of tides back to his people. There Hygd offered him hoard and kingdom, rings and a princely throne; now that Hygelac was dead, she did not trust that her son knew how to hold the throne of his homeland against foreign nations. Nevertheless the destitute people could not in any way persuade the prince to become lord

---

²³⁴⁰ helpan: MS he . . . .   ²³⁴¹ liþend: MS . . þend   ²³⁴⁷ þa: MS þā
²³⁵⁵ hondgemota: MS hondgemot   ²³⁶¹ eorla *restored*   ³²⁶² beag: MS . . ag
²³⁶³ þorfton: MS þorf . . .; Thorkelin B þorf . on

þæt he Heardrede   hlaford wære,   2375
oððe þone cynedom   ciosan wolde.
Hwæðre he hine on folce   freondlarum heold,
estum mid are,   oððæt he yldra wearð,
Weder-Geatum weold.
         Hyne wræcmæcgas
ofer sæ sohton,   suna Ohteres;   2380
hæfdon hy forhealden   helm Scylfinga,
þone selestan   sæcyninga
þara ðe in Swiorice   sinc brytnade,
mærne þeoden.   Him þæt to mearce wearð;
he þær for feorme   feorhwunde hleat   2385
sweordes swengum,   sunu Hygelaces.
Ond him eft gewat   Ongenðioes bearn
hames niosan,   syððan Heardred læg,
let ðone bregostol   Biowulf healdan,
Geatum wealdan.   Þæt wæs god cyning!   2390

XXXIIII   Se ðæs leodhryres   lean gemunde
uferan dogrum,   Eadgilse wearð,
feasceaftum freond;   folce gestepte
ofer sæ side   sunu Ohteres,
wigum ond wæpnum.   He gewræc syððan   2395
cealdum cearsiðum,   cyning ealdre bineat.
    Swa he niða gehwane   genesen hæfde,
sliðra geslyhta,   sunu Ecgðiowes,
ellenweorca,   oð ðone anne dæg
þe he wið þam wyrme   gewegan sceolde.   2400
Gewat þa twelfa sum,   torne gebolgen,
dryhten Geata   dracan sceawian.
Hæfde þa gefrunen   hwanan sio fæhð aras,
bealonið biorna;   him to bearme cwom
maðþumfæt mære   þurh ðæs meldan hond.   2405
Se wæs on ðam ðreate   þreotteoða secg,
se ðæs orleges   or onstealde,
hæft hygegiomor,   sceolde hean ðonon
wong wisian.   He ofer willan giong
to ðæs ðe he eorðsele   anne wisse,   2410
hlæw under hrusan   holmwylme neh,
yðgewinne,   se wæs innan full
wrætta ond wira.   Weard unhiore,
gearo guðfreca   goldmaðmas heold,
eald under eorðan;   næs þæt yðe ceap   2415

over Heardred or agree to accede to royal power. However, he upheld him among the people with friendly counsels, good-will with honour, until he became older and ruled the Weder-Geats.

Exiled men, the sons of Ohthere, sought him out from over the sea;* they had rebelled against the protector of the Scylfings, a famous prince, the best of the sea-kings, of those who distributed treasure in the Swedish kingdom. That was to mark his end; because of his hospitality, Hygelac's son received a mortal wound by strokes from a sword. And when Heardred lay dead, Ongentheow's son went back to seek his home again—allowed Beowulf to hold the princely throne, rule the Geats. That was a great king!

34   In later days he was mindful of requiting the prince's fall—became a friend to the destitute Eadgils; across the wide sea he advanced the cause of Ohthere's son among the people with fighters and weapons. Later he took vengeance with cold expeditions that brought sorrow—deprived the king of life.

Thus he, the son of Ecgtheow, had come safely through every conflict, dangerous onslaught, deeds of courage, until that particular day when he had to fight against the serpent. Then the leader of the Geats, swelling with rage, went as one of twelve to view the dragon. He had learned by then for what reason this feud had arisen, dire malice to men; the famous precious vessel had come into his lap through the hand of the informant. The thirteenth man in that band was he who had been responsible for the beginning of that strife, the slave who, mournful in mind, humiliated, had to lead the way from there to the place. Against his will he went to where he knew the singular earthen hall to be, a mound covered in soil near to the surging water, the tumult of the waves, which within was full of decorated objects and filigree. The hideous guardian, ready, bold in war, held the golden treasures, old

to gegangenne   gumena ænigum.
    Gesæt ða on næsse   niðheard cyning,
þenden hælo abead   heorðgeneatum,
goldwine Geata.   Him wæs geomor sefa,
wæfre ond wælfus,   wyrd ungemete neah,   2420
se ðone gomelan   gretan sceolde,
secean sawle hord,   sundur gedælan
lif wið lice;   no þon lange wæs
feorh æþelinges   flæsce bewunden.
Biowulf maþelade,   bearn Ecgðeowes: 2425
'Fela ic on giogoðe   guðræsa genæs,
orleghwila;   ic þæt eall gemon.
Ic wæs syfanwintre   þa mec sinca baldor,
freawine folca,   æt minum fæder genam.
Heold mec ond hæfde   Hreðel cyning,   2430
geaf me sinc ond symbel,   sibbe gemunde;
næs ic him to life   laðra owihte
beorn in burgum   þonne his bearna hwylc,
Herebeald ond Hæðcyn,   oððe Hygelac min.
Wæs þam yldestan   ungedefelice   2435
mæges dædum   morþorbed stred,
syððan hyne Hæðcyn   of hornbogan,
his freawine   flane geswencte,
miste mercelses   ond his mæg ofscet,
broðor oðerne,   blodigan gare.   2440
Þæt wæs feohleas gefeoht,   fyrenum gesyngad,
hreðre hygemeðe;   sceolde hwæðre swa þeah
æðeling unwrecen   ealdres linnan.
    Swa bið geomorlic   gomelum ceorle
to gebidanne,   þæt his byre ride   2445
giong on galgan.   Þonne he gyd wrece,
sarigne sang,   þonne his sunu hangað
hrefne to hroðre   ond he him helpe ne mæg,
eald ond infrod,   ænige gefremman.
Symble bið gemyndgad   morna gehwylce   2450
eaforan ellorsið;   oðres ne gymeð
to gebidanne   burgum in innan
yrfeweardas,   þonne se an hafað
þurh deaðes nyd   dæda gefondad.
Gesyhð sorhcearig   on his suna bure   2455
winsele westne,   windge reste
reote berofene.   Ridend swefað,
hæleð in hoðman;   nis þær hearpan sweg,

beneath the earth; it was no easy merchandise for any man to win.

Then the king, bold in conflict, sat on the headland, as the gold-friend of the Geats wished the companions of his hearth good fortune. His spirit was mournful, restless and ready for death—the fate very close which should meet the old man, seek out the soul's hoard, divide asunder life from body; the life of the prince was not wrapped in flesh for long then. Beowulf spoke, the son of Ecgtheow: 'In youth I came safely through many an onslaught in war, period of conflict; I remember it all. I was seven winters old when the commander of treasure, the lord and friend of the people, took me on from my father.* King Hrethel kept and maintained me, gave me treasure and banquet, remembering our relationship; I was no more hated by him as a warrior in the strongholds during his lifetime, than any of his sons: Herebald and Hæthcyn, or my Hygelac. A bed of violent death was spread for the eldest, inappropriately by the actions of a kinsman when Hæthcyn, his lord and friend, struck him with an arrow from a horn bow, missed the mark and shot his kinsman, one brother the other, with a bloody dart.* That was a conflict without compensation, a wicked crime wearying to ponder in the heart; but nevertheless, the prince had to relinquish life unavenged.

Just so, it is a sad thing for an old man to endure if his son should swing young on the gallows. Then he may recite a story, a sorrowful song, as his son hangs, a profit to the raven, and he, old and wise with years, cannot afford him any help. Regularly each morning he is reminded of his offspring's journey elsewhere; he does not care to wait for another heir within the stronghold when the first has completed his trial of deeds in the compulsion of death. Moved with sorrow, he sees in his son's chamber a deserted wine-hall, a windswept resting-place bereft of joy. The horsemen sleep,

2448 helpe: MS helpan

gomen in geardum,   swylce ðær iu wæron—

—gewiteð þonne on sealman,   sorhleoð gæleð,   2460
an æfter anum.   Þuhte him eall to rum,
wongas ond wicstede;   swa Wedra helm
æfter Herebealde   heortan sorge
weallinde wæg;   wihte ne meahte
on ðam feorhbonan   fæghðe gebetan;   2465
no ðy ær he þone heaðorinc   hatian ne meahte
laðum dædum,   þeah him leof ne wæs.
He ða mid þære sorhge,   sio þe him sare belamp,
gumdream ofgeaf,   Godes leoht geceas;
eaferum læfde,   swa deð eadig mon,   2470
lond ond leodbyrig,   þa he of life gewat.
    Þa wæs synn ond sacu   Sweona ond Geata,
ofer wid wæter   wroht gemæne,
herenið hearda,   syððan Hreðel swealt;
oððe him Ongenðeowes   eaferan wæran   2475
frome, fyrdhwate,   freode ne woldon
ofer heafo healdan,   ac ymb Hreosnabeorh
eatolne inwitscear   oft gefremedon.
Þæt mægwine   mine gewræcan,
fæhðe ond fyrene,   swa hyt gefræge wæs,   2480
þeah ðe oðer his   ealdre gebohte,
heardan ceape;   Hæðcynne wearð,
Geata dryhtne,   guð onsæge.
Þa ic on morgne gefrægn   mæg oðerne
billes ecgum   on bonan stælan,   2485
þær Ongenþeow   Eofores niosað;
guðhelm toglad,   gomela Scylfing
hreas heoroblac;   hond gemunde
fæhðo genoge,   feorhsweng ne ofteah.
    Ic him þa maðmas,   þe he me sealde,   2490
geald æt guðe,   swa me gifeðe wæs,
leohtan sweorde;   he me lond forgeaf,
eard, eðelwyn.   Næs him ænig þearf
þæt he to Gifðum   oððe to Gar-Denum
oððe in Swiorice   secean þurfe   2495
wyrsan wigfrecan,   weorðe gecypan.
Symle ic him on feðan   beforan wolde,
ana on orde;   ond swa to aldre sceall
sæcce fremman,   þenden þis sweord þolað,
þæt mec ær ond sið   oft gelæste,   2500

heroes in darkness; there is no sound of harp, mirth in the courts, as once there was—

35 —then he goes to his couch, chants a dirge for the lost one. The land and dwelling-place seemed all too roomy for him; so the Weders' protector felt sorrow welling in the heart for Herebeald; he could in no way settle the feud with the life-slayer; nor yet could he persecute the battle-warrior with acts of hatred, although he was not loved by him. Then with the sorrow which had befallen him he forsook the joys of men, chose God's light; when he passed from life he left his offspring, as a prosperous man does, land and the national stronghold.

After Hrethel died there was hostility and strife between Swedes and Geats, a mutual grievance across the broad water, severe warlike conflict; and the offspring of Ongentheow were brave, bold in war, wanted to keep no peace over the sea, but often committed dreadful malicious slaughter around Mares' Hill. As is well known, my dear kinsman avenged that feud and crime, although one of them bought it with his life, a hard bargain; the war was fatal to Hæth-cyn, leader of the Geats. I heard that then in the morning one kinsman took vengeance for the other with the edge of the sword on the slayer, when Ongentheow sought out Eofor;* the war-helmet split apart, the aged Scylfing fell, made pale by the sword; the hand remembered enough feuds, did not withold the mortal blow.

As it was granted me, I repaid with my bright sword in the battle the treasures he bestowed on me; he gave me estate, dwelling, delight in homeland. There was no need, not any cause, for him to seek out to hire for a price a worse fighting-man among the Gifthas* or among the Spear-Danes or in the Swedish kingdom. I would always go before him in the troop, alone in the van; and while life lasts I shall do battle for as long as this sword endures that has stood by me early and late, ever since I slew the Franks'

---

syððan ic for dugeðum   Dæghrefne wearð
to handbonan,   Huga cempan.
Nalles he ða frætwe   Frescyninge
breostweorðunge   bringan moste,
ac in campe gecrong   cumbles hyrde,   2505
æþeling on elne;   ne wæs ecg bona,
ac him hildegrap   heortan wylmas,
banhus gebræc.   Nu sceall billes ecg,
hond ond heard sweord   ymb hord wigan.'
Beowulf maðelode,   beotwordum spræc   2510
niehstan siðe: 'Ic geneðde fela
guða on geogoðe;   gyt ic wylle,
frod folces weard,   fæhðe secan,
mærðu fremman,   gif mec se mansceaða
of eorðsele   ut geseceð!'   2515
Gegrette ða   gumena gehwylcne,
hwate helmberend   hindeman siðe,
swæse gesiðas: 'Nolde ic sweord beran
wæpen to wyrme,   gif ic wiste hu
wið ðam aglæcean   elles meahte   2520
gylpe wiðgripan,   swa ic gio wið Grendle dyde;
ac ic ðær heaðufyres   hates wene,
oreðes ond attres;   forðon ic me on hafu
bord ond byrnan.   Nelle ic beorges weard
oferfleon fotes trem,   ac unc furður sceal   2525
weorðan æt wealle,   swa unc wyrd geteoð,
Metod manna gehwæs.   Ic eom on mode from,
þæt ic wið þone guðflogan   gylp ofersitte.
Gebide ge on beorge,   byrnum werede,
secgas on searwum,   hwæðer sel mæge   2530
æfter wælræse   wunde gedygan
uncer twega.   Nis þæt eower sið,
ne gemet mannes,   nefne min anes
þæt he wið aglæcean   eofoðo dæle,
eorlscype efne.   Ic mid elne sceall   2535
gold gegangan,   oððe guð nimeð,
feorhbealu frecne,   frean eowerne!'
Aras ða bi ronde   rof oretta,
heard under helme,   hiorosercean bær
under stancleofu,   strengo getruwode   2540
anes mannes;   ne bið swylc earges sið!
Geseah ða be wealle,   se ðe worna fela,
gumcystum god,   guða gedigde,

champion Dæghrefn with my hand in the presence of tried warriors. In no way could he bring to the Frisian king the ornament adorning the breast, but the standard-bearer fell in the contest, a prince with courage; nor was a sword-edge his slayer, but a warlike grip broke his heart's surge, his bone frame. Now the edge of the blade, hand and hard sword, must fight for the hoard.'

Beowulf spoke, uttered vaunting words for the last time: 'I engaged in many a war in my youth; an old guardian of the people, I will seek out the feud, achieve a deed of glory, if the wicked ravager will come out of the earthen hall to meet me!'

Then he addressed each of the men, bold helmet-bearers, dear companions, for the last time: 'I would not carry a sword, a weapon, against the serpent if I knew how else, in accordance with my boast, I could grapple with the monster as once I did with Grendel; but here I expect hot battle-fire and poisonous breath; therefore I have shield and mail-coat upon me. I will not retreat one footstep from the guardian of the barrow, but at the rampart it shall be for us both as fate, the Providence ruling every man, shall decree. I am resolute in spirit, so I will abstain from boasts against the war-flier. You wait on the barrow, men in armour, protected by mail-coats, to see which of us two can better endure wounds in the deadly onslaught. It is not your exploit, nor is it any man's measure but mine alone that he should pit strength against the monster, display heroism. I shall win the gold with courage, or else war, fierce deadly evil, will take your lord!'

Then the renowned champion rose, leaning on his shield, bold beneath his helmet, carried his mail-shirt beneath the rocky cliff, trusted in a single man's might—such is not the way of a coward! Then he who, great in manly virtues, had survived so many a war, crash of battle when troops clashed, saw arches of rock standing in

---

2503 Frescyninge: MS frescyning   2505 in campe: MS incempan   2514 mærðu: MS mærðū   2523 oreðes ond attres: MS reðes 7 hattres   2525 furður *supplied*   2532 nefne: MS nef . .; Thorkelin A and B nefu   2534 þæt: MS wat

hildehlemma,   þonne hnitan feðan,
stondan stanbogan,   stream ut þonan   2545
brecan of beorge;   wæs þære burnan wælm
heaðofyrum hat;   ne meahte horde neah
unbyrnende   ænige hwile
deop gedygan   for dracan lege.
Let ða of breostum,   ða he gebolgen wæs,   2550
Weder-Geata leod   word ut faran,
stearcheort styrmde;   stefn in becom
heaðotorht hlynnan   under harne stan.
Hete wæs onhrered,   hordweard oncniow
mannes reorde;   næs ðær mara fyrst   2555
freode to friclan.   From ærest cwom
oruð aglæcean   ut of stane
hat hildeswat;   hruse dynede.
Biorn under beorge   bordrand onswaf
wið ðam gryregieste,   Geata dryhten.   2560
Ða wæs hringbogan   heorte gefysed
sæcce to seceanne.   Sweord ær gebræd
god guðcyning,   gomele lafe,
ecgum ungleaw.   Æghwæðrum wæs
bealohycgendra   broga fram oðrum.   2565
Stiðmod gestod   wið steapne rond
winia bealdor,   ða se wyrm gebeah
snude tosomne;   he on searwum bad.
    Gewat ða byrnende   gebogen scriðan,
to gescipe scyndan.   Scyld wel gebearg   2570
life ond lice   læssan hwile
mærum þeodne   þonne his myne sohte;
ðær he þy fyrste   forman dogore
wealdan moste,   swa him wyrd ne gescraf
hreð æt hilde.   Hond up abræd   2575
Geata dryhten,   gryrefahne sloh
incgelafe,   þæt sio ecg gewac,
brun on bane,   bat unswiðor
þonne his ðiodcyning   þearfe hæfde,
bysigum gebæded.
                    Þa wæs beorges weard   2580
æfter heaðuswenge   on hreoum mode,
wearp wælfyre;   wide sprungon
hildeleoman.   Hreðsigora ne gealp
goldwine Geata;   guðbill geswac,
nacod æt niðe,   swa hyt no sceolde,   2585

the rampart through which a stream gushed out of the barrow; the surge of that brook was hot with deadly fire; because of the dragon's flame he could not survive for any length of time in the hollow near the hoard without being burned. Then, swollen with rage as he was, the prince of the Weder-Geats let a cry break forth from his breast: the stout-hearted stormed; clear in battle, the voice came roaring in beneath the grey rock. Hatred was aroused as the guardian of the hoard recognised human speech; there was no more time to sue for peace. First the monster's breath came out from the rock, a hot battle-vapour; the earth resounded. The man beneath the barrow, the leader of the Geats, swung his round shield against the terrible visitant. Then the heart of the coiled creature was incited to seek combat. The great war-king had already drawn his sword, an ancient heirloom very sharp of its edges. Each of them, intent on havoc, felt horror at the other. Resolute, the prince of friends stood by his tall shield while the serpent quickly coiled itself together; in his armour he waited.

Then burning, coiled, it went gliding out, hastened to its fate. The shield protected the famous prince well in life and limb for less time than he anticipated; there on that occasion for the first time he had to manage without fate assigning him triumph in battle. The leader of the Geats swung his hand, struck the patterned horror with the fine heirloom so that the burnished edge gave way on the bone, bit less strongly than the nation's king had need, hard-pressed by troubles.

Then as a result of the battle-blow the heart of the barrow's guardian was savage, threw out a deadly fire; the flames of battle sprang wide. The gold-friend of the Geats boasted of no glorious victories; the naked war-sword failed in combat as it should not

2545 stondan: MS stodan

iren ærgod.   Ne wæs þæt eðe sið,
þæt se mæra   maga Ecgðeowes
grundwong þone   ofgyfan wolde;
sceolde ofer willan   wic eardian
elles hwergen,   swa sceal æghwylc mon   2590
alætan lændagas.   Næs ða long to ðon,
þæt ða aglæcean   hy eft gemetton.
Hyrte hyne hordweard   —hreðer æðme weoll—
niwan stefne;   nearo ðrowode,
fyre befongen,   se ðe ær folce weold.   2595
   Nealles him on heape   handgesteallan,
æðelinga bearn   ymbe gestodon
hildecystum,   ac hy on holt bugon,
ealdre burgan.   Hiora in anum weoll
sefa wið sorgum;   sibb æfre ne mæg   2600
wiht onwendan   þam ðe wel þenceð.

XXXVI   Wiglaf wæs haten,   Weoxstanes sunu,
leoflic lindwiga,   leod Scylfinga,
mæg Ælfheres.   Geseah his mondryhten
under heregriman   hat þrowian.   2605
Gemunde ða ða are   þe he him ær forgeaf,
wicstede weligne   Wægmundinga,
folcrihta gehwylc,   swa his fæder ahte.
Ne mihte ða forhabban;   hond rond gefeng,
geolwe linde,   gomel swyrd geteah,   2610
þæt wæs mid eldum   Eanmundes laf,
suna Ohteres.   Þam æt sæcce wearð,
wræccan wineleasum,   Weohstan bana
meces ecgum,   ond his magum ætbær
brunfagne helm,   hringde byrnan,   2615
ealdsweord etonisc.   Þæt him Onela forgeaf,
his gædelinges   guðgewædu,
fyrdsearo fuslic;   no ymbe ða fæhðe spræc,
þeah ðe he his broðor bearn   abredwade.
He frætwe geheold   fela missera,   2620
bill ond byrnan,   oððæt his byre mihte
eorlscipe efnan   swa his ærfæder;
geaf him ða mid Geatum   guðgewæda
æghwæs unrim,   þa he of ealdre gewat,
frod on forðweg.   Þa wæs forma sið   2625
geongan cempan,   þæt he guðe ræs
mid his freodryhtne   fremman sceolde.

have done, iron of proven merit. It was no pleasant exploit, for the
famous kinsman of Ecgtheow would forsake the face of the earth;
against his will he must inhabit a dwelling in some other place,
just as every man must relinquish the days loaned him. It was
not long before they came together again, those terrible foes. The
guardian of the hoard took heart once again—its breast surged
with breath; encircled by fire, he who formerly ruled a nation
suffered severe straits.

In no way did his close companions, sons of princes, take up a
stand in a band around him with honour in battle, but they turned
to the wood, saved their lives. In one of them a spirit welled with
sorrows; nothing can ever set aside friendship in him who means
well.

36   He was called Wiglaf, son of Weohstan, a much-loved shield-
fighter, a prince of the Scylfings,* kinsman of Ælfhere. He saw
his leader of men suffer the heat beneath his war-visor. Then he
remembered the property which formerly he granted him, the
wealthy dwelling-place of the Wægmundings, each rightful share
of common land, such as his father possessed. He could not then
restrain himself; hand grasped shield, the yellow limewood, drew
an ancient sword that was known among men as an heirloom of
Ohthere's son Eanmund. In combat Weohstan had become his
slayer when a friendless exile, and carried off to his kinsmen a
brightly-burnished helmet, ringed mail, an ancient sword made by
ogres. Onela granted him all that—his relative's war-gear, ready
battle-trappings; he did not talk of a feud, although he had laid
low his brother's child. He kept the adornments, sword and coat
of mail, for many a season until his son was able to display heroism
like his father before him; then among the Geats he gave him
countless war-gear of all kinds when, aged, he passed away from
life on his journey hence. This was the first time for the young
champion that he had to stand the onslaught of war with his noble

2589 ofer *supplied*   2596 handgesteallan: MS heand gesteallan   2612 Ohteres:
MS ohtere   2613 wræccan: MS w . . . . .; Thorkelin A wræcca; Weohstan: MS
weohstanes

Ne gemealt him se modsefa,   ne his mæges laf
gewac æt wige.   Þæt se wyrm onfand,
syððan hie togædre   gegan hæfdon.   2630
   Wiglaf maðelode,   wordrihta fela
sægde gesiðum   —him wæs sefa geomor:
'Ic ðæt mæl geman,   þær we medu þegun,
þonne we geheton   ussum hlaforde
in biorsele,   ðe us ðas beagas geaf,   2635
þæt we him ða guðgetawa   gyldan woldon,
gif him þyslicu   þearf gelumpe,
helmas ond heard sweord.   Ðe he usic on herge geceas
to ðyssum siðfate   sylfes willum,
onmunde usic mærða,   ond me þas maðmas geaf,   2640
þe he usic garwigend   gode tealde,
hwate helmberend,   þeah ðe hlaford us
þis ellenweorc   ana aðohte
to gefremmanne,   folces hyrde,
forðam he manna mæst   mærða gefremede,   2645
dæda dollicra.
                  Nu is se dæg cumen
þæt ure mandryhten   mægenes behofað,
godra guðrinca.   Wutun gongan to,
helpan hildfruman,   þenden hyt sy,
gledegesa grim.   God wat on mec   2650
þæt me is micle leofre   þæt minne lichaman
mid minne goldgyfan   gled fæðmie.
Ne þynceð me gerysne   þæt we rondas beren
eft to earde,   nemne we æror mægen
fane gefyllan,   feorh ealgian   2655
Wedra ðeodnes.   Ic wat geare
þæt næron ealdgewyrht,   þæt he ana scyle
Geata duguðe   gnorn þrowian,
gesigan æt sæcce;   urum sceal sweord ond helm,
byrne ond beaduscrud   bam gemæne.'   2660
   Wod þa þurh þone wælrec,   wigheafolan bær
frean on fultum,   fea worda cwæð:
'Leofa Biowulf,   læst eall tela,
swa ðu on geoguðfeore   geara gecwæde
þæt ðu ne alæte   be ðe lifigendum   2665
dom gedreosan.   Scealt nu dædum rof,
æðeling anhydig,   ealle mægene
feorh ealgian;   ic ðe fullæstu!'
   Æfter ðam wordum   wyrm yrre cwom,

leader. His heart's spirit did not melt, nor did the heirloom of his kinsman fail in the fray. The serpent found that out after they had come together.

Wiglaf spoke, said many a fitting word to his companions—his spirit was mournful: 'I remember the occasion on which we drank mead, when in the beer-hall we promised our lord, who gave us these rings, that we would repay him for the war-equipment, the helmets and hard sword, if any such need as this were to befall him. For that reason he chose us of his own accord from the army for this adventure, thought us worthy of glories—and gave me these treasures—because he reckoned us good spear-fighters, bold helmet-bearers, though for our sake the lord, the people's guardian, thought to perform this deed of courage alone, since he of all men had achieved the greatest glories, audacious deeds.

Now the day has come when our leader of men has need of the strength of good warriors. Let us go forward, assist the battle-leader while the heat, the grim terrible fire, lasts. For myself, God knows that I would much prefer that coals of fire should embrace my flesh with my gold-giver. I do not think it proper that we should carry our shields back home unless we can first fell the foe, defend the life of the Weders' prince. I certainly know that his past deeds were not such that he alone among the tried warriors of the Geats should suffer distress, go down in combat; both of us shall together share sword and helmet, coat of mail and battle-clothing.'

Then he advanced through the deadly smoke, carried his war-helmet to the aid of his lord, spoke in few words: 'Beloved Beowulf, carry through all well, for long ago in the days of your youth you declared that you would never allow your reputation to decline for as long as you lived. Now, resolute prince, renowned for deeds, you must defend your life with all your might; I will aid you!'

After these words, the serpent, angry, a dreadful malicious

atol inwitgæst,   oðre siðe,   2670
fyrwylmum fah,   fionda niosian,
laðra manna.   Lig yðum for,
born bord wið rond;   byrne ne meahte
geongum garwigan   geoce gefremman;
ac se maga geonga   under his mæges scyld   2675
elne geeode,   þa his agen wæs
gledum forgrunden.   Þa gen guðcyning
mærða gemunde,   mægenstrengo sloh
hildebille,   þæt hyt on heafolan stod
niþe genyded.   Nægling forbærst;   2680
geswac æt sæcce   sweord Biowulfes,
gomol ond grægmæl.   Him þæt gifeðe ne wæs
þæt him irenna   ecge mihton
helpan æt hilde;   wæs sio hond to strong,
se ðe meca gehwane,   mine gefræge,   2685
swenge ofersohte,   þonne he to sæcce bær
wæpen wundum heard;   næs him wihte ðe sel.
    Þa wæs þeodsceaða   þriddan siðe,
frecne fyrdraca   fæhða gemyndig,
ræsde on ðone rofan,   þa him rum ageald;   2690
hat ond heaðogrim,   heals ealne ymbefeng
biteran banum;   he geblodegod wearð
sawuldriore;   swat yðum weoll.

XXXVII   Ða ic æt þearfe gefrægn   þeodcyninges
andlongne eorl   ellen cyðan,   2695
cræft ond cenðu,   swa him gecynde wæs.
Ne hedde he þæs heafolan,   ac sio hand gebarn
modiges mannes,   þær he his mæges healp
þæt he þone niðgæst   nioðor hwene sloh,
secg on searwum,   þæt ðæt sweord gedeaf,   2700
fah ond fæted,   þæt ðæt fyr ongon
sweðrian syððan.   Þa gen sylf cyning
geweold his gewitte,   wællseaxe gebræd,
biter ond beaduscearp,   þæt he on byrnan wæg;
forwrat Wedra helm   wyrm on middan.   2705
Feond gefyldan   —ferh ellen wræc—
ond hi hyne þa begen   abroten hæfdon,
sibæðelingas.   Swylc sceolde secg wesan,
þegn æt ðearfe!
                Þæt ðam þeodne wæs
siðast sigehwile   sylfes dædum,   2710

spirit, came on a second time, glowing with surges of fire, to seek out his enemies, the hated men. The fire advanced in waves, burned the shield right up to the boss; coat of mail could afford the young spear-fighter no help; but the young man courageously went behind his kinsman's shield when his own was destroyed by coals of fire. Then the war-king was again mindful of glorious deeds, struck with the war-sword in great strength so that, driven by violence, it stuck in the head. Nægling shattered; Beowulf's sword, old and patterned grey, failed in combat. It was not granted him that edges of iron might help him in the battle; the hand was too strong which, as I heard, over-taxed every blade with its stroke, when he carried into combat a weapon hardened with wounds; it was none the better for him.

Then a third time, when it had opportunity, the scourge of the nation, the dangerous fire-dragon, was mindful of feuds, rushed upon the brave man, hot and battle-grim, clenched his entire neck between sharp tusks; he became ensanguined with life-blood; gore welled up in waves.

37 Then, as I have heard, at the need of the nation's king the warrior by his side displayed courage, skill and daring, as was natural to him. He did not bother about the head, so the hand of the brave man, warrior in armour, was burned as he helped his kinsman by striking the spiteful creature somewhat lower down, so that the sword, shining and plated, sank in, so that thereupon the fire began to abate. Then the king himself, again in control of his senses, drew the deadly knife, keen and battle-sharp, that he wore on his mail; the protector of the Weders cut the serpent open in the middle. They felled the foe—courage had driven out its life—and they had cut it down together, kindred noblemen. That is what a man should be, a thane in time of need!

For the prince that was the moment of victory, brought about

---

worlde geweorces. Ða sio wund ongon,
þe him se eorðdraca   ær geworhte,
swelan ond swellan;   he þæt sona onfand,
þæt him on breostum   bealoniðe weoll
attor on innan.   Ða se æðeling giong,   2715
þæt he bi wealle,   wishycgende,
gesæt on sesse;   seah on enta geweorc,
hu ða stanbogan   stapulum fæste
ece eorðreced   innan healde.
Hyne þa mid handa,   heorodreorigne,   2720
þeoden mærne,   þegn ungemete till,
winedryhten his   wætere gelafede,
hildesædne,   ond his helm onspeon.

   Biowulf maþelode   —he ofer benne spræc,
wunde wælbleate;   wisse he gearwe   2725
þæt he dæghwila   gedrogen hæfde,
eorðan wynne;   ða wæs eall sceacen
dogorgerimes,   deað ungemete neah:
'Nu ic suna minum   syllan wolde
guðgewædu,   þær me gifeðe swa   2730
ænig yrfeweard   æfter wurde,
lice gelenge.   Ic ðas leode heold
fiftig wintra;   næs se folccyning,
ymbesittendra   ænig ðara,
þe mec guðwinum   gretan dorste,   2735
egesan ðeon.   Ic on earde bad
mælgesceafta,   heold min tela,
ne sohte searoniðas,   ne me swor fela
aða on unriht.   Ic ðæs ealles mæg,
feorhbennum seoc,   gefean habban;   2740
forðam me witan ne ðearf   Waldend fira
morðorbealo maga,   þonne min sceaceð
lif of lice.
            Nu ðu lungre geong
hord sceawian   under harne stan,
Wiglaf leofa,   nu se wyrm ligeð,   2745
swefeð sare wund,   since bereafod.
Bio nu on ofoste,   þæt ic ærwelan,
goldæht ongite,   gearo sceawige
swegle searogimmas,   þæt ic ðy seft mæge
æfter maððumwelan   min alætan   2750
lif ond leodscipe,   þone ic longe heold.'

by his own deeds—work in the world. Then the wound which the earth-dragon had inflicted on him earlier began to burn and swell; straight away he found that the poison within welled up with deadly evil in his breast. Then thinking deeply, the prince went till he sat on a bank by the rampart; he looked at the giant's work—how the enduring earthen hall held within it stone arches fast on pillars. Then with his hands that most excellent thane bathed his friend and leader, the famous prince, blood-stained, sated with battle, and unfastened his helmet.

Beowulf spoke—talked despite his hurt, pitiful mortal wound; he knew well enough that he had come to the end of his span of days, joy in the earth; then all the number of his days was passed away, death exceedingly near: 'I would have wanted to present the war-garb to my son, if it had been granted that any heir belonging to my body should succeed me. I held this nation for fifty winters; there was no nation's king among those dwelling around who dared approach me with allies in war, threaten with terror. At home I awaited what was destined, held well what was mine, sought no treacherous quarrels, nor did I unjustly swear many oaths. Sick with mortal wounds, I can rejoice in all this; indeed, when life passes from my body, the Ruler of men has no cause to blame me for the wicked murder of kinsmen.

Now you go quickly, beloved Wiglaf, to examine the hoard beneath the grey rock, now that the serpent lies low, sleeping from a grievous wound, bereft of treasure. Make haste now, so that I may appreciate the ancient wealth, gold possessions, may eagerly examine the brilliant precious jewels, so that because of the treasure's richness I may the more easily leave my life and country which I have held for so long.'

2714 bealoniðe: MS beal . . . . .; Thorkelin B bealoniði   2723 helm: MS he . .; Thorkelin A helo   2727 wynne: MS wyn . .; Thorkelin A wym, Thorkelin B wyni

XXXVIII   Ða ic snude gefrægn   sunu Wihstanes
aefter wordcwydum   wundum dryhtne
hyran heaðosiocum,   hringnet beran,
brogdne beadusercean   under beorges hrof.   *2755*
Geseah ða sigehreðig,   þa he bi sesse geong,
magoþegn modig   maððumsigla fealo,
gold glitinian   grunde getenge,
wundur on wealle   geond þæs wyrmes denn,
ealdes uhtflogan,   orcas stondan,   *2760*
fyrnmanna fatu,   feormendlease,
hyrstum behrorene.   Þær wæs helm monig,
eald ond omig,   earmbeaga fela,
searwum gesæled.   Sinc eaðe mæg,
gold on grunde,   gumcynnes gehwone   *2765*
oferhigian,   hyde se ðe wylle!
    Swylce he siomian geseah   segn eallgylden
heah ofer horde,   hondwundra mæst,
gelocen leoðocræftum;   of ðam leoma stod,
þæt he þone grundwong   ongitan meahte,   *2770*
wræte giondwlitan.   Næs ðæs wyrmes þær
onsyn ænig,   ac hyne ecg fornam.
Ða ic on hlæwe gefrægn   hord reafian,
eald enta geweorc   anne mannan,
him on bearm hladon   bunan ond discas   *2775*
sylfes dome;   segn eac genom,
beacna beorhtost.   Bill ær gescod
—ecg wæs iren—   ealdhlafordes
þam ðara maðma   mundbora wæs
longe hwile,   ligegesan wæg   *2780*
hatne for horde,   hioroweallende
middelnihtum,   oðþæt he morðre swealt.
    Ar wæs on ofoste,   eftsiðes georn,
frætwum gefyrðred;   hyne fyrwet bræc,
hwæðer collenferð   cwicne gemette   *2785*
in ðam wongstede   Wedra þeoden
ellensiocne,   þær he hine ær forlet.
He ða mid þam maðmum   mærne þioden,
dryhten sinne   driorigne fand,
ealdres æt ende.   He hine eft ongon   *2790*
wæteres weorpan,   oðþæt wordes ord
breosthord þurhbræc.
                    Þa se beorn gespræc,
gomel on giohðe   —gold sceawode:

38 Then, I heard, after this speech Weohstan's son quickly obeyed his wounded leader, injured in combat, carried his ring-mail, the woven battle-shirt, beneath the roof of the barrow. Then as he went along the bank, the brave young thane, exulting in victory, saw many a precious jewel, gold glittering lying on the ground, wonderful things on the wall throughout the lair of the serpent, the ancient pre-dawn flier, pitchers standing, the vessels of men of old, stripped of their ornaments, lacking a polisher. There was many an old and rusty helmet, many a bracelet skilfully twisted. Treasure, gold in the earth, can easily overwhelm any of the human race, hide it who will!

Also he saw hanging high above the hoard a banner, all gold, the finest of wonderful hand-wrought things, woven with the fingers' skill; from it there shone a light so that he could discern the level ground, survey the works of art. There was not any sign of the serpent there, for the blade's edge had carried him off. Then, I heard, one man plundered the hoard in the mound, the ancient work of giants, loaded his bosom with bowls and dishes at his own choice; he also took the banner, the brightest of signs. The aged lord's sword—its edge was iron*—had earlier injured that which for a long time had been guardian of the treasures, carried hot flaming terror for the sake of the hoard, fiercely welling up in the middle of the night, until it died a violent death.

The messenger made haste, eager to return, urged on by the ornaments; anxiety pricked him, a man bold in spirit, as to whether he would find the Weders' prince, deprived of strength, still alive in the place where earlier he had left him. Then with those treasures he found the famous prince his leader, dripping with blood, at the end of his life. Again he began to splash him with water, until the beginning of speech broke from his breast's hoard.

Then the hero spoke, an aged man in distress—examined the

---

²⁷⁵⁵ under: MS urder   ²⁷⁵⁹ geond: MS 7   ²⁷⁶⁵ grunde: MS gr . . . .; Thorkelin A and B grund   ²⁷⁶⁹ leoma: MS leoman   ²⁷⁷¹ wræte: MS wræce ²⁷⁷⁵ hladon: MS hlo . . .; Thorkelin B hlodon   ²⁷⁹²ᵇ *supplied*   ²⁷⁹³ giohðe: MS giogoðe

'Ic ðara frætwa   Frean ealles ðanc,
Wuldurcyninge,   wordum secge,   2795
ecum Dryhtne,   þe ic her on starie,
þæs ðe ic moste   minum leodum
ær swyltdæge   swylc gestrynan.
Nu ic on maðma hord   minne bebohte
frode feorhlege,   fremmað gena   2800
leoda þearfe;   ne mæg ic her leng wesan!
Hatað heaðomære   hlæw gewyrcean,
beorhtne æfter bæle   æt brimes nosan;
se scel to gemyndum   minum leodum
heah hlifian   on Hronesnæsse,   2805
þæt hit sæliðend   syððan hatan
Biowulfes biorh,   ða ðe brentingas
ofer floda genipu   feorran drifað.'
   Dyde him of healse   hring gyldenne
þioden þristhydig,   þegne gesealde,   2810
geongum garwigan,   goldfahne helm,
beah ond byrnan,   het hyne brucan well.
'Þu eart endelaf   usses cynnes,
Wægmundinga;   ealle wyrd forsweop
mine magas   to metodsceafte,   2815
eorlas on elne;   ic him æfter sceal.'
   Þæt wæs þam gomelan   gingæste word
breostgehygdum,   ær he bæl cure,
hate heaðowylmas;   him of hræðre gewat
sawol secean   soðfæstra dom.   2820

XXXIX   Ða wæs gegongen   guman unfrodum
earfoðlice,   þæt he on eorðan geseah
þone leofestan   lifes æt ende,
bleate gebæran.   Bona swylce læg,
egeslic eorðdraca,   ealdre bereafod,   2825
bealwe gebæded.   Beahhordum leng
wyrm wohbogen   wealdan ne moste,
ac hine irenna   ecga fornamon,
hearde, heaðoscearde,   homera lafe,
þæt se widfloga   wundum stille   2830
hreas on hrusan   hordærne neah.
Nalles æfter lyfte   lacende hwearf
middelnihtum,   maðmæhta wlonc
ansyn ywde;   ac he eorðan gefeoll
for ðæs hildfruman   hondgeweorce.   2835

gold: 'I give words of thanks to the Lord of all, the King of Glory, eternal Ruler, for these adornments which I gaze on here, that I was able to acquire such things for my people before the moment of death. Now that I have paid for the hoard of treasures with the life allotted me, you must attend to the people's needs henceforth; I can remain here no longer! Bid those famous for war to build a fine mound after the pyre on the headland by the sea; it shall tower high on Whale's Cape as a remembrance to my people, so that seafarers when they drive their tall ships from afar across the mists of the flood will thereafter call it Beowulf's Barrow.'

The valiant prince took the golden collar from his neck, presented to the thane, the young spear-fighter, gold-adorned helmet, ring and coat of mail, bade him make good use of them. 'You are the last left of our race, the Wægmundings; fate has swept away all my kinsmen, courageous warriors, as destiny decreed; I must follow them.'

That was the aged man's final word from the thoughts of his heart before he was to choose the pyre, hot, fierce surges; the soul passed from his breast to seek the glory of the righteous.

39 Then it went hard with the young man when he saw the most beloved on the ground at the end of his life in a pitiful condition. The slayer, the terrible earth-dragon, likewise lay dead, bereft of life, overwhelmed in destruction. The coiled serpent could no longer rule the ring-hoard, but edges of iron, hard, notched by battle, the hammers' legacy, had carried it off, so that the wide-flier, stilled by wounds, had sunk to the earth near the treasure-house. In no way did it whirl, playing in the air in the middle of the night, display its form, proud of precious possessions; but it fell to the ground as a result of the war-leader's handiwork. Yet, so

2814 forsweop: MS for speof   2819 hræðre: MS hwæðre   2821 *fitt number supplied*; guman: MS gumū   2828 hine: MS him

Huru þæt on lande   lyt manna ðah,
mægenagendra,   mine gefræge,
þeah ðe he dæda gehwæs   dyrstig wære,
þæt he wið attorsceaðan   oreðe geræsde,
oððe hringsele   hondum styrede,   2840
gif he wæccende   weard onfunde
buon on beorge.   Biowulfe wearð
dryhtmaðma dæl   deaðe forgolden;
hæfde æghwæðer   ende gefered
lænan lifes.
                    Næs ða lang to ðon   2845
þæt ða hildlatan   holt ofgefan,
tydre treowlogan   tyne ætsomne,
ða ne dorston ær   dareðum lacan
on hyra mandryhtnes   miclan þearfe;
ac hy scamiende   scyldas bæran,   2850
guðgewædu,   þær se gomela læg;
wlitan on Wilaf.   He gewergad sæt,
feðecempa,   frean eaxlum neah,
wehte hyne wætre;   him wiht ne speow.
Ne meahte he on eorðan,   ðeah he uðe wel,   2855
on ðam frumgare   feorh gehealdan,
ne ðæs Wealdendes   wiht oncirran.
Wolde dom Godes   dædum rædan
gumena gehwylcum,   swa he nu gen deð.
    Þa wæs æt ðam geongan   grim andswaru   2860
eðbegete   þam ðe ær his elne forleas.
Wiglaf maðelode,   Weohstanes sunu,
sec, sarigferð   —seah on unleofe:
'Þæt la mæg secgan,   se ðe wyle soð specan,
þæt se mondryhten   se eow ða maðmas geaf,   2865
eoredgeatwe,   þe ge þær on standað,
þonne he on ealubence   oft gesealde
healsittendum   helm ond byrnan,
þeoden his þegnum,   swylce he þrydlicost
ower feor oððe neah   findan meahte,   2870
þæt he genunga   guðgewædu
wraðe forwurpe,   ða hyne wig beget.
Nealles folccyning   fyrdgesteallum
gylpan þorfte;   hwæðre him God uðe,
sigora Waldend,   þæt he hyne sylfne gewræc,   2875
ana mid ecge,   þa him wæs elnes þearf.
Ic him lifwraðe   lytle meahte

far as I have heard, there was no man possessed of strength in the land, daring in every action though he were, whom it benefited to rush against the breath of the poisonous scourge, or to disturb the ring-hall with his hands, if he found the guardian awake who dwelt in the barrow. The mass of noble treasures was paid for by Beowulf with death; they had each come to the end of this transitory life.

It was not long then before those slow to do battle forsook the wood, ten frail faith-breakers together, who earlier did not dare bring darts into play at their leader's great need; but, ashamed, they carried their shields, battle-dress, to where the aged man lay dead; they gazed at Wiglaf. Exhausted he sat, the foot-soldier, by the shoulders of his lord, sought to rouse him with water; he did not succeed at all. Dearly though he would wish, he could not keep earthly life in the chieftain, nor turn aside anything ordained by the Ruler. The judgement of God would rule the actions of every man, as he still does.

Then it was easy to get from the young man a grim answer to him who earlier lost his courage. Wiglaf the son of Weohstan spoke, sick, sad in spirit—looked at the unloved ones: 'Well, he who wants to speak the truth can say that the leader of men who gave you those treasures, the war-equipment with which you stand there—when he, as a prince to his thanes, often presented helmet and mail-coat to those sitting on ale-benches in the hall, of the most splendid kind he could find anywhere, far or near— that, when conflict befell him, he had woefully completely thrown away the war-gear. The people's king had no reason at all to boast about comrades in arms; however, God, the Ruler of victories, granted him that when there was need for courage he avenged himself alone with the edge of the sword. I could do little to

---

2844 æghwæðer: MS æghwæðre   2854 speow: MS speop   2860 geongan: MS geongū   2863 secg: MS sec

ætgifan æt guðe,   ond ongan swa þeah
ofer min gemet   mæges helpan.
Symle wæs þy sæmra,   þonne ic sweorde drep   2880
ferhðgeniðlan,   fyr unswiðor
weoll of gewitte.   Wergendra to lyt
þrong ymbe þeoden,   þa hyne sio þrag becwom.
Nu sceal sincþego   ond swyrdgifu,
eall eðelwyn   eowrum cynne,   2885
lufen alicgean;   londrihtes mot
þære mægburge   monna æghwylc
idel hweorfan,   syððan æðelingas
feorran gefricgean   fleam eowerne,
domleasan dæd.   Deað bið sella   2890
eorla gehwylcum   þonne edwitlif!'

XL   Heht ða þæt heaðoweorc   to hagan biodan
up ofer ecgclif,   þær þæt eorlweorod
morgenlongne dæg   modgiomor sæt,
bordhæbbende,   bega on wenum,   2895
endedogores   ond eftcymes
leofes monnes.   Lyt swigode
niwra spella,   se ðe næs gerad,
ac he soðlice   sægde ofer ealle:
'Nu is wilgeofa   Wedra leoda,   2900
dryhten Geata   deaðbedde fæst,
wunað wælreste   wyrmes dædum.
Him on efn ligeð   ealdorgewinna
siexbennum seoc;   sweorde ne meahte
on ðam aglæcean   ænige þinga   2905
wunde gewyrcean.   Wiglaf siteð
ofer Biowulfe,   byre Wihstanes,
eorl ofer oðrum   unlifigendum,
healdeð higemæðum   heafodwearde,
leofes ond laðes.
                    Nu ys leodum wen   2910
orleghwile,   syððan underne
Froncum ond Frysum   fyll cyninges
wide weorðeð.   Wæs sio wroht scepen
heard wið Hugas,   syððan Higelac cwom
faran flotherge   on Fresna land,   2915
þær hyne Hetware   hilde genægdon,
elne geeodon   mid ofermægene,
þæt se byrnwiga   bugan sceolde;

protect his life in the battle, but nevertheless I undertook beyond my measure to help my kinsman. When I struck the deadly foe with the sword it was ever the weaker, the fire surged less strongly from its head. Too few defenders thronged about the prince when the evil time came upon him. Now the receiving of treasure and giving of swords, all delight in native land, beloved home, must cease for your race; once princes afar off should hear of your flight, inglorious action, every man of the tribe will have to wander, stripped of rights in the land.* To any warrior death is better than a life of disgrace!'

40 Then he commanded that the deed of battle be announced to the enclosure high on the cliff-edge, where the warriors, troop of shield-bearers, sat mournful at heart all morning long, expecting one of two things: the last day or the return of the beloved man. He who rode to the headland kept back little of the new tidings, but spoke truthfully in the hearing of them all:

'Now he who grants the desires of the people of the Weders, the leader of the Geats, is fast on his death-bed, lies on a couch of slaughter, as a result of the serpent's actions. At his side lies the deadly enemy stricken with knife-wounds; with his sword he could not inflict injury of any kind on the monster. Wiglaf son of Weohstan sits by Beowulf, one warrior by the lifeless other, in weariness of heart keeps watch by the heads of friend and of foe.

Now the people can expect a period of conflict, once the fall of the king becomes openly known abroad among Franks and Frisians. The bitter grievance against the Hugas was brought about when Hygelac came journeying with a sea-borne army into the land of the Frisians, where the Hetware subdued him in battle, with greater forces brought it about that the mailed fighter had to bow

---

2882 Wergendra: MS fergendra   2884 Nu: MS hu   2911 underne: MS under
2916 genægdon: MS gehnægdon

feoll on feðan,   nalles frætwe geaf
ealdor dugoðe.   Us wæs a syððan   2920
Merewigingas   milts ungyfeðe.

Ne ic te Sweoðeode   sibbe oððe treowe
wihte ne wene;   ac wæs wide cuð
þætte Ongenðio   ealdre besnyðede
Hæðcen Hreþling   wið Hrefnawudu,   2925
þa for onmedlan   ærest gesohton
Geata leode   Guð-Scilfingas.
Sona him se froda   fæder Ohtheres,
eald ond egesfull,   ondslyht ageaf,
abreot brimwisan,   bryd ahredde   2930
gomela iomeowlan   golde berofene,
Onelan modor   ond Ohtheres;
ond ða folgode   feorhgeniðlan,
oððæt hi oðeodon   earfoðlice
in Hrefnesholt   hlafordlease.   2935

Besæt ða sinherge   sweorda lafe,
wundum werge;   wean oft gehet
earmre teohhe   ondlonge niht,
cwæð he on mergenne   meces ecgum
getan wolde,   sume on galgtreowum   2940
fuglum to gamene.   Frofor eft gelamp
sarigmodum   somod ærdæge,
syððan hie Hygelaces   horn ond byman,
gealdor ongeaton,   þa se goda com
leoda dugoðe   on last faran.   2945

XLI   Wæs sio swatswaðu   Sweona ond Geata
wælræs weora   wide gesyne,
hu ða folc mid him   fæhðe towehton.
Gewat him ða se goda   mid his gædelingum,
frod felageomor   fæsten secean;   2950
eorl Ongenþio   ufor oncirde.
Hæfde Higelaces   hilde gefrunen,
wlonces wigcræft;   wiðres ne truwode,
þæt he sæmannum   onsacan mihte,
heaðoliðendum,   hord forstandan,   2955
bearn ond bryde;   beah eft þonan
eald under eorðweall.
            Þa wæs aht boden
Sweona leodum,   segn Higelaces
freoðowong þone   forð ofereodon,

in death; the chieftain fell in the troop, in no way gave adornments to tried warriors. The favour of the Merovingian has been denied us ever since.*

Nor do I expect the least friendship or loyalty from the Swedish nation;* for it was widely known that Ongentheow took the life of Hæthcyn Hrethling near Ravenswood when the men of the Geats in their arrogance first went looking for the War-Scylfings. Straight away Ohthere's wise father, old and terrible, struck a return blow, cut down the sea-king; he rescued the aged woman, his wife of former years, the mother of Onela and Ohthere, stripped of gold; and then he pursued his mortal enemies until with difficulty they escaped into Ravenswood without their lord.

Then with a great army he besieged those whom the swords had left, exhausted with wounds; frequently throughout the night he promised miseries to the wretched band, said that in the morning he would cut them to pieces with the blade's edge—some on gallows-trees as sport for the birds. Together with daybreak comfort returned to their grieving minds when they heard Hygelac's battle-cry, horn and trumpet, as the great man came following their track with the tried warriors of the people.

41 The bloody trail of Swedes and Geats, the deadly onslaught of men, was widely visible—how those peoples had awakened the feud between them. Then old, mourning much, the great man went with his kinsmen to seek his stronghold; the warrior Ongentheow turned aside to higher ground. He had heard of Hygelac's warfare, the proud man's skill in battle; he did not trust in resistance, that he could fight off the seamen, defend hoard, women and children from the war-voyagers; thence the old man drew back behind an earthen rampart.

Then pursuit was given to the people of the Swedes, Hygelac's banners over-ran the place of refuge once the Hrethlings pressed

---

2921 Merewigingas: MS mere wio ingas   2929 ondslyht: MS hondslyht   2930 bryd ahredde: MS bryda heorde   2940 sume on galgtreowum: MS sum on galg treowu   2941 fuglum *supplied*   2946 Sweona: MS swona   2958 Higelaces: MS higelace   2959 forð: MS ford

syððan Hreðlingas   to hagan þrungon.   2960
Þær wearð Ongenðiow   ecgum sweorda,
blondenfexa   ond bid wrecen,
þæt se þeodcyning   ðafian sceolde
Eafores anne dom.   Hyne yrringa
Wulf Wonreding   wæpne geræhte,   2965
þæt him for swenge   swat ædrum sprong
forð under fexe.   Næs he forht swa ðeh,
gomela Scilfing,   ac forgeald hraðe
wyrsan wrixle   wælhlem þone,
syððan ðeodcyning   þyder oncirde.   2970
Ne meahte se snella   sunu Wonredes
ealdum ceorle   ondslyht giofan,
ac he him on heafde   helm ær gescer,
þæt he blode fah   bugan sceolde,
feoll on foldan.   Næs he fæge þa git,   2975
ac he hyne gewyrpte,   þeah ðe him wund hrine.
Let se hearda   Higelaces þegn
bradne mece,   þa his broðor læg,
ealdsweord eotonisc,   entiscne helm
brecan ofer bordweal;   ða gebeah cyning,   2980
folces hyrde   wæs in feorh dropen.
    Ða wæron monige   þe his mæg wriðon,
ricone arærdon,   ða him gerymed wearð,
þæt hie wælstowe   wealdan moston.
Þenden reafode   rinc oðerne,   2985
nam on Ongenðio   irenbyrnan,
heard swyrd hilted   ond his helm somod;
hares hyrste   Higelace bær.
He ðam frætwum feng   ond him fægre gehet
leana mid leodum,   ond gelæste swa;   2990
geald þone guðræs   Geata dryhten,
Hreðles eafora,   þa he to ham becom,
Iofore ond Wulfe   mid ofermaðmum;
sealde hiora gehwæðrum   hund þusenda
landes ond locenra beaga
                        —ne ðorfte him ða lean oðwitan 2995
mon on middangearde—   syððan hie ða mærða geslogon;
ond ða Iofore forgeaf   angan dohtor,
hamweorðunge,   hyldo to wedde.
    Þæt ys sio fæhðo   ond se feondscipe,
wælnið wera,   ðæs ðe ic wen hafo,   3000
þe us seceað to   Sweona leoda,

forward to the enclosure. There the white-haired Ongentheow was
brought to bay by the edges of swords, so that the nation's king
had to consent to the sole decree of Eofor. Wulf Wonreding had
struck him angrily with his weapon so that as a result of the blow,
blood spurted forth from the veins beneath his hair. However, he
was not afraid, the aged Scylfing, but once he turned towards him,
the nation's king swiftly repaid the deadly blow with a worse
exchange. Wonred's brave son could not give the old fellow a
return blow, for he had first sheared through the helmet on his head,
so that he had to sink down, stained with blood—fell to the ground.
He was not yet doomed, for he recovered, though the wound hurt
him. As his brother lay there, the stern thane of Hygelac let his
broad blade, an ancient sword made by ogres, break the gigantic
helmet behind the shield-wall; then the king sank down, the
people's guardian was mortally stricken.

When it was open to them that they might control the place of
slaughter, there were many who bandaged his kinsman, speedily
lifted him up. Meanwhile, one warrior plundered the other, took
from Ongentheow iron coat of mail, hard hilted sword, and his
helmet as well; he carried the grizzled man's equipment to
Hygelac. He accepted the trappings and courteously promised him
rewards among the people, and fulfilled it thus; when he came home
the leader of the Geats, Hrethel's offspring, repaid Eofor and Wulf
for that battle-onslaught with copious treasures; he bestowed on
each of them a hundred thousands'-worth* of land and linked
rings—no man on earth need reproach him for those rewards—
after they had achieved fame by fighting; and then he gave Eofor
his only daughter, an ornament to the home, as a pledge of good
faith.

That is the feud and the enmity, deadly hatred of men, for
which I expect the people of the Swedes will come looking for us,

2961 sweorda: MS sweordū   2972 ondslyht: MS hondslyht   2978 bradne:
MS brade   2989 ðam: MS ð . .   2990 mid *restored*; gelæste: MS gelæsta
2996 syððan: MS syðða   3000 wen *supplied*

syððan hie gefricgeað   frean userne
ealdorleasne,   þone ðe ær geheold
wið hettendum   hord ond rice
æfter hæleða hryre,   hwate Scildingas,   3005
folcred fremede   oððe furður gen
eorlscipe efnde.
                    Nu is ofost betost
þæt we þeodcyning   þær sceawian
ond þone gebringan,   þe us beagas geaf,
on adfære.   Ne scel anes hwæt   3010
meltan mid þam modigan,   ac þær is maðma hord,
gold unrime,   grimme geceapod;
ond nu æt siðestan   sylfes feore
beagas gebohte.   Þa sceall brond fretan,
æled þeccean   —nalles eorl wegan   3015
maððum to gemyndum,   ne mægð scyne
habban on healse   hringweorðunge;
ac sceal geomormod,   golde bereafod,
oft, nalles æne,   elland tredan,
nu se herewisa   hleahtor alegde,   3020
gamen ond gleodream.   Forðon sceall gar wesan
monig morgenceald   mundum bewunden,
hæfen on handa,   nalles hearpan sweg
wigend weccean,   ac se wonna hrefn
fus ofer fægum   fela reordian,   3025
earne secgan   hu him æt æte speow,
þenden he wið wulf   wæl reafode.'
    Swa se secg hwata   secggende wæs
laðra spella;   he ne leag fela
wyrda ne worda.   Weorod eall aras;   3030
eodon unbliðe   under Earnanæs
wollenteare,   wundur sceawian.
Fundon ða on sande   sawulleasne
hlimbed healdan,   þone þe him hringas geaf
ærran mælum;   þa wæs endedæg   3035
godum gegongen,   þæt se guðcyning,
Wedra þeoden,   wundordeaðe swealt.
    Ær hi þær gesegan   syllicran wiht,
wyrm on wonge   wiðerræhtes þær,
laðne licgean;   wæs se legdraca,   3040
grimlic gryrefah,   gledum beswæled.
Se wæs fiftiges   fotgemearces
lang on legere;   lyftwynne heold

once they hear that our lord has lost his life—he who earlier held
hoard and kingdom against those who hated us, after the fall of
heroes furthered the good of the people, the bold Scyldings,* and
displayed still more heroism.

Now it is best to make haste that we may look there upon the
nation's king and bring him, who gave us rings, on his way to the
pyre. Not just a single share shall melt away with the brave man,
for there is a hoard of treasures, countless gold, grimly purchased;
and now in the end he has bought these rings with his own life.
These the fire shall devour, flame enfold—no warrior to wear a
jewel in remembrance, no bright girl to have the adornment of rings
about her neck; but mournful at heart, stripped of gold, they will
have to tread an alien land, not once but often, now that the leader
of armies has laid aside laughter, merriment and joyful mirth.
Wherefore many a spear, chill in the morning, shall be grasped
with the fists, lifted in the hand—in no way shall the sound of the
harp awaken the fighting-men, but the dark raven, eager for the
doomed, shall speak of much, tell the eagle how he fared at
the meal when with the wolf he plundered the slain.'

Thus the bold man was the teller of grievous news; he did not
much lie in respect of facts or words. The whole company rose up;
unhappy, they went below Eagles' Crag to gaze on the wondrous
sight with welling tears. Then they found the lifeless man on the
sand, keeping to his bed of rest, he who had given them rings in
former times; the final day had come to pass for the great man then,
when the war-king, the prince of the Weders, perished by a
wondrous death.

First they saw there a very remarkable creature, the loathsome
serpent lying on the open ground there opposite; the fiery dragon,
terrible patterned horror, was scorched with live coals. It measured
fifty feet long as it lay; at one time it had delight in the air by night,

nihtes hwilum,   nyðer eft gewat
dennes niosian;   wæs ða deaðe fæst,   3045
hæfde eorðscrafa   ende genyttod.
    Him big stodan   bunan ond orcas,
discas lagon   ond dyre swyrd,
omige, þurhetone,   swa hie wið eorðan fæðm
þusend wintra   þær eardodon.   3050
Þonne wæs þæt yrfe   eacencræftig,
iumonna gold,   galdre bewunden,
þæt ðam hringsele   hrinan ne moste
gumena ænig,   nefne God sylfa,
sigora Soðcyning,   sealde þam ðe he wolde   3055
—he is manna gehyld—   hord openian,
efne swa hwylcum manna   swa him gemet ðuhte.

XLII   Þa wæs gesyne   þæt se sið ne ðah
þam ðe unrihte   inne gehydde,
wræce under wealle.   Weard ær ofsloh
feara sumne;   þa sio fæhð gewearð
gewrecen wraðlice.   Wundur hwar þonne
eorl ellenrof   ende gefere
lifgesceafta,   þonne leng ne mæg
mon mid his magum   meduseld buan.   3065
Swa wæs Biowulfe,   þa he biorges weard
sohte, searoniðas;   seolfa ne cuðe
þurh hwæt his worulde gedal   weorðan sceolde.
Swa hit oð domes dæg   diope benemdon
þeodnas mære,   þa ðæt þær dydon,   3070
þæt se secg wære   synnum scildig,
hergum geheaðerod,   hellbendum fæst,
wommum gewitnad,   se ðone wong strude.
Næs he goldhwæte   gearwor hæfde
agendes est   ær gesceawod.   3075
    Wiglaf maðelode,   Wihstanes sunu:
'Oft sceall eorl monig   anes willan
wræc adreogan,   swa us geworden is.
Ne meahton we gelæran   leofne þeoden,
rices hyrde   ræd ænigne,   3080
þæt he ne grette   goldweard þone,
lete hyne licgean   þær he longe wæs,
wicum wunian   oð woruldende;
heold on heahgesceap.
                        Hord ys gesceawod,

came down again to seek out its den; then it was fixed by death, had made its last use of earthen caverns.

Beside it stood bowls and pitchers, dishes and precious swords lying rusty, eaten through, as if they had rested a thousand winters there in the bosom of the earth. Moreover, that exceedingly great heritage, the gold from men of years gone by, was bound by an incantation, so that no man could touch the ring-hall unless God himself, the true King of victories—he is the protection of men—should grant to him whom he wished, whatever man seemed fit to him, power to open the hoard.

42 It was evident then that the venture had not benefited the creature that wrongfully kept hidden within, in misery beneath the rampart. Earlier the guardian had slain a man like few others; the feud was then cruelly avenged. It is a mystery where a warrior renowned for courage may meet the end of his destined life, when a man may no longer dwell in the mead-hall with his kinsmen. So it was with Beowulf when he sought out the barrow's guardian, a treacherous contest; he himself did not know by what means his departure from the world should be brought about. The famous princes who put it there had laid a curse,* that until doomsday the man who should pillage the place would be guilty of sin, confined in pagan shrines, fast in hell-bonds, punished with evils. He had never before examined more eagerly the owner's legacy, abundant gold.*

Wiglaf spoke, the son of Weohstan: 'Often many a warrior has to endure distress owing to the will of one man, as has befallen us. By no counsel could we persuade the beloved prince, guardian of the kingdom, not to approach the keeper of the gold, but let it lie where it had long been, to live in its dwelling until the world's end; he kept to his great destiny.

The hoard, grimly acquired, has been examined. The fate

³⁰⁶⁵ magum: MS . . . ū: Thorkelin B . gum   ³⁰⁷³ strude: MS strade   ³⁰⁷⁸ adreogan: MS adreogeð

grimme gegongen.   Wæs þæt gifeðe to swið   3085
þe ðone þeodcyning   þyder ontyhte!
Ic wæs þær inne   ond þæt eall geondseh,
recedes geatwa,   þa me gerymed wæs,
nealles swæslice   sið alyfed
inn under eorðweall.   Ic on ofoste gefeng   3090
micle mid mundum   mægenbyrðenne
hordgestreona,   hider ut ætbær
cyninge minum.   Cwico wæs þa gena,
wis ond gewittig.   Worn eall gespræc
gomol on gehðo,   ond eowic gretan het,   3095
bæd þæt ge geworhton   æfter wines dædum
in bælstede   beorh þone hean,
micelne ond mærne,   swa he manna wæs
wigend weorðfullost   wide geond eorðan,
þenden he burhwelan   brucan moste.   3100
    Uton nu efstan   oðre siðe
seon ond secean   searogimma geþræc,
wundur under wealle.   Ic eow wisige,
þæt ge genoge   neon sceawiað
beagas ond brad gold.   Sie sio bær gearo,   3105
ædre geæfned,   þonne we ut cymen,
ond þonne geferian   frean userne,
leofne mannan,   þær he longe sceal
on ðæs Waldendes   wære geþolian.’
    Het ða gebeodan   byre Wihstanes,   3110
hæle hildedior,   hæleða monegum,
boldagendra,   þæt hie bælwudu
feorran feredon,   folcagende,
godum togenes: ‘Nu sceal gled fretan
—weaxan wonna leg—   wigena strengel,   3115
þone ðe oft gebad   isernscure,
þonne stræla storm   strengum gebæded
scoc ofer scildweall,   sceft nytte heold,
fæðergearwum fus,   flane fulleode.’
    Huru se snotra   sunu Wihstanes   3120
acigde of corðre   cyniges þegnas,
syfone ætsomne,   þa selestan,
eode eahta sum   under inwithrof
hilderinca;   sum on handa bær
æledleoman,   se ðe on orde geong.   3125
Næs ða on hlytme   hwa þæt hord strude,
syððan orwearde,   ænigne dæl,

that impelled the nation's king towards it was too great! I have been in there and gazed around at all the precious trappings of the building, once the way was open to me—the journey within beneath the earthen rampart not allowed in any friendly fashion. In haste, I seized in my hands a huge great load of hoarded treasures, and carried it out here to my king. He was still alive then, alert and conscious. The aged man spoke many things in his distress, and commanded me to address you, asked that in remembrance of your friend's deeds you should construct at the site of the pyre a high barrow, huge and glorious, because as long as he could still rejoice in a prosperous stronghold he was the worthiest fighter among men throughout the wide world.

Let us now make haste to seek out and see for a second time the heap of precious jewels, the wonder beneath the rampart. I will direct you so that you may examine close up rings and thick gold in plenty. Let the bier be ready, rapidly prepared, when we come out, and then let us carry our lord, the beloved man, to where he must long abide in the keeping of the Ruler.'

The son of Weohstan, a hero brave in battle, then bade them command many a hero, those who possessed buildings, that they carry wood for the pyre from afar to where he who possessed the nation, the great man, lay: 'Now live coals must devour the commander of fighters—the flame grow dark—him who often endured the iron shower when, driven from strings, the storm of arrows passed over the shield-wall, when shaft, eager with feathered flights, did its duty, urged on the barb.'

Well, Weohstan's prudent son called forth together seven men from the king's bodyguard of thanes, the noblest, and as one of eight battle-warriors went in beneath the evil roof; the one who walked in front carried a flaming torch in his hand. There was no lottery then to decide who should pillage that hoard, once the

---

3086 þeodcyning *supplied*   3101 siðe *supplied*   3102 searogimma geþræc: MS
searo ge þræc   3119 fæðergearum: MS fæder gearū   3122 ætsomne *restored*
3124 hilderinca: MS hilde rinc

secgas gesegon   on sele wunian,
læne licgan;   lyt ænig mearn
þæt hi ofostlice   ut geferedon   3130
dyre maðmas.   Dracan ec scufun,
wyrm ofer weallclif,   leton weg niman,
flod fæðmian   frætwa hyrde.
Þa wæs wunden gold   on wæn hladen,
æghwæs unrim,   æþelingc boren,   3135
har hilderinc   to Hronesnæsse.

XLIII   Him ða gegiredan   Geata leode
ad on eorðan   unwaclicne,
helmum behongen,   hildebordum,
beorhtum byrnum,   swa he bena wæs.   3140
Alegdon ða tomiddes   mærne þeoden
hæleð hiofende,   hlaford leofne.
Ongunnon þa on beorge   bælfyra mæst
wigend weccan;   wudurec astah
sweart ofer swioðole,   swogende leg   3145
wope bewunden   —windblond gelæg—
oðþæt he ða banhus   gebrocen hæfde,
hat on hreðre.   Higum unrote
modceare mændon,   mondryhtnes cwealm.
Swylce giomorgyd   Geatisc meowle   3150
bræd on bearhtme   bundenheorde
song sorgcearig   swiðe geneahhe,
þæt hio hyre heofungdagas   hearde ondrede,
wælfylla worn,   werudes egesan,
hynðo ond hæftnyd.   Heofon rece swealg.   3155
   Geworhton ða   Wedra leode
hlæw on hoe,   se wæs heah ond brad,
wegliðendum   wide gesyne,
ond betimbredon   on tyn dagum
beadurofes becn;   bronda lafe   3160
wealle beworhton,   swa hyt weorðlicost
foresnotre men   findan mihton.
Hi on beorg dydon   beg ond siglu,
eall swylce hyrsta,   swylce on horde ær
niðhedige men   genumen hæfdon;   3165
forleton eorla gestreon   eorðan healdan,
gold on greote,   þær hit nu gen lifað
eldum swa unnyt   swa hit æror wæs.
   Þa ymbe hlæw riodan   hildedeore,

men saw that any part of it remained unguarded in the hall, lay wasting; little did anyone grieve that they should hastily carry the precious jewels outside. Also they pushed the dragon, the serpent, over the cliff, let the wave take it, the flood embrace the guardian of the ornaments. Then twisted gold was loaded on a wagon, a countless number of things, and the prince, the grizzled battle-warrior, carried to Whale's Cape.

43   Then the people of the Geats prepared a pyre for him on the earth, unstinted, hung about with helmets, battle-shields and bright coats of mail, as his wish was. In the midst the lamenting heroes then laid down the famous prince, the beloved lord. Then on the mount the fighting-men began to kindle the greatest of funeral-fires; wood-smoke climbed up, black over the blaze, roaring flame mingled with weeping—the swirling wind fell still—until it had broken the bone frame, hot at the heart. With cheerless spirits they bewailed their souls' sorrow, the death of their leader. Likewise, a Geatish woman,* sorrowful, her hair bound up, sang a mournful lay, chanted clamorously again and again that she sorely feared days of lamentation for herself, a multitude of slaughters, the terror of an army, humiliation and captivity. Heaven swallowed up the smoke.

Then the people of the Weders constructed on the promontory a mound which was high and broad, to be seen far and near by those voyaging across the waves, and in ten days had built up a monument to the man renowned in battle; they surrounded the remains of the fire with a rampart, the finest that the most skilful men could devise. In the barrow they placed rings and brooches, all such trappings as men disposed to strife had earlier taken from the hoard; they let the earth keep the warriors' treasure, gold in the dust, where it still remains now, as useless to men as it was before.

Then those brave in battle, the children of princes, twelve in all,

---

3130 ofostlice: MS ofostl . . . ; Thorkelin B ofostlic .   3134 Þa: MS Þ   3135 æþelingc: MS æþelinge   3136 hilderinc: MS hilde   3139 helmum: MS helm   3144 wudurec: MS w . . . rec; Thorkelin A wud . rec   3145 swioðole: MS swicðole   3145 leg: MS le; Thorkelin A and B let   3149 cwealm: MS . . . . lm; Thorkelin A cw . aln   3150–5a extensively restored after Pope   3155 swealg restored from Thorkelin A and B sealg   3158 wegliðendum: MS . egliðendum   3168 hit æror: MS hi . . . . r

æþelinga bearn,   ealra twelfe,   3170
woldon ceare cwiðan,   kyning mænan,
wordgyd wrecan   ond ymb wer sprecan.
Eahtodan eorlscipe   ond his ellenweorc
duguðum demdon.   Swa hit gedefe bið
þæt mon his winedryhten   wordum herge,   3175
ferhðum freoge,   þonne he forð scile
of lichaman   læded weorðan.
Swa begnornodon   Geata leode
hlafordes hryre,   heorðgeneatas;
cwædon þæt he wære   wyruldcyninga   3180
manna mildust   ond monðwærust,
leodum liðost   ond lofgeornost.

rode round the mound, would lament their grief, bewail their king, recite a lay and speak about the man.* They praised his heroism and acclaimed the nobility of his courageous deeds. It is fitting that a man should thus honour his friend and leader with words, love him in spirit, when he must needs be led forth from the flesh. Thus the people of the Geats, the companions of his hearth, mourned the fall of their lord; they said that among the world's kings he was the gentlest of men and the most courteous, the most kindly to his people and the most eager for renown.

3170 twelfe: MS twelfa   3171 ceare *restored*   3172 wer: MS w . .   3174 gedefe: MS ge . . . .   3177 læded *restored*   3179 hryre: MS . . yre   3180 wyruldcyninga: MS wyruldcyni . . .   3181 manna: MS . anna; monðwærust: MS . . . . ust; Thorkelin A and B mondrærust

Notes

4ff   Scyld is well known in Scandinavian tradition as the eponymous ancestor of the Scyldings and true founder of the Danish fortunes. His mysterious arrival, as a young child alone in a boat, is peculiar to *Beowulf*. But the same story is commonly told of the hero Scef, whom early tradition regards as the father of Scyld.

5   *meodosetla ofteah*. The mead-bench—the most prominent feature of any hall—is a symbol of success and security in heroic Germanic society. The free warrior is assured of a place in the companionship of the hall, feasting and receiving gifts from his leader. For this to be denied him is a mark of his subjection and distress.

6   *egsode Eorle*. MS *eorl* is both grammatically and stylistically unsatisfactory. The Eruli (Lat. *Heruli*) were a Germanic people originally inhabiting the Danish islands; notorious for their ferocity, they were valued as mercenary auxiliaries in the Roman army, and had been used among others by Theodosius to put down the British revolt of 367–8 A.D. If Scyld was to consolidate Danish power, he must first have subdued the Eruli. The sixth-century historian Jordanes states that they were driven from their original homelands by the Danes (*Getica*, XXIII, 117–18), and afterwards they seem to have wandered as mercenaries in various parts of Europe until early in the fifth century they disappear from recorded history as an identifiable unit.

14–15   *Fyrenðearfe . . . aldorlease*. The distress Scyld was sent to remedy apparently resulted from the activities of the wicked and avaricious King Heremod, who was eventually driven into exile by his people. See note to lines 901–15.

18   *Beowulf*. Probably an error for *Beow* or *Beaw*, the form the name takes in the West Saxon and other genealogies. This is Beowulf Scylding (cf. 53) not to be mistaken for Beowulf the Geat, the hero of the poem. This Beowulf is not referred to again in the body of the text.

32f   The employment of a ship for the journey to the afterlife is an ancient concept in northern Europe and elsewhere. There are literary parallels in the Scandinavian sagas for the kind of sea-burial accorded Scyld, and a particularly interesting analogue in a probably ninth-century *Life of St Gildas*, in which this sixth-century Welsh saint instructs that his body is to be cast adrift in an open boat to be assigned a final resting place wherever God wills (*M.G.H. Auct. Ant.* XIII, 101). Pseudo ship-burials in which the outline of the boat is formed by massive upright stones were common at this time in Scandinavia, several examples being known at Lejre (the site of Heorot, cf. note to line 78). True ship-burials on land are archaeologically attested from the sixth and seventh centuries in central Sweden and along the coast of East Anglia. Particularly richly equipped was that found at Sutton Hoo in Suffolk, which presents a pertinent parallel to that described in *Beowulf*, especially in respect of its trappings, which included pieces of Swedish armour, presumably heirlooms brought into the country by Redwald's forbears.

62   *Yrse wæs Onelan cwen.* The only known member of the Scylfings with a name ending -*ela* is Onela, so this restoration seems highly probable. The name of the girl is less certain; but conventional alliteration in the Old English line indicates that it began with a vowel, and a good case can be made for Yrse, the mother of Hrothulf. (See generally Kemp Malone, *The Literary History of Hamlet*, Heidelberg, 1923, pp. 101f, 230–41.)

78   *Heort.* Already important houses, like swords, were given names. Heor(o)t means 'Hart, Stag'; the figure of a stag surmounted the Sutton Hoo sceptre, and is well attested as a quasi-religious Germanic symbol of nobility (cf. Swanton, *Antiquity*, XLVIII, 1974, 313–15). The Utrecht Psalter *c.* 800 depicts a king (David) seated outside his palace, which is decorated with a stag's mask and antlers set in the gable (cf. *banfag*, 780).

The site of Heorot is probably identifiable with the modern village of Lejre, which lies near to the north coast of Zealand, three miles from the sea and some five miles from Roskilde, the seat of later medieval Danish kings.

82–5 *heaðowylma bad . . . scolde.* We are left in no suspense as to the ultimate fate of Heorot. As the Scandinavian sources confirm, Hrothgar's palace would be destroyed by fire during the course of the Danish–Heathobard feud. The son-in-law and father-in-law in question are Ingeld and Hrothgar (see note to lines 2024–69).

106f The story of Cain and Abel, the archetypal instance of brother slaying brother, is told in Genesis IV. The Old English *Maxims I*, 192f show that this incident was regarded as the symbolic source of violence and disorder in human society. The notion that all monsters, hobgoblins and evil progenies were descended from Cain was a medieval commonplace, although in this instance the direct source is not clear (cf. lines 1261f). For the giants who warred against God and were destroyed in the Flood (cf. lines 1688f) see Genesis VI, 4; Job XXVI, 5 (Vulgate, *gigantes*); Revelation XIII, 1.

139–40 *Gerumlicor ræste sohte, bed æfter burum.* Excavations at Cheddar, Yeavering and elsewhere show that the Migration-Age hall was surrounded by a number of smaller ancillary buildings (*buras*), with various domestic functions. One or another may have represented private apartments for the owner, or for an important guest (cf. lines 1299–1301, and the implied description of the manor at Merton, *Anglo-Saxon Chronicle*, s.a. 755). But most provided lodging for women ('bower'), or for cattle ('byre'). Since it was customary for members of the *comitatus* to sleep in the hall, the demoralising effect of Grendel's depredations is clear.

168–69 An apparently inept parenthetic remark, made doubly difficult by numerous ambiguities. The major problems are: (*a*) does *he* refer to Hrothgar or Grendel? (*b*) is the *gifstol* that of Hrothgar or God? (*c*) does *gretan* mean 'to approach' or 'to attack'? (*d*) does *for* mean 'because of' or 'in the presence of'? (*e*) does *myne* mean 'mind' or 'purpose' or 'love'?

175–88 Possibly the poet knew that Heorot (Hleiðr, Lejre) was the site of an ancient heathen sanctuary. His strictures on the religious practices of the Danes (who were not in fact converted until the eleventh century) is the most pointedly 'Christian' passage in the poem. The personal intrusion of the author (or interpolator) is interesting for the cultural perspective it provides.

For Anglo-Saxon reversion to paganism in response to natural afflictions such as the outbreak of plague, see Bede, *Historia Ecclesiastica*, III 30, IV 27.

204 *hæl sceawedon*. For the ancient Germanic practice of sortilege, telling the auguries by casting lots, see generally Tacitus, *Germania* x. A collection of astragali perhaps intended for such use, belonging to the late fifth century, was found in the pagan Anglo-Saxon cemetery at Caistor-by-Norwich (J. N. L. Myres and Barbara Green, *The Anglo-Saxon Cemeteries of Caistor-by-Norwich and Markshall, Norfolk*, London, 1973, pp. 114–17).

219 *ymb antid oþres dogores*. Travelling coast-wise from Geatland (presumably from a point somewhere in the region of Göteborg) to a convenient spot on the coast of Zealand, is little more than 160 miles. With favourable conditions, a ship of the forty-oared Sutton Hoo type could have managed such a journey with ease.

303 *Eoforlic scionon* . . . The use of boar-crests on Migration-Age helmets is illustrated on a probably sixth-century bronze metalworker's die from Torslunda, Öland, and one such helmet was worn by the seventh-century Mercian warrior buried at Benty Grange, Derbyshire (Sheffield Museum). The boar was anciently sacred to the Vanir, the Germanic fertility gods; and that such decoration originally had religious significance is attested by Tacitus, speaking of the Baltic Aestii: 'They worship the mother of the Gods, and wear as emblems of this cult the masks of boars, which stand them in stead of armour or human protection and ensure the safety of the worshipper even among his enemies' (*Germania*, XLV). Cf. lines 1453–4 below. Warriors wearing tusked visors are depicted in plates on a sixth-century helmet from Vendel, and evidence for an actual visor of this kind has been found in a seventh-century warrior grave nearby at Valsgärde. A boar-standard is referred to in line 2152.

320 *Stræt wæs stanfah*. While short lengths of metalled roadway were not unknown in Iron Age Scandinavia, the word 'street' suggests that the poet may have had in mind fine Roman roads familiar in Britain. Cf. note to 725. The distance from Lejre to the most obvious landing-point, Köge Bay on the east coast of Zealand, is about ten miles, although it is little more than three or four miles to the head of Ise or Roskilde Fjords to the north.

348 *Wulfgar . . . þæt wæs Wendla leod*. Hrothgar's *comitatus* was clearly prestigious enough to attract noblemen from distant regions. Possibly some remnants of Vandal people may have remained in their original homelands in East Germany, or scattered in various parts of Scandinavia (cf. Vendel, Uppland; Vendill, North Jutland), but by this time in the fifth century the greatest part of the Vandals had migrated via Spain to North Africa, where they had established a kingdom centred on Carthage—to be destroyed by Byzantine forces in 534–5 A.D.

404   *heorðe.* MS *heoðe.* The compound form *hel-heoðo* in the Old English poem *Christ and Satan* 699 suggests that here *heoð* may mean something like 'hall' or 'interior' of a hall; but the etymology is far from clear, and in the absence of any other evidence most editors prefer to emend to *heorð*, 'hearth', although in this case the preposition *on* looks odd.

446   *hafalan hydan.* Possibly this is merely a metaphor for burial, although it may well contain an allusion to the early funerary practice of covering the head of the dead with a cloth.

451   *lices feorme.* Since Beowulf is, as it were, seconded to Hrothgar's *comitatus*, his upkeep would temporarily represent a charge on Heorot. *Feorm* means literally 'sustenance' and possibly the phrase ironically alludes to the meal Grendel may make of the hero.

455   *Welandes geweorc.* Any piece of armour or weapon attributed to the legendary Germanic smith Weland clearly laid claim both to extreme antiquity and superb craftmanship. The stories associated with the figure of Weland survive in their most extended form in The Old Norse *Vǫlundarkviða*, but that they were familiar in early Anglo-Saxon England is indicated by allusions in the opening stanzas of the Old English poem *Deor* and by scenes from the legend depicted in the front panel of the early eighth-century whalebone Franks Casket.

489–90 The exact interpretation of Hrothgar's exhortation poses several difficulties, the chief of which depend on the MS spacing, which as usual offers no certainty as to intended meaning. 489b–90a are usually transcribed 7 *on sæl meoto sige hreð secgū.*

Meoto has been construed either (*a*) as the imperative singular of a verb **meotian*, postulated as an Anglian form of *metian*, 'to ponder, think about', hence 'attend, listen to', or (*b*) as the accusative plural of an otherwise unrecorded noun **meotu*, 'thought, meditation'. As separated in the manuscript, the phrase *on sæl* might mean 'in due season', 'in the hall', or even 'joyfully', although *on sælum* is the poet's usual form; alternatively read as one word, *onsæl* might be taken as the imperative singular of the verb *onsælan* 'to unloose', i.e. 'reveal'. *Hreð* might be attached either to the preceding word or that following, reading thus *sigehreð*, 'triumphant victories', or *hreðsecgum*, 'to the triumphant warriors'.

The reading preferred in the text: *on sælum eow sige hreðsecgum* has the advantage of avoiding speculation over the hypothetical form **meoto* in favour of two forms well known to the poet: *on sælum* (607, 643, 1170), and *eow*, sg. imp. of *ywan*, 'display, reveal' (1738 etc.), but assumes the scribe's preservation of an archaic *w* in place of the normal *wynn* graph.

499f   *Unferð.* While Unferth's structural role in the poem is clear, his function in Heorot is less obvious. He is a man of undoubted influence in the court, sharp-witted and well-informed. He is twice called *þyle* ?'spokesman, orator' (1165, 1456). The compound *þelcræft* is used to gloss *rethorica*, and certainly Unferth proceeds to engage Beowulf in a 'flyting' or a verbal testing.

506ff The account of Beowulf's swimming-contest with Breca is clearly subject to heroic exaggeration, and the geographical details should not be pressed too closely. The land of the Heatho-Ræmas where Breca came ashore apparently lay around Oslo Fjord (cf. the province of Romerike north of Oslo), while Beowulf claims to have swum, admittedly driven by bad weather, as far as the land of the Lapps (Finnaland), normally identified either with Finmarken in the north of Norway, or with some part of the north Baltic, the former involving a distance of well over a thousand miles, and the latter at least seven hundred. If the name can be associated with Finnheden in south-west Sweden, however, the feat becomes more plausible.

612f *Eode Wealhþeow forð* . . . Noble ladies played an important role in heroic Anglo-Saxon society, both at the feast and in council. For the respect accorded women among the early *Germani*, as compared with their treatment in contemporary Roman society, see Tacitus, *Germania* VIII, XVIII-XX. The queen's office as cupbearer in hall ceremonies is described in the Old English *Maxims I*, 88–92.

703f That Beowulf's *comitatus* should all fall asleep under those circumstances is strange; possibly they had been entertained too well! Certainly it serves to enhance the hero's bold watchfulness. Perhaps it reflects early versions of the story in which a series of unsuccessful attempts to ward off the demon intruder are associated with sleepiness on the part of a succession of heroes; similarly this might account for Beowulf's apparent hesitation to come immediately to the aid of his comrade when attacked, 736f.

725 *on fagne flor.* Possibly the poet has in mind a tessellated floor of the Roman type. In Britain and on the continent these may have been common where Germanic halls were built over the sites of earlier Roman villas, although material evidence for this is as yet lacking. The name *fag flor* occurs occasionally in Anglo-Saxon land-charters, however; and in one instance—at Fawler, Oxfordshire—a Roman mosaic has been discovered. Such floors will certainly have been familiar in urban settings such as Canterbury, where early Kentish kings probably held court in one of the larger public buildings.

769 *ealuscerwen.* A difficult word, because unique. Its general context indicates a sense implying panic, misery or distress, and the author of the Old English poem *Andreas*, who imitated much that he found in *Beowulf*, coined the parallel form *meoduscerwen* for a similar situation, where feasting and happiness are followed by the terror of a destructive flood: *Meoduscerwen wearð æfter symbeldæge* (1526–7). The first element *ealu* means 'ale'. A hypothetical **ealu*, meaning 'good fortune', has been postulated. But the *Andreas*-poet certainly understood it in the former sense, replacing 'ale' by 'mead' apparently for the sake of alliteration. The second element, *scerwen*, is otherwise unrecorded. It may be formed from a verb **scerwan*, with a meaning similar to that of *bescerwan*, 'to deprive'. Or it may be related to the noun *scearu*, 'a sharing'. In the former case the compound *ealuscerwen* would mean 'deprivation of ale', a ready metaphor for consternation (cf. note to line 5). In the latter case *ealuscerwen* would mean 'the serving of ale'—a bitter drink, and hence a metaphor for distress, despite the fact that this is not the normal view of ale in the poem. Although mead (the *Andreas*-poet's alternative) is not bitter, it parallels *biter beorþegu*, 'bitter beer-drinking', a line or two later (1533). Probably we should assume an ironic use here.

867–74. *Hwilum cyninges þegn . . . wordum wrixlan*. These lines offer a convenient description of Old English verse composition: the major poetic techniques of alliteration (*soðe gebunden*) and elegant variation (*wordum wrixlan*). The minstrel is the repository of ancient legends and, as evinced in the stories which follow, characteristically incorporated allusions to them in his poetry.

874–97 The comparison of Beowulf with Sigemund at this point not only enhances the hero in the estimation of the audience but also anticipates Beowulf's future dragon-slaying exploit and, ironically, its tragic consequences.

The story of Sigemund Wælsing occurs in its most extended form in the Old Norse *Vǫlsunga Saga*, composed *c.*1200 and, later, Wagner's *Der Ring des Nibelungen*. Sigmundr (Sigemund) is the eldest son of king Vǫlsungr (Wæls). His twin sister Signý is unhappily married to Siggeirr, king of Gautland. While visiting Siggeirr's court, Vǫlsungr and his men are treacherously slain; but Sigmundr escapes into the forest. Signý nurses her disaffection, and believing that only a true Vǫlsung son could accomplish her revenge, visits her brother in the forest, disguised as a witch. In due course the fruit of their incestuous relationship, Sinfjǫtli (Fitela), is born. When he is of an age, his mother sends him to join Sigmundr in the forest, and together they engage in numerous heroic deeds, living for a time as werewolves. Eventually Vǫlsung vengeance is accomplished when Sigmundr and Sinfjǫtli burn down Siggeirr's hall with the king and his entire court inside.

That the Sigemund–Fitela stories were well-known in Anglo-Saxon England is suggested by the discovery at Winchester of a fragmentary tenth- or eleventh-century bas-relief which apparently depicts a scene from this legend (*Antiquaries Journal* XLVI, 1966, 329–32, pl. LXIIa).

The ascription of a dragon-fight to Sigemund is peculiar to *Beowulf*. In the, admittedly much later, Old Norse and German versions, the dragon-fight is said to be the work of Sigmundr's son Sigurðr (Wagner's Siegfried). But it is probable that the Old English account, which was set down in written form several centuries before the Old Norse versions, preserves the older tradition. Whatever may be the case, it represents the archetype of various dragon-fights in Germanic literature, and is important in understanding certain details of Beowulf's dragon-fight.

As recounted in the *Vǫlsunga Saga*, its significant details are as follows: The mischievous god Loki has occasion to compensate a giant called Hreiðmarr, having accidentally slain one of his sons.

Loki makes payment with gold—including a certain ring—which he forces from the dwarf Andvari. Before finally relinquishing his treasure, the dwarf declares that to possess the ring, or any of the gold, will result in death. Later Hreiðmarr's avaricious son Fáfnir kills his father for the sake of the gold, drives away a third son, Reginn, and goes off to live in the wilds, where eventually he turns into a dragon and lies guarding the treasure. Reginn, cheated of his share of the compensation, eventually persuades the hero Sigurðr to slay the dragon Fáfnir, presenting him with a fine sword with which to do the deed. Sigurðr accomplishes this by standing in a pit dug in the path the dragon is accustomed to take on his way to drink at the water, and stabbing him in the softer underparts. Before dying, Fáfnir repeats the dwarf's curse on the gold. Realising that Reginn intends treachery, Sigurðr kills him. Finally Sigurðr himself dies during the course of a conflict between the Burgundians and the Huns, thus fulfilling the curse, albeit belatedly.

Arguably it is scenes from the Sigurðr legend that are carved on the problematic right-hand side of the Franks Casket (cf. note to line 455).

901–15 *Heremod.* The association of Sigmundr with a certain Hermoðr occurs in Scandinavian literature, but apart from the fact that both were patronised by the god Oðinn, the exact nature of their connection is unclear. We know little of the hero Hermoðr, and the story of Heremod which may be deduced from *Beowulf* is obscure— merely a series of allusions intended for an audience who were familiar with the tale. The significant passages occur here and in 1709–22, in both of which the career of Heremod is contrasted with that which may be anticipated for the exemplary young Beowulf.

The major burden of the allusion is this: Heremod was an ancient king of the Danes who had in his youth showed promise of a brilliant career but in the event proved a bad ruler. Miserly and bloodthirsty, slaying even members of his own *comitatus*, he proved too sore a burden to his people, and (like the Swede Eanmund who seeks refuge with his traditional enemies the Geats, only to be killed there, cf. note to lines 2922-98), Heremod was eventually forced to flee to his enemies, and is there betrayed and killed. It was apparently after this that Scyld was sent to restore the fortunes of the leaderless Danish people (cf. note to lines 14–15).

MS *mid eotenum* (902) should mean 'among the *eotenas*, giants', but unless 'giants' is employed figuratively to describe Heremod's foes, which seems unlikely in this context, it seems reasonable that the poet should have intended to refer to the Eote, the Jutes, neighbours and traditional enemies of the Danes. According to the seventeenth-century Swedish historian Messenius, this was certainly what happened to a certain King Lotherus, whom some scholars have confidently identified with Heremod.

926   *stod on stapole.* On his way from Wealhtheow's *bur* Hrothgar has apparently paused outside the hall to gaze up at some point beneath the roof—probably on the gable—where Grendel's limb has been nailed—perhaps a customary place for such trophies (cf. note to line 78). The primary sense of *stapol*, 'column, pillar' or 'post' (cf.

2718), is scarcely appropriate here, where the poet apparently has in mind some kind of erection standing close to or against the hall. *Stapol* is also found as a gloss to *basis* and *petronus*, so that a secondary meaning 'raised platform' or 'short staircase leading up to a house' must be assumed. Heavy stone or wooden thresholds raised above floor-level are known from several Germanic house-sites; and a ninth-century house at Hedeby (Schleswig) was approached by steps leading to a small landing (H. Jankuhn, *Haithabu*, Neumünster, 1956, p. 103, plan II).

However, a royal centre like Heorot may have boasted a variety of ancillary structures which could have afforded Hrothgar a suitable vantage-point. The seventh-century Anglo-Saxon palace at Yeavering (Northumberland) was provided with a platform facing a kind of grandstand, apparently used for open-air ceremonies, while the foundations of free-standing watchtowers were found in the palace of a contemporary British chieftain at Castle Dore (Cornwall).

1018–19 nalles facenstafas Peod-Scyldingas penden fremedon. And cf. the ironic anticipatory allusions: 1164f, 1180f, 1228f. The author of *Widsith* returns to the same theme: 'For a very long time did Hrothgar and Hrothulf, uncle and nephew, keep peace together' (45–6). The relationship between Hrothgar and Hrothulf was well known to the English audience, and presumably they knew the story of how the two finally fell out. It is possible to piece together from early Danish historians the fact that Hrothulf usurped and slew Hrethric, who apparently succeeded his father Hrothgar to the Danish throne. Scandinavian tradition remembers Hrothulf (Hrólfr Kraki) as the leader of a *comitatus* at Lejre which was to become the model of chivalry for northern Europe, as Arthur's court was for the west.

1020 brand Healfdenes. The primary sense of *brand* is 'burning, fire', and metaphorically 'sword' (e.g. 1454), the occasional poetic use of which occurs in Middle English and down to the present day. A few lines later Hrothgar is described simply as *Healfdenes hildewisa* (1064), so that although unusual, this sense is perfectly appropriate here, parallel with the more common description of the king as *helm Scyldinga*, 371 etc.

1033 scurheard. Apparently a metalworking image. In the previous line the sword had been described as *fela laf*, 'the files' legacy' (cf. 'the hammers' legacy', 2829). In such a context it might be supposed that 'shower-hardened' refers to the usual tempering of blades by quenching in water, although it is possible that the intended reference is to the 'showers of battle', which would result in the blade's hardening not only figuratively but actually by the process known as 'work-hardening'. It is not without interest that Heroic Age warrior–smith stories occasionally described newly-forged swords being tempered in the blood of enemies. The seax Hrunting is said to be 'hardened in the gore of battle', 1459–60.

1046f For this characteristic gift of arms, horses and treasure (and cf. the presents later given by Beowulf to Hygelac and Hygd, 2152f) compare what Tacitus says of the early *Germani*: 'The companions are prodigal in their demands on the generosity of their chiefs. It is always "Give me that war-horse", or "Give me that bloody and victorious spear" . . . The chiefs take particular pleasure in gifts from neighbouring states, such as are sent not only by individuals, but by the community as well—choice horses, splendid arms, metal rings and collars' (*Germania*, XIV, XV).

1068–1159. The Finnsburh story is unknown outside *Beowulf* and the fragment of a second heroic poem we call simply *The Fight at Finnsburh*, but its main details are plain—dealing with a familiar and tragic conflict of loyalties in heroic society: the duty of revenge and of loyalty to a sworn oath. The allusion is utilised ironically at this point in the poem, when the glory of Heorot is apparently once more secure, to emphasise that any great house might be destroyed as a result of a bloody feud between relatives—even between uncle and nephew—thus paralleling the circumstances under which Heorot was eventually to fall (cf. notes to lines 82–5, 1018–19).

Finn is king in Frisia and it is around his palace, Finnsburh, that the events take place. He has in his service not only Frisians, but Jutes, who archaeological evidence argues settled these parts during the earlier fifth century. Finn has married a Danish princess, Hildeburh. Possibly this alliance had been arranged in an attempt to secure peace between the two peoples, although if this were the case the poet later shows himself well aware of the futility of such a hope, 'however worthy the bride may be' (2024–31). There is certainly evidence for ancient antagonism between Danes and Jutes (cf. note to 901–15). But whether or not there had existed a lengthy history of hostility between Danes and Frisians, violence flares up during a visit to Finnsburh by Hildeburh's brother Hnæf, leading a party called variously Danes, Half-Danes, or Scyldings. Hnæf and his men are attacked by night in a hall within Finnsburh. (It is this episode that the 'Fragment' treats.) After a lengthy battle Hnæf and many of his men, together with many of Finn's followers including his son by Hildeburh, lie dead. At the end of the day uncle and nephew lie side by side on the same funeral pyre, mourned over by Hildeburh, sister and mother.

A warrior called Hengest assumes leadership of the surviving Danes. Both sides having fought to the point of exhaustion, the stalemate is acknowledged; a treaty is concluded. Hengest's Danes will join Finn's sadly depleted *comitatus* on the understanding that they are accorded honourable and equal treatment, and that no-one will allude to the circumstances that led to this situation. For to follow the man responsible for the death of one's own leader—however practical it might seem—struck at the heart of the heroic ethic (cf. Tacitus, *Germania*, XIV, or the account of the 'putsch' at Merton given in *The Anglo-Saxon Chronicle*, s.a. 755). A winter passes, but eventually two Danes, Guthlaf and Oslaf, are unable to keep silent, and Hengest is stirred into action by the sight of an old sword—perhaps one that had belonged to Hnæf. In the ensuing conflict Finn is killed, his treasure seized and his wife carried back to her own people by the victorious Danes. We may assume also that, like Heorot, Finnsburh was burned.

Possibly it was this Hengest who subsequently brought his *comitatus* to the aid of the British king Vortigern *c.* 499 A.D., and founded the Anglo-Saxon kingdom of Kent.

For an up-to-date summary of opinion concerning this episode, and a full discussion of its various problems, see D. K. Fry, ed., *Finnsburh Fragment and Episode*, London, 1974.

1197–1201 The significant details of this allusion may be pieced together thus. Eormenric was a historical Ostrogothic king who flourished in the middle years of the fourth century, dying by his own hand following an invasion by the Huns, *c.* 375. In heroic literature he came to represent the type of a savage tyrant; and the extent of his treasury was famous (cf. the early Old English poems *Deor*, 21f and *Widsith*, 8f, 88f).

The story of Hama survives in the late *Þiðreks Saga af Bern*. In this Hama (Heimir) is a warrior owing loyalty to the Ostrogothic leader Theodoric and also, by implication, to Theodoric's uncle Eormenric. When uncle and nephew quarrel, Hama sides with Theodoric and, in company with his friend Wudga, is obliged to flee the enmity of Eormenric. There is no mention of him having taken with him Eormenric's gold, although he certainly acquires such treasures by violent means in later incidents. We may assume that a more pristine version was familiar to the early Anglo-Saxons, however, from the *Widsith*-poet's having linked together the names of Hama and Wudga in an heroic allusion (124–30).

The *Brosinga mene* which the *Beowulf*-poet suggests Hama stole from Eormenric can be identified with the legendary *Brísinga men*, of Scandinavian literature, the necklace made by the Brísing dwarfs and which was acquired by the goddess Freyja. (Grimms' fairy-tale 'Snow White and the Seven Dwarfs', which must have ancient Germanic origins, reflects one version of this.)

geceas ecne ræd (120–1), 'chose eternal gain', is unlikely to refer, as some scholars have supposed, to the *Þiðreks Saga*'s account of Hama having entered a monastery. Of course the 'historical' Hama could no more have been a monk than Hrothgar; and writing as early as he did, and with such a feeling for antiquity, it seems unlikely that our poet should have had recourse to the later Christianised version of the story. Almost exactly the same words are used by Hrothgar in urging Beowulf to choose lasting benefits for himself in this world (1759–60).

1202–14 Allusion to Hygelac's final fatal adventure, which indirectly led to Beowulf's assuming the throne, recurs repeatedly in the poem: 2354–66, 2501–8, 2913–20. Hygelac's death is the one major incident used by the poet which is verifiable from sound historical sources: the late sixth-century *Historia Francorum* of Gregory of Tours, III, 3, and the early eighth-century *Gesta Francorum*, XIX.

Apparently flushed with success following his defeat of the Swedes at Ravenswood (cf. notes to 2922–98), Hygelac rashly turned his attention to the Franks. In about 521 A.D. he set out on a ship-borne raid up the Rhine, ravaging the territory of the Hetware (*Chattuarii*) who formed part of the general Frankish hegemony, at that time under the rule of the Austrasian king Theuderich. The main force had re-embarked, taking with them much plunder and many captives, when the rearguard led by Hygelac himself was overtaken by a powerful Frankish army led by Theuderich's son Theudebert. (At least some of these Franks went under the by-name of Hugas.) There takes place a violent struggle in which Beowulf plays a prominent part, crushing to death with his bare hands the Frankish standard-bearer Dæghrefn and taking his sword Nægling for himself (2499–508). Hygelac is killed together with most of his followers, the Geatish fleet is routed and the plunder restored. But Beowulf manages to escape (2359–68).

A probably eighth-century English *Liber Monstrorum* states that Hygelac's bones were still to be seen preserved as marvels on an island in the mouth of the Rhine.

1357–76 For his description of the surroundings to Grendel's lair, the poet seems to have drawn on features of the Christian Hell as it was described in the *Visio Pauli*. Although the frosty northern scene does not occur in any known version of the *Visio*, this, together with several verbal parallels, is found in the account retailed by the author of the probably ninth-century Blickling homily No. 17: 'As St Paul was gazing towards the northern part of this world, where all waters pass below, he also saw there above the water a certain grey stone. And to the north of the stone there had grown very frosty groves; and there were dark mists; and beneath the stone was the dwelling place of water-monsters and evil spirits. And he saw that on that cliff many black souls bound by their hands were hanging in the icy groves; and the devils in the shape of water-monsters were clutching at them, just like ravenous wolves. And the water under the cliff below was black; and between the cliff and the water was about twelve miles. And when the twigs broke, the souls which hung on the twigs dropped below and the water-monsters seized them. These were the souls of those who had sinned wickedly here in the world, and would not turn from it before their life's end.' The rhythmic quality of the author's prose suggests that he appreciated vernacular poetry; very probably he knew this passage and drew on its phraseology.

For the stag (1368–9), symbol of nobility and purity, see note to line 78.

1457 hæftmece. This word, used to describe Unferth's remarkable weapon Hrunting, is otherwise unrecorded. It is interesting that in the same place in the paradigm in the Old Norse *Grettis Saga*, the same kind of strange weapon occurs, described there as a *heptisax*, a word similarly otherwise unknown. But in *Grettis Saga* the weapon is wielded not by the hero Grettir but by the underwater troll he fights, and much more is made of the hafted nature of the weapon— referred to only casually in *Beowulf*. Later Grettir returns from his adventure, bringing with him to give to his friend a wooden rod (apparently the haft of the troll's *heptisax*, which the hero clove in two) carved in runes with a poetic account of his exploit. This is paradigmatically identifiable with the inscribed sword-hilt which Beowulf carries back from his adventure and gives to Hrothgar (cf. note to lines 1688–98). In this detail at least, we may assume that *Grettis Saga* contains the more pristine account, despite its later date.

The kind of weapon referred to is presumably the larger war-seax which became popular in England during the seventh century, and which was provided with a specially long hilt so as to be grasped with both hands, *mid mundum* (1461).

1688–98. That the name of the person for whom the weapon was made should be inscribed on the hilt is quite appropriate. A number of hilt-inscriptions are known, both in runes and in Roman lettering, which apparently give either the name of the weapon or its owner. Probably the most apposite example is the late sixth-century hilt from a pagan grave at Gilton, Kent, where the pommel is lightly engraved with runes which may be interpreted 'Sigimer named the blade'. However, there would scarcely have been room, nor would it have been usual, for a story to have been written on the hilt, however briefly. The poet presumably has in mind a sword-hilt like that found in a rich sixth-century grave at Snartemo, Vest Agder, bearing a graphic illustration of some kind. Germanic art of the kind applied to sword-hilts, jewels and so forth at this period characteristically took the form of a pattern of disjected zoomorphic and anthropomorphic writhings, which could well have been interpreted as a monstrous conflict at the time the *Beowulf*-poet was writing—when such art had been superseded.

1743–4 It would be tempting to recognise here an echo of the biblical images of the arrows of the devil and spiritual armour (cf. Ephesians, VI, 13–17), but the metaphor is a perfectly natural one; it occurs casually in such eighth-century Anglo-Saxon writers as Eddius Stephanus (*Vita Wilfridi*, XXIV) or Boniface (*Epistolae*, LXXIII).

1801–2 Like the 'mournful cuckoo' in *The Seafarer* and *The Husband's Message*, the employment of a 'happy raven' at this point strikes the modern reader as bizarre. A bird intimately linked with Woden, god of war, the raven is usually associated with carnage (cf. lines 2448, 3024). However, there is good evidence in both Norse and Latin literature that the raven was considered a prophetic bird which might augur either good or evil; and that the Anglo-Saxons shared in this tradition is indicated by early penitentials. Ravens characteristically herald daybreak, and the fifth-century Gallo-Roman poet Sidonius Apollinaris found the sound pleasing (*Epistolae*, II, 2).

1931–62 The contrast between the young and virtuous Hygd and the imperious young Thryth is introduced abruptly. The 'taming of the shrew' is a common Germanic motif, found typically in Brunhild of the *Nibelungenlied*. Thryth is said to have changed her character upon marriage to the young Offa, a king of the Angles some time during the later fourth century. Prior to their migration to Britain, the Angles lived south of the Danes in Schleswig. We are told nothing of Thryth's background save that she was a foreign princess who agreed to this marriage at the instance of her father (1949–51). Stories about Offa would naturally have been introduced into Britain with the fifth-century settlements; some are alluded to in *Widsith*, 35–44.

As the direct ancestor of Offa II of Mercia, in whose reign the poem *Beowulf* in the form we have it may have been composed, it is arguable that this allusion was introduced as an oblique compliment to the English king. That Offa of Mercia was commonly compared with his ancestor Offa of Angeln is suggested both by historical events in the life of the two kings and by parallel stories told about them in the twelfth-century *Lives of the Two Offas* preserved by a monk of St Albans. In this historical romance incidents originally attributed to one king are ascribed to the other. In particular the significant detail of Offa I's wife has been transferred to Offa II. Thryth (Drida), a beautiful but wicked girl related to Charlemagne, is condemned to be cast adrift on the sea in an open boat. Cast up on the English coast, she is led to King Offa. She claims that her banishment was the result of intrigue on the part of suitors whose offers of marriage she had rejected. Deceived by the girl's beauty, Offa marries her. From this point, however, the stories diverge. In *Beowulf* Thryth is transformed into the model of a virtuous queen, whereas in the St Albans version Thryth is said to show her true colours and after a wicked life meets a violent death. The reason for this transference is apparently the fact that the name of Offa's real queen was Cwenthryth; and although she herself seems to have led a relatively blameless life for one in her position, her daughter Eadburg certainly acquired a deserved reputation for wickedness.

The allusion has caused considerable speculation among certain critics as to the possible moral intention of the poet. See generally *Modern Philology* II (1904–5), 29–48, 321–76.

1968 bonan Ongenþeoes. The Swedish king was actually killed by Eofor (2484f, 2961f), not Hygelac, but it was conventional for the members of a *comitatus* to ascribe their own individual deeds of prowess to its leader (Tacitus, *Germania*, XIV).

2000f Beowulf's own account of his adventures includes detailed information not mentioned in the earlier narrative: the presence in Heorot of Freawaru and the fact of her betrothal to Ingeld (2020f), the name of the member of Beowulf's *comitatus* killed by Grendel— Hondscioh (2076), Grendel's *glof* (2085f), and Hrothgar's gift to Beowulf of King Heorogar's armour (2155f).

2024–69 The story of the son of Froda (Ingeld) was well known to the Anglo-Saxon audience; it was this story which Alcuin chose to specify when rebuking the monks of Lindisfarne *c.* 797 for paying more attention to the minstrel's tales than the words of Scripture: "What has Ingeld to do with Christ?" Froda and Ingeld belonged to the Heathobards, who seem to have lived on the lower Elbe; perhaps originally a remnant of the Langobards (the *Bardi bellicosissimi* of Helmold), who migrated from here during the course of the fifth century, they were probably later subsumed with the Saxons.

An Ingeld–Froda story is preserved in the writings of the twelfth-century Danish chronicler Saxo Grammaticus—although he assumes the two men to be Danes, and their foes to be Saxons. When Froda is killed during a feud with the Saxons, his son Ingeld is given a Saxon princess in marriage, in an attempt by her brothers to prevent vengeance being exacted. But finally, as the result of the reproaches of an old companion, Ingeld is stung into taking revenge, and during a feast bloodily destroys his father's killers, including his wife's brothers. This might be additional to the event alluded to by the *Beowulf*-poet, or a confused version of it. The Anglo-Saxon tradition, which is earlier and probably more pristine than the Scandinavian, makes it clear that there had existed an ancient feud between Hrothgar's Danes and Froda's Heathobards. Probably Froda has been killed; in any event, Hrothgar attempts to buy peace by marrying his daughter to Froda's son, Ingeld. Beowulf declares himself sceptical as to the likely success of this plan. And the Anglo-Saxon audience knew well what the outcome would be. In due course Ingeld revives the feud (apparently during a visit to his father-in-law), and is there destroyed. The *Widsith*-poet tells how: "Hrothulf and Hrothgar . . . humbled Ingeld's battle-array, cut down at Heorot the power of the Heathobards" (45–9).

2085–8 *Glof hangode . . . dracan fellum.* In *Grettis Saga* the female troll carries a trough in which to carry her victims; and in Scandinavian tradition a hideous, pouch-like glove is commonly attributed to such creatures, serving to emphasise their awesomeness.

2183f *Hean wæs lange . . .* This allusion to Beowulf's sluggish youth seems at odds with the hero's own account (408f), but is a common folkloristic motif, attributed for instance to the heroes of at least two Old Norse analogues to *Beowulf*: *Grettis Saga* and *Orms þáttr Stórólfssonar.*

2195 *seofan þusendo.* The term *þusend* is commonly used in Old English without expressing the unit of value (cf. 2994–5). In this case, referring to an estate, it is presumably the unit of land known as a 'hide', originally as much land as would support one family. If this is the case, Beowulf's estate must have been very extensive; according to Bede, seven thousand hides was the size of North Mercia (*Historia Ecclesisastica*, III, 24).

2200–8 The events of succeeding years, leading to Beowulf's coming to the throne, briefly alluded to here, are expanded upon later in the poem, especially 2354–96. See notes to lines 1202–14, 2922–98.

2231f The dragon's hoard has a complicated background; an earlier phase in its history is recounted later in the poem, 3049f. (For certain features in the story compare the parallel account of Sigemund's dragon-fight, note to lines 874–97.) Long ago the treasure had been consigned to the earth by noble princes. A curse is laid on it. In time it is discovered by a warrior race, who make use of it, but apparently succumb to the curse. Mourning, the lone survivor of this people eventually commits the treasure to the earth once again, using an ancient funeral mound for the purpose. The poet seems to imply that the mound had been newly made (2241–3), but later it seems clear that what the poet visualises is a prehistoric megalithic chambered tomb of the kind regarded in early medieval times as 'the work of giants' (2717, 2774; cf. Saxo Grammaticus, *prefatio*). There the hoard is found by a dragon, who keeps watch over it for three hundred years, until the theft of a cup rouses his anger and brings about the tragic denouement of the poem.

2359–62 When Beowulf turned back to the coast, he carried with him the war-gear presumably of those Frankish warriors he had slain and plundered. 'Thirty' may be an arbitrary number, simply meaning 'much, many' (cf. 123, 379–80). Beowulf's reputation as a remarkable swimmer is already well established in the poem (cf. 506ff), so possibly he should be visualised actually carrying this heap of war-gear with him across the water. Earlier Germanic warriors from the lower Rhine were renowned for their ability to swim powerful rivers while wearing full armour (Dio Cassius, LXIX, 9), and the epitaph of one named Soranus alludes to such an exploit crossing the Danube in terms which suggest it was considered an heroic feat (*C.I.L.*, III, 3676).

2379–96 For the details of this allusion, expanded later in the poem, see note to lines 2922–98.

2428f Ic wæs syfanwintre . . . It was customary among Germanic peoples for youths to be sent to another household, away from the overprotective influence of their parents, to be trained in the customs of heroic society. Often they will have been sent to their mother's brother or father, which must represent the basis of the close relationship between uncle and nephew at this time (cf. Tacitus, *Germania*, XX). The training of youth ordinarily began at the age of seven—which was when Bede says he was sent to be brought up by Abbot Benedict (*Historia Ecclesiastica*, V, 24). In the case of Beowulf, whose family was related to the ruling house of the Geats, the most obvious foster-father was Hrethel.

2435 The accidental killing of one brother by another was particularly tragic. While manslaughter normally invoked the same punitive compensation as murder, in this case Hrethel was the father of both slayer and the slain, so that neither compensation nor bloody vengeance can assuage his distress. The example of an old man who sees his son hanged is parallel, since neither compensation nor retribution could be exacted for those killed by legal process.

2484–5 mæg oðerne, 'One kinsman (Hygelac) avenged the other (Hæthcyn)'; we have no evidence that the actual slayer of Ongentheow (Eofor) was yet related to the Hrethlings. Cf. note to line 1968.

2494 The *Gifðas* (Lat. *Gepidae*) were an East Germanic people living near the mouth of the Vistula in the south-east Baltic. Following the Gothic movement south-east, the majority of the Gifthas had migrated to the Hungarian steppes by the end of the third century, where they established a kingdom which was to be annihilated by Langobards and Avars in the mid sixth century. But the Gifthas were notable warriors, instrumental in the mid fifth century in destroying Attila's Hunnish empire. From this reference it seems probable that some remnants survived in the north to form part of the Danish hegemony.

2603 leod Scylfinga. That Weohstan, a relative of Beowulf, could be regarded in some way as a Swedish prince is a further witness to the complex tribal relationships of the Migration Age. Certainly (2611f), he fought on behalf of King Onela, slaying the king's rebellious nephew Eanmund, whom the Geats were then supporting (see note to lines 2922–98). In return for this service Onela presented him with Eanmund's armour. It is clear from the cosmopolitan character of Hrothgar's court, and from the implications of lines 2493–96, that ordinarily a king might look for followers from any tribe, personal rather than ethnic loyalties being a characteristic feature of heroic society. And young heroes like Beowulf himself customarily sought out such service (*Germania*, XIV). In the same way Beowulf is dubbed the Scylding's 'patron' (3003–5), although there is no suggestion that he was in fact Danish. Any debate as to the exact ethnic antecedents of the Wægmundings is misleading. Archaeological evidence suggests that the Germanic tribes of the Migration Age were far more 'mixed' and mongrel a population than the names used by Classical historians would suggest.

2778   ecg wæs iren. This seems a rather gratuitous remark; but possibly it reflects an earlier stage when iron was relatively rare among Germanic peoples (cf. *Germania*, VI).

2884–91 For Wiglaf's imputation of cowardice and consequent shame to those of Beowulf's *comitatus* who did not go to their leader's aid, see Tacitus, *Germania*, XIV. Reflecting the poet's association by alliteration of 'shame' and 'shields', *hy scamiende scyldas bæron*, 2850, Tacitus remarks: "To throw away one's shield is the supreme disgrace; the guilty wretch is debarred from sacrifice or council. Men have often survived battle only to end their shame by hanging themselves" (VI).

2920–1 'Merovingian' is a generic term applied to the ruling house of the Franks, founded by the eponymous hero Merovech; the identity of the particular ruler in question would depend upon the exact date of Beowulf's death.

2922–98 After the death of the powerful King Hrethel, the Swedes had atacked the Geats, sending raiding-parties south across the great lakes led by Ohthere and Onela, the sons of the aged Swedish king Ongentheow, inflicting great damage on the Geats and notably around their centre at Hreosnaburh (the site unidentified, but possibly Hyssna bro, two dozen miles inland from Göteborg), 2472–8. Later—or sufficiently later for it to be considered a separate campaign (cf. *ærest* 2926)—Hrethel's sons Hæthcyn and Hygelac mounted a reprisal raid, at first successful, even capturing Ongentheow's aged queen. But the Swedish king fell upon Hæthcyn's army, inflicting a savage defeat upon it at Ravenswood. The Geat king is killed and the Swedish queen rescued; and the Geatish survivors are besieged in the forest until relieved next morning by the timely appearance of Hygelac's army. The tables turned, Ongentheow is pursued and finally confronted by two Geatish warriors, the brothers Wulf and Eofor, the latter striking the blow which finally kills the Swedish king. (The notion that a two-to-one fight is in some way shameful, is a later, chivalric supposition, as found in Saxo's rather confused version of the incident.)

Subsequent events in Swedish–Geat relations had been alluded to earlier in the poem, 2379–96, 2611–19. After Ongentheow was killed at Ravenswood, Ohthere had taken the Swedish throne, and in due course, upon his death was succeeded by his brother Onela. Ohthere's sons, Eanmund and Eadgils, likely contenders for the throne, were obliged to seek refuge with the Geats, now ruled by Heardred under Beowulf's guidance. Onela invaded Geatland, killing the Geatish king and one of the Swedish princes, Eanmund, before returning to Sweden, and allowing Beowulf finally to succeed to the throne. It is interesting that it was a Geatish warrior Weohstan, father of Wiglaf and a relative of Beowulf himself, who should have sided with Onela at this point, and become personally responsible for the death of Eanmund (2611–19; and cf. note to 2603). A few years later Eadgils, with the aid of Geatish troops, invades Sweden, kills Onela and seizes the throne.

At the stage of Geatish history reached at this point in the poem it must be assumed that Eadgils is either dead or no longer powerful in matters of state, or that he considered former Geatish assistance in assuming the throne to be a matter for personal loyalty to Beowulf rather than to the Geats as a whole.

2994–5 hund þusenda landes and locenra beaga. See note to 2195. The hide can scarcely be referred to here, since a hundred thousand hides would amount to more than the whole of Geatland. In this case the unit of value must be applicable to both land and bullion, and was presumably therefore monetary. In early Anglo-Saxon England the monetary unit was the *sceatt*. The poet Widsith says that a valuable ring, *beah*, given him by Eormenric (see note to lines 1197–201) was worth 6000 *sceattas* (*Widsith*, 89–92). Interlocking rings were a convenient and customary manner of dividing bullion.

3003–5 Beowulf had properly been called 'champion of the Scyldings', *freca Scyldinga*, earlier in the poem (1563). But it is unclear why the hero should be singled out in this way as a patron of the Scyldings at this stage in his career. Possibly it harks back to his dealings with Grendel and Grendel's mother—admittedly important in the poem, but now rather remote. Or it may refer to a period after the death of Hrothgar, or of Hrothulf, when the hero might once again have intervened in events in Denmark—the story of which is lost to us. Beowulf had certainly promised to look after the interests of Hrothgar's sons, and although there is no evidence that he attempted to secure their claims against Hrothulf, he may have done so belatedly, in the same way as he took vengeance on the Swedes for the death of Heardred. In view of these possibilities, it seems best to allow the MS to stand, although the line in question: *æfter hæleða hryre, hwate Scildingas* (3005) exactly echoes line 2052, and it is tempting to suppose that this may have resulted in an error of *Scildingas* for *Scylfingas* (scarcely more appropriate but cf. note to 2603), or *Sæ-Geatas*, or the more general *scildwigan*, 'shield-warriors'.

3051f In view of the date at which the poem was written down, the Christian complexion of the curse laid on the 'heathen' gold (2216, 2276) is almost inevitable (cf. note to lines 175–88).

3074–5 Næs he goldhwæte gearwor hæfde / agendes est ær gesceawod. The exact import of these lines is obscure. Probably we should assume that *he* refers to Beowulf rather than *se secg* (3071). In this case, however, what exactly does *goldhwæte* mean, and does *agendes* refer to God, or the dragon, or one of the original owners of the gold?

Compounds in -*hwæte*, 'active, vigorous, successful', suggest that *goldhwæte*, otherwise unrecorded, means 'rich', or 'abounding in gold', although in view of the cursed nature of the treasure here, it is tempting to suppose that *hwæte* is associated with *hwata*, *hwatung*, 'diviner, augury'.

If the 'owner' of the gold is supposed to be God, then *est* should probably be understood as 'grace' and the whole rendered: 'Never before had he beheld more fully the gold-abounding grace of God', i.e. God had never given Beowulf a greater treasure than this one. If on the other hand, as seems more likely, the owner referred to is one or other of its earthly possessors, then *est* would better be understood as 'legacy' or 'liberality', and the whole rendered either as given, or alternatively: 'he had not first examined well enough the owner's legacy.'

A variety of other interpretations have been suggested, some of them requiring textual emendation, but none is convincing.

3150 *Geatisc meowle.* It might be thought appropriate that this female mourner should be Beowulf's wife, although we do not know that he married. It has been suggested that the term 'Geatish woman' refers to the aged queen Hygd who, as was the case in several historical instances, may have been taken on together with the throne (cf. 2369f); her advanced age might then account for Beowulf's lack of a direct heir. The general obsequies associated with Beowulf's funeral are parallelled in the literature. Tacitus says of the early *Germani*: 'There is no pomp about their funerals. The one rule observed is that the bodies of famous men are burned with special kinds of wood. When they have heaped up the fire they do not throw robes or spices on the top; but only a man's arms, and sometimes his horse too, are cast into the flames. The tomb is a raised mound of turf. They disdain to show honour by laboriously rearing high monuments of stone; they would only lie heavy on the dead. Weeping and wailing are soon abandoned—sorrow and mourning not so soon. A woman may decently express her grief in public; a man should nurse his in his heart' (*Germania*, XXVII).

3169 Jordanes says of the funeral of Attila (*c.* 453) that before the king's body was placed in the barrow, the finest horsemen of the Hunnish nation rode round and round the place where the body lay, while they proclaimed his deeds in a funeral dirge (*Getica*, XLIX).

Peoples and genealogies

The Danes: Bright-, Half-, Ring-, Spear-, North-, South-, East-, West-Danes; Scyldings, Honoured-, Victorious-, War-Scyldings; Friends of Ing.

The Danish ruling house

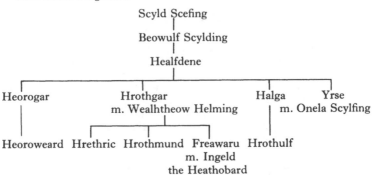

Scyld Scefing
|
Beowulf Scylding
|
Healfdene

Heorogar   Hrothgar   Halga   Yrse
m. Wealhtheow Helming   m. Onela Scylfing

Heoroweard   Hrethric Hrothmund Freawaru Hrothulf
m. Ingeld
the Heathobard

The Geats: Sea-, War-, Weather-Geats.

The Geatish ruling house

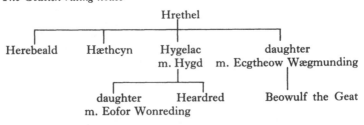

Hrethel

Herebeald   Hæthcyn   Hygelac   daughter
m. Hygd   m. Ecgtheow Wægmunding

daughter   Heardred   Beowulf the Geat
m. Eofor Wonreding

The Swedes: Scylfings: Battle-, War-Scylfings.

The Swedish ruling house

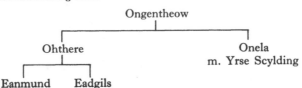

Ongentheow

Ohthere   Onela
m. Yrse Scylding

Eanmund   Eadgils

Glossary of proper names

Abel. Old Testament character; killed by his brother Cain (Genesis, IV). 108.

Ælfhere. Kinsman of Wiglaf Wægmunding. 2604.

Æschere. Comrade in arms and councillor of Hrothgar; elder brother of Yrmenlaf; killed by Grendel's mother. 1323f; 1420; 2122.

Ar-Scyldingas. Honoured Scyldings, a by-name for the Danish ruling house. 464; 1710.

Beanstan. Father of Breca. 524.

Beorht-Dene. 'Bright Danes'. 427; 609.

Beowulf the Dane. An early Danish king, son of Scyld Scefing, father of Healfdene. 18; 53ff.

Beowulf, Biowulf, the Geat. Chief protagonist of the poem; son of Ecgtheow Wægmunding, nephew and thane of King Hygelac, and himself later king of the Geats. 194 *et passim.*

Breca. Son of Beanstan and leader of the Brondingas; as a youth had engaged in a famous swimming-contest with Beowulf. 506f.

Brondingas. A people apparently living in southern Sweden or Norway, but unidentified. 521.

Brosingas. A race of dwarfs, makers and owners of a particularly valuable necklace. 1199.

Cain. Old Testament character; killer of his brother Abel and subsequently outcast by God (Genesis, IV). 107; 1261.

Dæghrefn. Warrior and standard-bearer of the Hugas; killed by Beowulf. 2505.

Dene. The Danes; many compound by-forms. *Passim.*

Eadgils. Swedish prince, son of Ohthere and brother of Eanmund. 2379ff.

Eafor. See *Eofor*

Eanmund. Swedish prince, son of Ohthere and brother of Eadgils. 2611.

Earnanæs. Eagles' Crag, a headland in southern Sweden near the scene of the dragon-fight, possibly identifiable with Örnäs on the Göta älv, Västragötland. 3031.

East-Dene. East Danes. 392; 616; 828.

Ecglaf. Father of Unferth the Dane. 499 *et passim.*

Ecgþeow. Father of Beowulf; a Wægmunding, married into the ruling house of the Geats; killer of Heatholaf the Wylfing and subsequently given sanctuary by the young Danish king Hrothgar. 262f; 373f; 460f *et passim*.

Ecgwela. An early Danish king, otherwise unknown. 1710.

Eofor, Eafor, Iofor. Geatish warrior, son of Wonred and brother of Wulf; killer of the Swedish king Ongentheow, and rewarded by marriage to the daughter of the Geatish king Hygelac. 2486f; 2964; 2977f.

Eomer. Anglian prince, son of Offa, grandson of Garmund and kinsman of Hemming. 1960f.

Eorle. The Heruli, a warlike people formerly living in Denmark. 6.

Eormenric. A powerful Ostrogothic king of the later fourth century. 1201.

Eote. The Jutes; followers of the Frisian king Finn. 902; 1072f; 1141f.

Fin(n). King of the East Frisians, son of Folcwalda; married to Hildeburh the sister of Hnæf the Half-Dane. 1068f; 1146.

Finnas. The Lapps, living in northern Sweden and Norway. 580.

Fitela. Nephew (and son) of the dragon-slayer Sigemund. 879f.

Folcwalda. Father of the Frisian king Finn. 1089.

Francan, Froncan. The Franks. 1210f. 2912f.

Freawaru. Hrothgar's daughter, given in marriage to the Heathobard leader Ingeld in an attempt to end the Danish–Heathobardan feud. 2020f.

Fresan, Frysan. The Frisians East 1093; 1104; and West 1207; 2912f.

Frescyning. King of the West Frisians. 2503.

Freslond. Land of the Frisians, East 1126; and West 2357.

Freswæl. Description of a battle-field, the site of a confrontation between Frisians and Half-Danes. 1070.

Froda. King of the Heathobards and father of Ingeld; killed fighting the Danes. 2025f.

Froncan. See *Francan*.

Frysan, Frysland. See *Fresan, Freslond*.

Gar-Dene. Spear-Danes. 1 *et passim*.

Garmund. Father of the Anglian king Offa. 1960f.

Geatas. The Geats, a people living in what is now southern Sweden, to the south of the great lakes; several compound by-forms. 205 *et passim*.

Geatmæcgas. Men of the Geats. 829.

Gifðas. The Gepidae, an East Germanic people. 2494.

Grendel. The monster which ravages Heorot, and is killed by Beowulf. 102 *et passim*.

Guð-Geatas. War-Geats. 1538.

Guðlaf. A Danish warrior, follower of Hnæf and later Hengest. 1148.

Guð-Scilfingas. War-Scylfings, a by-name for the Swedish ruling house. 2927.

Hæreð. Father of the Geatish queen Hygd. 1929; 1981.

Hæðcyn, Hæðcen. Geatish king, the second son of Hrethel; accidental slayer of his elder brother Herebeald; killed fighting the Swedes. 2434f; 2474f.

Hæðnas. A people living in south-eastern Norway; apparently associated with the Geats. 1983.

Halga. Danish prince, the younger brother of Hrothgar. 61.

Hama. A hero of the Eormenric legends. 1198.

Healfdene. Danish king, son of Beowulf Scylding and father of Hrothgar. 57 *et passim.*

Healf-Dene. Half-Danes, a people ruled by Hnæf. 1069.

Heardred. Geatish king, son of Hygelac and Hygd; supported by Beowulf and killed by the Swedes. 2202; 2375f.

Heaþobardan, Heaðabardan. A Germanic people, unidentified but possibly a remnant of the Langobards; engaged in a destructive feud with the Danes. 2032f.

Heaþolaf. A Wylfing killed by Beowulf's father Ecgtheow. 459f.

Heaþo-Ræmas. A people living in south-eastern Norway (Romerike). 519.

Heaðo-Scilfingas. Battle-Scylfings, a by-name for the Swedish ruling house. 63; 2205f.

Helmingas. The family to which Hrothgar's queen Wealhtheow belonged; apparently part of the Wylfingas. 620.

Hem(m)ing. An Anglian kinsman of Eomer and Offa. 1944f.

Hengest. Leader of the Half-Danes after the death of Hnæf; possibly the historical Hengest who founded the Anglo-Saxon kingdom of Kent in the mid-fifth century. 1083; 1127.

Heorogar, Heregar, Hiorogar. Danish king, son of Healfdene and elder brother of Hrothgar. 61; 467; 2158.

Heorot, Heort, Hiorut. The hall of the Danish king Hrothgar; probably situated near Lejre in Zealand. 78 *et passim.*

Heoroweard. Son of the Danish king Heorogar, but apparently too young to succeed him. 2161.

Herebeald. Eldest son of the Geatish king Hrethel; accidentally killed by his younger brother Hæthcyn. 2434f.

Heregar. See *Heorogar.*

Heremod. An early Danish king, who gave promise of a brilliant career but subsequently proved a notoriously bad ruler; it was after Heremod's death at the hands of the Jutes that Scyld Scefing was sent to restore the Danish fortunes. 901f; 1709f.

Hereric. Uncle of the Geatish king Heardred, and probably the brother of queen Hygd. 2206.

Here-Scyldingas. War-Scyldings, descriptive by-name for the Danish ruling house. 1108.

Hetware. The Chattuarii, a warlike people, at this time apparently part of the Frankish hegemony on the Lower Rhine. 2363; 2916.

Higelac. See *Hygelac.*

Hildeburh. Daughter of Hoc and sister of Hnæf the 'Half-Dane'; married to the Frisian king Finn. 1071f; 1114f.

Hildeleoma. 'Battle-flame', a sword used by Hengest, possibly once belonging to Hnæf. 1143.

Hiorot. See *Heorot.*

Hnæf. Leader of the Half-Danes; son of Hoc and brother of Hildeburh; killed in the fight at Finnesburh. 1069; 1114f.

Hoc. Father of Hildeburh and Hnæf. 1076.

Hondscioh. Geatish warrior and member of Beowulf's *comitatus*; killed by Grendel. 2076f.

Hrædla. See *Hreðel.*

Hrefnawudu (also *Hrefnesholt*). 'Ravenswood', a forest in Sweden; site of a battle in which the Swedish king Ongentheow killed the Geatish king Hæthcyn. 2925f.

Hreosnabeorh. Mares' Hill, an unidentified hill in Geatland; site of an attack by the Swedes on the Geats. 2477.

Hreðel, Hrædel, Hrædla. Geatish king, father of Hygelac and maternal grandfather of Beowulf. 374 *et passim*.

Hrepling. 'Son of Hrethel' (e.g. Hygelac), and in the plural extended to the whole Geats. 1923; 2925; 2960.

Hreðric. Elder son of Hrothgar and Wealhtheow. 1189; 1836.

Hring-Dene. 'Ring-Danes'. 116; 1279; 1769.

Hronesnæs(s). 'Whale's Cape', a headland on the Geatish coast; the site of Beowulf's funeral. 2805; 3136.

Hroðgar. Danish king and lord of Heorot; son of Healfdene. 61 *et passim*.

Hroðmund. Younger son of Hrothgar and Wealhtheow. 1189.

Hropulf. Hrothgar's nephew, the offspring of an incestuous relationship between Yrse and Halga; later king of the Danes. 1014f; 1163f.

Hrunting. Unferth's weapon, loaned to Beowulf. 1457; 1490; 1659; 1807.

Hugas. By-name for the Franks. 2501f; 2914f.

Hunlafing. 'Son of Hunlaf', a member of Hengest's *comitatus*. 1143.

Hygd. Wife of the Geatish king Hygelac; daughter of Hæreth and mother of Heardred. 1926f; 2172f; 2369f.

Hygelac, Higelac. Geatish king; youngest son of Hrethel, and uncle to Beowulf; killed fighting the Franks on the Lower Rhine A.D. 521. 194 *et passim*.

Ingeld. Heathobard prince, son of Froda. 2064.

Ingwine. 'The Friends of Ing', a name applied to the whole Danish people; identifiable with the Ingvaeones of Tacitus. 1044; 1319.

Iofor. See *Eofor*.

Merewiging. The Merovingian; leader of the ruling house of the Franks. 2921.

Nægling. Beowulf's sword; originally belonging to the Frankish standard-bearer Dæghrefn. 2680; 2499f.

Norð-Dene. North Danes. 783.

Offa. King of the Continental Angles living in the later fourth century. 1949f.

Ohthere, Ohtere. Swedish king; elder son of Ongentheow and father of Eanmund and Eadgils. 2380f; 2612; 2928f.

Onela. Swedish king; younger son of Ongentheow; married to the Geatish princess Yrse; killed by Eadgils. 62; 2616f; 2932.

Ongenþeow, Ongenðiow. Swedish king, father of Ohthere and Onela; killed by the Geatish warrior Eofor. 1968; 2387; 2475f; 2924ff.

Oslaf. A Danish warrior, follower of Hnæf and later Hengest. 1148.

Sæ-Geatas. Sea-Geats, a by-name perhaps referring to the maritime position and seafaring character of the people. 1850; 1968.

Scedeland, Scedenig. Skåne, the southernmost part of what is now Sweden, at that time under Danish suzerainty. 19; 1686.

Scefing. 'Son of Scef', or 'with a sheaf'; applied to Scyld. 4.

Scyld. Legendary founder of the Danish ruling house, the Scyldings. 4ff.

Scyldingas, Scildingas, Scildungar. 'Sons of Scyld', the name of the Danish ruling house, and applied generally to the Danes; several compound by-forms. 53 *et passim.*

Scylfingas, Scilfingas. Name of the Swedish ruling house, applied to the Swedes generally; several compound by-forms. 63 *et passim.*

Sigemund. Legendary dragon-slayer; son of Wæls, uncle (and father) of Fitela. 875f.

Sige-Scyldingas. Victorious-Scyldings, a by-name for the Danish ruling house. 597; 2004.

Suð-Dene. South Danes. 463; 1996.

Sweon. The Swedes, living in the east-central part of what is now Sweden, to the north of the great lakes. 2472; 2946ff.

Sweoðeod. The Swedish people. 2922.

Swerting. Maternal uncle or maternal grandfather of the Geatish king Hygelac. 1203.

Swiorice. The Swedish realm. 2383; 2495.

þeod-Scyldingas. The race of Scyldings, the Danish ruling house. 1019.

Pryðo. Wife of the Anglian king Offa. 1931f.

Unferð. Literally 'Discordia, Lacking-spirit'; the son of Ecglaf, and an officer (*þyle*) at the Danish court; responsible for the death of his brother. 499; 530; 1165; 1488.

Wægmundingas. The family to which Beowulf, Wiglaf and Wihstan belong; apparently related to the Geatish ruling house. 2607; 2814.

Wæls. Father of the dragon-slayer Sigemund. 897.

Wælsing. 'Son of Wæls', i.e. Sigemund. 877.

Wealhþeo(w). Wife of the Danish king Hrothgar, and mother of Hrethric and Hrothmund. 612 *et passim.*

Wederas, Weder-Geats. Weather- ?Storm-loving-Geats, a by-name perhaps referring to the maritime position and seafaring character of the people. 341 *et passim.*

Wedermearc. Land of the Weder(-Geatas). 298.

Weland. The famous weapon-smith of Germanic legend. 455.

Wendlas, Wendle. The Vandals, remnants of whom remained in the Baltic region, at Vendel in central Sweden and elsewhere. 348.

Weohstan, Weoxstan. See *Wihstan.*

West-Dene. The West Danes. 383; 1578.

Wiglaf. A Wægmunding (the last), son of Wihstan, a kinsman and heir to Beowulf; kinsman of Ælfhere. 2602 *et passim.*

Wihstan, Weohstan, Weoxstan. A Wægmunding, father of Wiglaf. 2602 *et passim.*

Wilfingas. See *Wylfingas.*

Wiðergyld. Heathobard warrior. 2051.

Wonred. Father of the Geatish warriors Eofor and Wulf. 2971.

Wonreding. 'Son of Wonred', i.e. Wulf. 2965.

Wulf. Geatish warrior; son of Wonred and brother of Eofor. 2965; 2993.

Wulfgar. Vandal prince, and an officer at the Danish court. 335f.

Wylfingas, Wilfingas. A Germanic people living along the southern Baltic coast. 461f.

Yrmenlaf. A Dane, younger brother of Æschere. 1324.

Yrse. Daughter of the Danish king Healfdene, married to the Swedish king Onela. 62.